Praise for
SLEEPER AGENT

"Many Americans are familiar with the names of the Soviet assets Alger Hiss, Klaus Fuchs, and Julius and Ethel Rosenberg. Few, however, have heard of George Koval, a devastatingly effective atomic spy during World War II who walked away from his exploits completely undetected by U.S. intelligence. Now writer Ann Hagedorn has told his story in *Sleeper Agent*, a historical page-turner of the highest order."

—*The Wall Street Journal*

"Ann Hagedorn has gifted us with a dazzling, gripping, most timely reflection of the Cold War era—and the ongoing legacy of hateful anti-Semitism driving the quest for sanctuary, education, and peace. This captivating, profoundly researched book is required reading for everyone concerned about history and the future."

—Blanche Wiesen Cook, author of *Eleanor Roosevelt* (Vols. 1–3), and *The Declassified Eisenhower*

"An eye-opening account of perhaps the Soviet Union's most successful sleeper agent."

—*Kirkus Reviews*

"Ann Hagedorn is one of those rare writers I trust to keep me reading in these times when the competition for our attention can be overwhelming. But with the fascinating *Sleeper Agent*, Ms. Hagedorn has once again captivated me with the focus and depth of her superlative investigative talents."

—Bob Shacochis, National Book award recipient, author of *The Woman Who Lost Her Soul*

"*Sleeper Agent* is both an important work of history and a story that's hard to put down. Ann Hagedorn might have been a master spy herself, so brilliantly has she assembled myriad specks of information into this extraordinary map of an underground America below the surface of World War II and the Cold War."

—James Tobin, author of *The Man He Became: How FDR Defied Polio to Win the Presidency*

"Compelling. . . . Hagedorn's well-researched account employs a host of primary and secondary sources to convincingly connect the dots between Koval, the Soviet spy network, and the creation of the atomic bomb."

—*Booklist*

"From 1940 to 1948, George Koval hid in plain sight, using his real name while gathering intelligence for the Soviet Union about the American atomic project. Ann Hagedorn tells this incredible story and more: Hagedorn's account of this life is a gripping page-turner, almost unbelievable yet true."

—Stephen M. Norris, Director, Havighurst Center for Russian and Post-Soviet Studies, Miami University

"Ann Hagedorn, who is a masterful historical sleuth and a superb writer, has told the riveting and previously untold story of an atomic spy. Hagedorn has not only penetrated the inner life of a 'sleeper agent,' she also has transformed our understanding of the origins of the nuclear arms race."

—Bill Tuttle, author of *Race Riot: Chicago in the Red Summer of 1919* and *"Daddy's Gone to War": The Second World War in the Lives of America's Children*

"Enlivened by its brisk pace and lucid scientific details, this is a rewarding introduction to a noteworthy episode in the history of Soviet espionage."

—*Publishers Weekly*

"Hagedorn draws from decades of scholarship, thorough archival research, and deftly FOIA'd F.B.I. reports to reconstruct the intricate network of

Russian cells in midcentury America, a world of handlers and honey traps and tradecraft worthy of a prequel *to The Americans.* . . . Hagedorn is an impressive reporter, sparing no detail from the elements of the story to which she has access. And it's without question a great story."

—*Airmail*

"*Sleeper Agent* is an enthralling tale to read."

—*Michigan Today*

"A great read."

—*Cincinnati Business Courier*

"A good adventure story, well told . . . worthy of John Le Carré."

—*The New York Journal of Books*

"Hagedorn has written another gripping, impeccably researched work of history."

—*Dayton Daily News*

"Ann Hagedorn's book is entirely true but so compelling that it reads like a classic spy novel."

—*Columbia* magazine

"In Hagedorn's deft hands, Koval's remarkable story—about a spy that we'd never even heard of—is one that we'll never forget."

—*Northern Kentucky Tribune*

"Hagedorn's research, drawing on FBI archives, Russian materials, and an array of secondary sources, is prodigious. . . . This spy tale is both remarkable and troubling."

—*The Forward* magazine

"A meticulously researched portrait of Koval."

—*The Columbus Dispatch*

ALSO BY ANN HAGEDORN

The Invisible Soldiers: How America Outsourced Our Security

Savage Peace: Hope and Fear in America, 1919

*Beyond the River: The Untold Story
of the Heroes of the Underground Railroad*

Ransom: The Untold Story of International Kidnapping

*Wild Ride: The Rise and Tragic Fall of Calumet Farm, Inc.,
America's Premier Racing Dynasty*

SLEEPER AGENT

THE ATOMIC SPY IN
AMERICA WHO GOT AWAY

ANN HAGEDORN

SIMON & SCHUSTER PAPERBACKS

NEW YORK   LONDON   TORONTO   SYDNEY   NEW DELHI

Simon & Schuster Paperbacks
An Imprint of Simon & Schuster, Inc.
1230 Avenue of the Americas
New York, NY 10020

First Simon & Schuster trade paperback edition June 2022

SIMON & SCHUSTER PAPERBACKS and colophon are
registered trademarks of Simon & Schuster, Inc.

For information about special discounts for bulk purchases,
please contact Simon & Schuster Special Sales at 1-866-506-1949 or
business@simonandschuster.com.

The Simon & Schuster Speakers Bureau can bring authors
to your live event. For more information or to book an event,
contact the Simon & Schuster Speakers Bureau at 1-866-248-3049
or visit our website at www.simonspeakers.com.

Interior design by Kyle Kabel

Manufactured in the United States of America

1   3   5   7   9   10   8   6   4   2

Library of Congress Cataloging-in-Publication Data is available.

ISBN 978-1-5011-7394-3
ISBN 978-1-5011-7395-0 (pbk)
ISBN 978-1-5011-7396-7 (ebook)

In memory of
Elizabeth, Dwight, Janet, Harry, Ethel, and Cyrus

CONTENTS

CONTENTS

PART III: THE HUNT

The powerful play goes on, and you may contribute a verse.

—Walt Whitman,
"O Me! O Life!",
Leaves of Grass

PROLOGUE

Sometimes the clues that should have been warnings are lost in a blur, only to be seen in hindsight. Caught in the need to move ahead, most people rush, like speeding trains, past the truths and half-truths tucked into the terrain they thought they knew. And so it would be for a man and a woman one evening in 1948 at New York City's Grand Central Palace, each soon to learn the timeless cost of missing clues.

It was September 19, the last day of the Golden Anniversary Exposition commemorating the 1898 consolidation of the city's five boroughs, a celebration that had begun in late August with one of the most memorable opening ceremonies in New York history. After a black-tie dinner at the Waldorf-Astoria Hotel, a torchlight procession of invited guests walked east to Lexington Avenue where for ten blocks, from Forty-Second Street north, all electric signs were turned off and street lamps dimmed to the level of gaslights fifty years before. Led by their hosts, New York mayor William O'Dwyer and David E. Lilienthal, the head of the US Atomic Energy Commission, the men and women, at least a hundred, stopped at the Forty-Seventh Street entrance to the Grand Central Palace where they joined thousands of opening-night guests along with fifty thousand or more spectators crowding the sidewalks of Lexington

Avenue. Then, all at once it seemed, everyone looked up. At the top of the Empire State Building were two planetarium-projector-size telescopes aimed at Alioth, the brightest star in the Big Dipper.

What happened next was a new atomic-age ribbon-cutting. At exactly 8:30 p.m., the light streaming from Alioth activated photo-electric cells in the eyepiece of each telescope. This energy pulse moved through telegraph wires to the fourth floor of the Grand Central Palace where it excited a uranium atom, causing a switch to flip and current to be sent to ignite a mass of magnesium woven into a block-long strip of ribbon on Lexington Avenue. The flaming magnesium cut through the ribbon, making loud crackling sounds, as bright lights returned to the area and the mayor announced the official start of the anniversary celebration: "It is highly appropriate that we open this Golden Anniversary Exposition with energy from the uranium atom. One of the biggest features here is 'Man and the Atom,' the most complete exhibit on atomic energy ever assembled."

To be sure, the multifaceted exhibit on the fourth floor of the Palace was extraordinary, especially in the way that it explained the erudite topic of the atomic bomb in layman's language, demon-strating how atom smashers and nuclear fission worked and even linking the most fear-laden weapon in human history to the cause of peace. Throughout the month of the Golden Anniversary, the exit polls revealed that the most popular exhibit was the one that took the narrative of the atomic bomb from fear to fascination. "'Man and Atom': Best Show in New York" one September news-paper headline read.

Such rave reviews may have inspired the man and the woman meeting for a date at the Grand Central Palace to visit the exhibition before it shut down on the nineteenth. Or their interest may have been instigated by the current relevance of atomic energy issues, such as the hot debates over international control of nuclear power or by the ever-mounting allegations of Soviet espionage during the war at the labs where the first US atomic bombs were developed. Nearly every day in the month of September there had been news about the suspected wartime spies. On the Saturday when the man, whose name was George Koval, invited Jean Finkelstein to the exhibit, the *New York Times* lead story centered on a soon-to-be-released report that would unveil "a shocking chapter in Communist espionage in the atomic field," exposing previously unknown individuals allegedly tied to a spy ring partly based in New York City.

But Koval told his date that his reason for wanting to visit the Palace exhibits was to meet old friends there, former colleagues from the war years when he worked at the atomic energy plants in Oak Ridge, Tennessee. He was certain they would come to see "Man and the Atom"—and see it with him. Out of respect for the man she believed she might marry, Jean agreed to his suggestion. And, having read reviews of the exhibits, such as the scale model of the Oak Ridge gaseous diffusion lab and the animated panels demonstrating how plutonium, a highly radioactive element, was produced, Jean was eager to go. Oak Ridge. Plutonium. Radioactivity. These were things her boyfriend knew a lot about, but she did not. And she wanted to know everything about this man: his interests, his past, and whatever part of his scientific knowledge she could learn.

Jean had first met George Koval one night in March 1948 at a bowling alley near the campus of the City College of New York. She was a twenty-one-year-old part-time student at CCNY and he was a thirty-four-year-old member of the same honorary fraternity in which her brother Leonard was active, both men having been recent classmates in CCNY's department of electrical engineering. That night the fraternity was competing for a bowling league title. And Leonard wanted his sister to meet his "interesting and rare friend," an electrical engineer who could recite verses from Walt Whitman and Henry Wadsworth Longfellow.

Years later when asked about that evening, Jean said only, "It was serious from the start." She would remember Koval as slender with broad shoulders, standing about six feet, appearing very masculine. He had short, straight brown hair, brown eyes, and very full lips, making his broad smile all the more attractive. A clean-cut guy, only two years out of the US Army, he typically wore a dark navy blazer and khaki trousers. And though he never seemed to be clothes conscious, he looked smart, urbane, more like a seasoned New York intellectual than a former soldier born and raised in Iowa, which he was. Still, it must have been his Midwest upbringing that caused traces of innocence to seep through his streetwise exterior. Or perhaps it was his curiosity about everyone and everything that surrounded him. Koval was like a cat, always watching and ready to act, with a playful mix of enthusiasm and caution.

When asked about Koval, Jean would say he was suave and spirited, but also cut from rugged rock. Few people knew his solemn side, which she believed may have been rooted in a distressed childhood. That also would have explained why he avoided detailed discussions about his past. However, he did tell her that he was born in Sioux City on Christmas day in 1913, that he was seventeen when he left home, and that shortly thereafter both of his parents had died. As an only child, that was the end of his family, he told her. She listened and had no reason to doubt his story. Besides, there was so much more to talk about, such as baseball, his ultra-passion. Koval could reel off the history and complete stats of every big-league pitcher in 1948. He was even renowned among friends for his skills as a shortstop.

During the months of planning her life around him, Jean was not on the hunt for evidence of anything negative. Why would she be? Occasionally she noticed that he went out of his way to validate his sincerity. He also had a tendency to suddenly be silent, as though a part of his machinery had abruptly shut down. He was always precise, never diverging from the norm and never saying more than he meant to. And he was very punctual.

But on September 19, he was late—and he seemed quite agitated about it. From the start of the evening, he was not the smooth, charming companion Jean had known thus far, and the longer they stayed at the Grand Central Palace the more troubled he seemed to be. Possibly to ease his anxiety, they were on the move constantly, visiting every exhibit, but always returning to "Man and the Atom," likely to be certain they hadn't missed the arrival of his friends. Nothing could distract him, not even the popular model of a 200,000-volt generator, used in atomic experiments, which had the capability of creating fierce electrical energies; it was on display in a compartment where viewers could enter and watch their hair stand on end.

Koval wasn't interested. He seemed like an actor who had forgotten his lines. Anxious. Distant. Alone. The exposition shut down at midnight and the couple stayed until the last second. No friends, no former colleagues from Oak Ridge, no war buddies ever arrived. Then, taking the subway back to the borough of the Bronx, where each of them lived, they had what Jean would later describe as "a lovers' quarrel, which had never happened before." With time, the reason for the spat would fade, but not the memory of how he "seemed to be picking a fight." When he walked her to the apartment where she lived with her parents, whether he said "good night" or "goodbye" was a detail she could never recall.

In the weeks ahead, Jean left him alone, as advised by her brother Leonard and guided by her own instincts. Such a standstill must have required remarkable discipline, especially considering the exchanges they could have been having about the two rousing battles consuming front-page news: one in sports and one in politics. In baseball, two underdog teams were headed to the 1948 World Series: the Boston Braves, which hadn't won a pennant since 1914; and the Cleveland Indians, absent from the winner's circle since

1920. It was the kind of contest that Koval, as a dedicated champion of the underdog, would closely follow. And in politics, there was a continuing blast of intriguing headlines about Soviet espionage in New York, including atom bomb spy networks. One headline read, "Spies in U.S. Are 'On Run.'"

Still, Jean resisted a daily urge to hear his voice. And when she finally had to talk to him and made the call, the landlady answered, telling her that Koval wasn't there and wouldn't be back for a while, a long while—perhaps never again. He didn't live there anymore, she said, and at that very moment he was on a ship heading to Europe. He had left "yesterday morning, with only a duffle bag."

For Jean, it must have seemed like sudden thunder on a clear day. After calling her brother, who said he knew nothing about Koval's leaving town, she contacted the man she believed to be Koval's closest friend, Herbie Sandberg. He confirmed that Koval had departed from New York on October 6, with a plan to work as a manager at the construction site of an electric power plant in Poland. Sandberg didn't know when his friend would return nor did he have a forwarding address to offer her. He did know that Koval left on a transatlantic liner called the SS *America*, from Pier 61, and he remembered that it had rained that day. But nothing more.

Though documents and interviews would someday expose parts of the truth about Koval's escape from America, some questions would never be answered, like what he was thinking as he watched the New York skyline diminish and the ocean's vast expanse draw near. Was he remembering the last time he had left America, in May 1932, with his parents and his two brothers on a ship leaving from Pier 54, bound eventually for the Soviet Union, or the details of his father's stories about being a Russian immigrant and seeing America for the first time in 1910? Did he have the manner of a professional, lacking last-minute hesitations or sentimentality, as the ship passed by the great statue symbolizing the freedoms of the country that was his birthplace? And did he struggle to push back all thoughts of what and whom he was leaving behind?

By November, Koval would be living in the Soviet Union, in Moscow, with his wife of twelve years, Lyudmila Ivanova Koval, and he would soon reunite with his sixty-five-year-old father, Abram; his mother, Ethel, then fifty-eight; and Isaiah, one of his two brothers. What he told them about his past eight years in America on a "business trip" for Soviet military intelligence is unknown. But one certain fact is that George Koval left the US just in time. And, as anyone who knew him would likely say, his timing was always nearly perfect.

PART I

THE LURE

If it were possible for any nation to fathom another people's bitter experience through a book, how much easier its future fate would become and how many calamities and mistakes it could avoid. But it is very difficult. There always is this fallacious belief: "It would not be the same here; here such things are impossible."

—Aleksandr Solzhenitsyn,
The Gulag Archipelago

CHAPTER ONE

THE DREAM ON VIRGINIA STREET

The first Sioux City residents to greet Abram Koval must have been the newsboys peddling the latest editions of Iowa dailies in a high-pitched "buy-a-paper-mister" cry while pushing across a crowded train platform. It was early May in 1910 and Abram was coming from Galveston, Texas, where he had just entered America for the first time. A month before, at dawn, he had departed from the Russian village of his birth, leaving behind his parents and siblings, and his future wife who would one day be the mother of his children, among them their son George Abramovich Koval. In a nearby town, Abram had boarded a train with dozens of men, women, and children, pressed against windowless walls, shoulder to shoulder, back to back, for an eight-hour trip to Bremen, Germany. There he registered for the April 7 transatlantic trip to America on the SS *Hannover* and spent two nights in a dormitory, most distinctive for its walls blackened with swarms of flies and its rows of tightly connected cots crammed with people of both genders and all ages—mere practice for his upcoming five-thousand-mile journey to Galveston in steerage with nearly 1,600 closely lodged passengers.

On April 28, Abram walked down the gangplank of the S.S. *Hannover* at the port of Galveston, known as the Ellis Island of the West, where he was officially listed as "Abram Berks Kowal" on an immigration form noting his destination as "Sioux City, Missouri." One week later, he deboarded the train at his new home in Sioux City, Iowa—on the Missouri River—where the sight of the newsboys and the hum of their high energy must have refueled his sense of purpose.

At the time of his journey, twenty-seven-year-old Abram Berko Koval was an experienced carpenter whose tireless work ethic and solid reputation had made him the very marrow of what was known as the Galveston Movement. This was a cause organized largely by prominent Jews in New York City, such as Jacob Schiff and Cyrus Sulzberger, who were trying to protect the rights of Jewish immigrants to enter America by diverting them to towns far west of New York City. Their goal was to prevent immigration restrictions that were under discussion because of prejudices rising out of the recent influx of Jewish immigrants to the US: one hundred thousand a year, beginning in 1905, and mostly crowding into the Lower East Side of Manhattan.

By the summer of 1906, their plan had begun. Galveston was chosen because it was in the West and it had a direct passenger shipping line, the North German Lloyd Shipping Company, from Bremen. Also, Galveston was a large terminus for railroad lines to and from every major city in the West and Midwest. By 1910, Schiff and his colleagues had placed nearly ten thousand Russian immigrants in sixty-six cities and eighteen states, all coming through Galveston, often after being recruited back home.

Working out of the Jewish Emigration Society, which was Schiff's organization based in Kiev, the Russian recruiters were looking for young men, like Abram Koval, who would adjust well and contribute to communities across America: healthy, under the age of forty, and skilled as ironworkers, tailors, butchers, shoemakers, and carpenters.

To attract them, the society offered vouchers to cover most of the costs of the journey, including the travel from hometowns to Bremen, plus the lodging for a night or two there, and the ship passage.

And for Abram, the decisive push to leave home may have been the visits of the society's recruiters, who must have stirred his hopes for a better life as they presented an array of opportunities in America. His village of Telekhany, in Belarus on the outskirts of Pinsk, was located within the Pale of Settlement, a tier of provinces in European Russia and Russian-held Poland where nearly four million Jews lived. In the Pale, there were restrictions that stifled the lives of Jews, especially their economic progress, including the inability to purchase land, to own businesses, and to enter professions. Their education was limited by a 10 percent Jewish quota in the secular schools, diminishing their chances to earn degrees that could lead to financial security. And for the men, there was also the six-year requirement to serve in the Russian army, plus nine years in the reserves.

To leave or not to leave was a timeless question, echoing out of the pasts of all oppressed people. How to escape, where to go, and when. The answers would come to Abram as the recruiters of the Galveston Movement offered hope and the realities surrounding him generated fear. Leaving Russia in 1910 meant escaping the pervasive anti-Semitism of Czar Nicholas II's Russia and the ongoing threat of violence against Jews. What most compelled Abram's departure were likely the same brutalities that had driven the unprecedented influx of Russian Jews to New York beginning in 1905.

In October that year, the czar had signed a document to end a general strike that was paralyzing his vast Russian empire. Known as the October Manifesto, it would, if implemented, require the czar to surrender the basic rights of his supreme power and transform his autocracy into a constitutional monarchy with the freedoms of speech, assembly, and conscience. No longer could one man alone make the laws that governed the lives of his people. There would be a parliament out of his control and elected by all classes, including workers like Abram whose voice could then be heard, as the manifesto assured Jews the right to vote and to be elected.

The next day thousands upon thousands of Russians who viewed the manifesto as the first Russian constitution took to the streets in hundreds of towns and cities to celebrate the triumphant outcome of what would be known as the Russian Revolution of 1905. But in the Pale, the joy was exceptionally brief. For there, by midafternoon, the rejoicing masses were silenced by mobs of armed ruffians and local police, causing the storied day to be described in the Pale not as a victory for the masses but as a *pogrom*, a storm of human violence targeting the Jews of the Russian Empire.

In the weeks that followed, there were 694 pogroms in 660 Russian towns—the majority occurring within the Pale. At least 3,000 Jews were killed and 2,000 critically injured. Reports of the wounded reached levels of more than 15,000 men, women, and children. In most afflicted towns, Jewish homes were robbed and burned; shops and synagogues were looted; and witnesses reported murders of babies and rapes of women and girls.

Russian authorities denied any secret plans to punish Jews in the aftermath of the czar's signing of the manifesto. Instead, they claimed that the pogroms were a mobilization of the Russian people in support of the czar and that the violence had erupted from the passion of his followers expressing what they did not want to lose: their czar and imperial Russia. But with time, the truth would surface: the massacres had to have been planned in advance by anti-Semitic, counterrevolutionary leaders. And it would one day be clear that false information created to set the blame on the Jews for the many failures of the czar's regime was at the core of the pogroms—for example, the discovery of a printing press hidden at police headquarters in Saint Petersburg producing anti-Semitic pamphlets during October and November 1905.

This was an age-old scenario: Repress the unwanted and when they revolt, blame them, the victims, for the ensuing carnage while allowing counterrevolutionary thugs to kill them and be lauded for saving the empire. The unseen irony beneath the thick crust of denial in czarist Russia was that oppression was and always would be the fuel for awakening class consciousness, inciting revolts against oppressors and crushing empires. To be sure, with the mounting anti-Semitism, Jewish radicalism in Russia only grew stronger. By 1906 many Jews in Russia hoped for and worked toward the collapse of the Russian autocracy, some as part of revolutionary organizations dedicated to the overthrow of the czar and even trained in armed resistance to defend Jewish communities against mob violence. One major player in the upsurge of political activism was the General Jewish Labor Union, known as the Bund. Abram Koval had been a member since his late teens.

What drove the young to the Bund was its uplifting solidar- ity. Their discriminated ethnicity, their working-class roots, their impoverished conditions were no longer shameful. These were not weaknesses, but rather the traits that could empower them as they pledged to change the world by ending oppression. Through solidar- ity, they could develop an identity based in dignity and hope—not fear and disgrace. This was a generation that would plot to overthrow the czar, who was the symbol of Jewish oppression.

Another member of that fiery generation was Abram's future wife, Ethel Shenitsky. Born in Telekhany, she was the daughter of a rabbi who did not want his daughter mingling in any rebel group promoting socialism—like the Bund. But to young Ethel, social- ism had effectively replaced the religion her father had spent years teaching her. As her son George would one day write: "My mother was a socialist long before most people knew the meaning of the word." This was disgraceful to Ethel's father, whose anger was deep enough that on one occasion he grabbed his daughter's thick brown hair and dragged her across a yard into the local synagogue. Neither time nor age would ease the tensions.

Ethel's beliefs only grew stronger as Russian authorities tightened the rules for Jews. Year after year, there was more surveillance, bringing daily dangers to those who were active in what might be considered revolutionary activities. Curfew was at 8 p.m. No assembly was allowed. And there were growing numbers of arrests, mostly of so-called revolutionaries. Worse still, there were vile efforts to force Jews out of the empire. For example, there were accounts of families pulled from their beds in the middle of the night and, with scarcely any time to dress, driven to a central police station, then herded out of the city in groups by soldiers on horseback. By 1910, there had been reports of local authorities "even taking babies from their mothers, leaving the parents the choice of abandoning their homes or their children." Such expulsions were later referred to as the "bloodless pogroms," but their power in pushing Jews out of Russia was as painfully mighty as the bloodiest pogroms.

When and where Abram and Ethel first met isn't known. But they were together by the time the recruiters from Kiev had reached out to Abram. And soon they had a plan. About ten months after Abram first arrived in Iowa, Ethel joined him. Then on June 3, 1911, they were married in Sioux City, a fast-growing trade center whose early-twentieth-century investors envisioned its potential as a second Chicago. For the Kovals, it was a smart start.

By 1911, one hundred passenger trains moved daily through Sioux City's three railway stations. It housed the second-largest stockyard in the nation and three major meatpacking plants. It had a population of nearly fifty thousand. And for the city's Jews, of whom there were three thousand, Sioux City had become a regional nucleus. In this town surrounded by the cornfields and tall grass of America's Great Plains, there were four Orthodox synagogues; more than a hundred Jewish-owned businesses; hundreds of Jewish tradesmen supplying some of the city's best carpenters, blacksmiths, tailors, bakers, masons, and electricians; and dozens of Jewish newsboys helping to support their immigrant families.

Until Ethel had arrived, Abram rented a small, sparsely furnished room at a boardinghouse about a half mile from what was known as the East Bottoms, where new immigrants, Jewish and non-Jewish, often lived in tenement-style apartment buildings. Then, after their marriage, the Kovals moved to a small house on Virginia Street, even farther from the ghetto-like settlements and four blocks from the off-white three-story wood-frame Victorian duplex they soon would share with one of Abram's sisters and her husband, also recent émigrés. This was the house at 619 Virginia Street, which the Kovals would one day own. It was where they would raise their three boys: Isaiah, born on July 22, 1912; George, December 25, 1913; and Gabriel, January 25, 1919.

For a while, the Kovals would be among the best examples of what the Galveston Movement recruiters had envisioned. From the Pale of Settlement to the house on Virginia Street, they were living what many thought was the American Dream.

CHAPTER TWO

"NOTHING BUT THE TRUTH"

George Koval grew up in a family who believed learning was the key to all dreams. His parents and aunts and uncles set the examples by reading, apprenticing, listening, and storytelling. Yiddish was often spoken at home, though both Ethel and Abram learned English and they instructed their sons to read English out loud, even to recite verses of poetry. They also encouraged the boys to attend plays and musicals, vaudeville shows and skits, as well as sporting events at Sioux City's Jewish Community Center, which was walking distance from their house and adjacent to a ballpark.

George may have learned the rules of baseball in the alley behind Virginia Street or on the often muddy playing field near the Jewish center. Sioux City baseball fans still talked about the 1891 "world series" when the Sioux City Huskers beat the Chicago Colts in a tie-breaking game. There was also the time when his high school principal let students leave early to attend a 2:30 p.m. exhibition game at the Sioux City Stock Yards Ball Park that featured the "home run twins" of the New York Yankees, Babe Ruth and Lou Gehrig. At the end of the seventh inning, Ruth called the game and then, with Gehrig, motioned the young fans to the outfield where the kids caught fly balls with their heroes.

In a setting of baseball, newsboys, skits, and plays, George's childhood appeared to be quite normal. But as he would later realize, as a Jew of Russian descent coming of age in America during the early decades of the twentieth century, there was a continuous reel of politics and prejudice running in the background of his life from the start.

He was three years old when the Russian revolutions of 1917 headlined the Sioux City newspapers. In March, there were the stories about the end of the imperial autocracy, the demise of Czar Nicholas II, and the bloody struggle to define a new Russia. "COMPLETE END TO THE REIGN OF ROMANOFF DYNASTY IN RUSSIA," read the banner headline in the *Sioux City Journal* on March 17. Though he likely wouldn't remember any details, he must have felt a jarring wave of high emotions in the Koval household, for the collapse of the empire meant the end of the Pale of Settlement. Then in early November—late October on the Russian calendar—in what would be known as the October Revolution, the radical socialist party, the Bolsheviks, seized power and began to usher in the world's first attempt to create a Communist system, which, under the leadership of Vladimir Lenin, pledged to criminalize anti-Semitism and to allow Jews full participation in society.

In America, however, only a few months later, George's parents appeared to be trapped once again in a tangle of distorted biases, for in the aftermath of the October Revolution, Russian Jews in America were quickly labeled as Bolsheviks—America's new enemies. The allegation was that the Jews in Russia, as activists for workers' rights and socialism, were the wicked plotters of the revolution and now must be conspiring to overthrow the American government. The alleged Jewish participation in the Bolshevik revolution, and the equating of Russian Jews with Bolsheviks, would spark a new generation of anti-Semitic hatred in America—targeting people like the Kovals, who were socialists and firm believers that capitalism could never eliminate poverty or oppression.

By the end of 1919, when George turned six, the post–World War I paranoia known as the Red Scare had begun to escalate. This new war was against Bolsheviks, socialists, Communists, trade unionists, and immigrants. And by the 1920s, hysteria, like a heavy fog, blocked any vision of the truth. America was off-balance and edgy, with the postrevolution suspicions taking hold and anti-Semitism as well as xenophobia invading America—not Bolshevism.

Part of the xenophobia took the form that Jacob Schiff and his colleagues in the Galveston Movement had fought so hard to prevent: immigration quotas that could significantly diminish Jewish entry into the US. In 1924, the restrictionists gained considerable ground with a law that radically reduced the arrival of people fleeing oppression from Eastern Europe and Russia. In Sioux City, it nearly halted the Jewish community's growth. And worse still, the Ku Klux Klan was on the rise in the Great Plains states.

Soon, as many as five million Americans were drawn to the racist, anti-Catholic, and anti-Semitic dogma of the Klan. Clad in white robes and peaked hoods, Klan members flaunted their supposed superiority over "other" Americans. And in the heart of the new "Ku Klux Klan belt" was Iowa, where the Klan was warning residents of Des Moines and Sioux City to beware of the Jewish conspiracy trying to control America.

By the summer of 1924, when George was ten years old, Iowa could estimate about forty thousand Klan members statewide in more than a hundred "klaverns," the Klan name for local branches. In Sioux City, where the number of new recruits was growing, fiery pine crosses could be spotted on the summits of hills where initiation ceremonies would take place shortly after dark. One Saturday that summer, Klansmen assembled on a highway at the east end of Sioux

City for a giant parade of floats, banners, and masked participants, who moved through the main streets of town, as they would do multiple times in 1924.

So it was that George's childhood introduced him to the ignorance and biases that would surround him for many years of his life. In the 1920s, American Jews were rejected for jobs at banks, public utilities, and at large local companies owned by non-Jews. Newspapers carried ads for jobs specifically stating "Christians Only Need Apply." An array of clubs denied their entry. And there was what historians would describe as "the greatest barrage of anti-Semitism in American history": a ninety-one-part series about "the Jewish menace" published in the *Dearborn Independent*, the personal weekly newspaper of industrialist Henry Ford.

During the nearly two-year run of the series, front-page stories exposed what the publication defined as "Jewish-inspired evil." The most toxic of these alleged "exposés" were reprinted by Ford in a four-volume set of books called *The International Jew*, which sold an estimated ten million copies in America and millions more in Europe, South America, and the Middle East. Each 225-page volume cost twenty-five cents and was translated into sixteen languages, including Arabic. Ford called it his "chronicle of neglected truth."

Quite the opposite: Ford had been swayed by a fabricated document called the *Protocols of the Learned Elders of Zion*, which had been used years before in Russia as propaganda to incite pogroms. Based largely on a mid-nineteenth-century French novel, it outlined a Jewish international plot to destroy all Aryan nations. In the tenth article of the *Independent*'s series, the *Protocols* book was introduced to readers.

To assure a vast readership for his paper, Ford had informed the company's dealers that if they wanted to continue selling Ford cars and trucks, they had to distribute his *Dearborn Independent* in their showrooms. The newspaper, they were boldly told, was a Ford product, just like the vehicles. Because of this requirement, nation-wide circulation of the publication soared. But some dealers refused to cooperate, among them the Barish brothers of Sioux City, Iowa.

The Barish brothers shut down their Ford showrooms and published a full-page ad in the *Sioux City News* announcing that they were sorry that Henry Ford viewed the paper as a Ford product. And if they were required to sell all Ford products in order to continue selling cars and trucks, then they would take their savings and launch a new enterprise. "We are Jewish and we are successful. And money is less important than loyalty, dignity and truth. Stop the lies and we'll return. But until you do, we will find another way to make an honest living," the brothers wrote.

By the late 1920s, Ford, as part of a settlement in a highly publicized lawsuit against the *Dearborn Independent*, issued a six-hundred-word retraction that was published in every major newspaper in the nation. By then the Klan had lost its credibility after the Grand Dragon of the Indiana Klan was charged with kidnapping, drugging, and raping a woman. But the lies perpetrated by Klansmen as well as the four-volume *The International Jew* lived on, sinking deeply into the American consciousness and affecting the lives of many Jews, including young George. The biases and uncertainties of his early years may have nurtured his special mix of charm and secrecy, teaching him caution. As his childhood friends would later say, he was popular and outgoing, but always intensely private about his personal life.

George attended Sioux City's Central High, from 1926 to 1929. Early in his senior year, he was appointed to the National Honor Society where members were chosen by the faculty for their superior leadership and character. He was the secretary of the Chrestomathian Literary Society, which claimed its ideals to be "uprightness, loyalty and democracy." And he was active in the theater, his most acclaimed role being in the senior class play, "Nothing But the Truth." In it, George played a skeptical, effusive young man who didn't believe it was possible for anyone to have the discipline or courage to tell the truth for a full day. "Honesty is not the safest policy," his character warned.

On June 13, 1929, fifteen-year-old George became the youngest person ever to graduate from the "castle on the hill," as Central High was known. He was an exemplary student. A local reporter wrote about him: "Interscholastic debater, Honor Society student and youngest member of the June graduating class are three honors held by George Koval, popular member of the June class at Central high school. . . . He played an important part in the interscholastic debate last fall, being judged one of the best speakers on the squad. . . . He is the son of Mr. and Mrs. Abe Koval."

Under his name beneath his picture in the school yearbook were his list of club memberships and honors, and a quote: "A mighty man is he." The line comes from the first stanza of Henry Wadsworth Longfellow's "The Village Blacksmith." In the poem, the blacksmith pounds the iron on the anvil, symbolizing a world in which people must shape their lives through their actions. The blacksmith is a metaphor for living a purposeful life, though there is also the fact that "koval" is the Ukrainian word for "blacksmith."

A few months after graduation, George moved to Iowa City, where he enrolled at the University of Iowa in the College of Engineering. Then, barely two months into his first semester, share prices on the New York Stock Exchange plummeted for five days in a row, causing the crash that launched a twelve-year economic depression affecting all Western industrialized nations. Soon, George began giving lectures on street corners in Iowa City about how the Great Depression would not affect the Soviet Union, as it was not connected to the world economy. He told his audiences that, in fact, the USSR was entering a period of unstoppable industrial expansion and that the socialist world was taking off, while capitalism appeared to be collapsing. For the believers of Soviet promises, this was a positive time, he said.

The following year, George was elected as Iowa's delegate to the Young Communist League (YCL) at the Iowa State Convention of the Communist Party. Held in Chicago in mid-August, the YCL convention was well attended. Detailed reports of the event were sent to two organizations: the Iowa Communist Party headquarters in Des Moines, and the office of the American Vigilant Intelligence Federation (AVI) in Chicago.

George likely knew little about the AVI, a private anti-Communist organization that compiled extensive reports on persons and groups considered subversive. Nor is it likely that he knew about the informer sent to observe the convention and take detailed notes. The AVI's information was made available to businesses, for an annual fee; and to any government intelligence agency or congressional committee requesting it, for free. The AVI was part of a network of privately funded intelligence sources established during the First World War and active in the Red Scare that followed. During the 1920s its volunteer informers sent monthly reports to the US Justice Department's Bureau of Investigation, forerunner of the FBI. Though this was unofficial intelligence activity, it had been acknowledged by the bureau's director J. Edgar Hoover in a memo he wrote to the Justice Department in 1925: "When information concerning Communist activities in the United States is voluntarily furnished to field offices of the Bureau, by parties not connected therewith, the information is forwarded to this office."

That was still true in 1930. But who might be spying for whom at the Chicago YCL convention, and where reports may have been filed, were matters of little concern to sixteen-year-old George Koval, an enthusiastic young Communist in America.

CHAPTER THREE

THE ARREST

One morning in late July 1931, massive, dark clouds blocked the rising sun in Sioux City as millions of flying grasshoppers swarmed northwest Iowa, hitting buildings and houses like hailstones, denuding trees and devouring everything in sight, from harnesses on stall doors to garments on clotheslines to the outlying fields of corn and alfalfa. More than a million acres of crops were decimated in a region already in the grip of an escalating crisis: endless drought. Farm foreclosures. Gangs of bandits terrorizing the countryside. And an unemployment rate at 15.9 percent, up from 8.7 percent the year before. This was the hard year of 1931.

The cause of what experts claimed to be the most devastating hopper attack in the history of the continent was the extreme dryness and heat in America's farm belt. The higher the temperature, the more grasshopper eggs were laid; the drier the days, the scarcer the fungus that would have killed the eggs. And the impact would add to the devastating new normal of the 1930s: more farm foreclosures. In Iowa more than a thousand farms were lost in 1931 alone because of unpaid taxes and mortgages, causing some farmers to take

direct action, such as blocking foreclosures by intimidating potential
buyers, or bringing the price of land and equipment down to a level
where better-off neighbors and friends could buy and return them
to the owners. Or joining radical rural groups. For Communists in
America, all of this spelled opportunity.

As a decade of desperation began to unfold, the casualties of a
capitalist system appeared to be spreading across a fragile America,
stirring an ideology opposed to capitalism. One way for Communists to capture the momentum was to organize an unemployment
movement on a national scale that would build organizations to
take regional and local action on behalf of the unemployed—such as
protests before city councils and state legislatures. What were called
Unemployed Councils were set up to fight foreclosures and evictions.
Members of these councils would organize marches to stand up for
the homeless and, if necessary, to confront local and regional officials.

By the summer of 1931, Abram Koval's work as a carpenter had
fallen off significantly. George quit his Iowa City jobs peeling pota-
toes at a local restaurant and working as a custodian, and returned
home for several months to bring in extra money for the family by
doing handyman work. He also volunteered for Iowa's Unemployed
Council, which the *Sioux City Journal* described in a front-page
article on September 4, 1931, as "a Communist group." This charac-
terization appeared in a story about the arrest of George Koval for
allegedly inciting a "raid" at the office of the county's overseer of
the poor to demand food and lodging for two middle-age homeless
women.

On the afternoon of September 3, George was arrested, accused
of "threatening violence in the office of the Overseer," and locked in
a county jail cell for twenty-four hours. The arrest card filed in the
Woodbury County Sheriff's Office in Sioux City read: "Address 617
[*sic*] Virginia Street, sex male, race white, age 17, height 6', weight 175
pounds, brown hair, brown eyes, medium complexion, marital status

single, occupation unemployed, nativity Sioux City, Iowa, criminal charge investigation, date of arrest September 3, 1931, committed by Sheriff Davenport, released September 4, 1931."

Upon his release, he agreed to tell the *Journal* reporter his side of what had happened. And out of that came another front pager bearing the headline "Freed Youth Tells Story: Asserts He Threatened No One in Office of Poor Overseer." George was quoted as saying that he and his group of fifty followers wanted only to obtain a stipend to support the women while they looked for work. "It was not until confronted by a mass delegation," George told the reporter, "that [the overseer] gave any promises of help."

For George, as well as his parents, the only country in the world in 1931 that was dedicated to ending poverty and oppression was the Soviet Union. To them, post-czarist Russia was the hope of mankind, the solution to problems of injustice and inequality. Fascism and anti-Semitism, while spreading elsewhere, were illegal in the Soviet system. And while few of the Kovals' fellow Sioux City residents likely agreed with them, their beliefs grew stronger by the day, bolstered by the tragedies that surrounded them and also by the influence of IKOR (Idishe Kolonizatsye Organizatsye in Rusland), the Association for Jewish Colonization in Russia.

This organization was formed in 1924, in part to enlighten Americans about the Soviet Union's new commitment to relocate Jews to an area known as the Jewish Autonomous Region, also called Birobidzhan, in the Soviet Far East, near the border with China. Its purpose was to attract as many Jews as possible to this new land of Jewish unity and to fight the Zionist call for Jews to move to Palestine. In America, it sought to inform the Jewish masses of the meaning of Jewish colonization in the USSR, and to raise funds to send American machinery and tools to the colonization sites. It also recruited regional leaders throughout the US, one of whom was Abram Koval, who headed the Sioux City chapter beginning in 1925.

IKOR's publications, in English and Yiddish, and its US confer-
ences and representatives tried to disseminate hope-filled ideas in
the bewildering tangle of America's current woes. Articles lauded
the Soviet government's efforts to provide Jews with a Soviet homeland and discussed the ways Jewish colonization would carry out
the Soviet Union's "determined struggle against bloody Fascism." In
one IKOR pamphlet entitled "Why the Jewish Masses Must Rally
to the Defense of the Soviet Union," the author positioned capitalist
America as a USSR enemy and stressed the importance of the victory
of the workers and peasants bringing "the Jewish masses liberty,
equality, and equal share in the Socialist construction, a new life of
creative effort and untold promise." Simply put: the revolution freed
you, now return to Russia and live in that freedom.

In the spring of 1929, IKOR had sent a commission of scientists,
sociologists, and marketing specialists, headed by the president of
Utah's Brigham Young University, to Birobidzhan to study its conditions and challenges. The commission's report of approval, published
in several publications in 1931 and 1932, described Birobidzhan as
an empire in the making with enough natural resources for "great
agricultural and industrial wealth. There seems to be no reason
why this region should not develop into a well-populated area and
its settlers into a prosperous people. The Commission states this
with a confidence which comes as a result of earnest open-minded
investigation."

The total number of IKOR followers in Sioux City by 1932 is
unknown but, by most accounts, all of them had been expelled
from the Jewish Community Center, including the Kovals, despite
being hardworking citizens of the town for more than twenty years.
While many Jews in Sioux City were striving to project an image
as true and loyal Americans, the Kovals chose to remain loyal to
their socialist beliefs, which they saw as the only way to end the
oppression of Jews. Their socialist principles set the Kovals apart

from their Jewish brethren in Sioux City. They must have felt more protected by the credos of IKOR than by the Americanization of their local Jewish community. A friend who had been the president of Sioux City's Jewish Community Center in the early 1930s later recalled, "Wasn't easy to be for [IKOR], not at all, but the Kovals were and they said so, often."

And so once again the question of whether or not to leave their home consumed Ethel and Abram, swayed by the crushing realities of the Great Depression and the growing perils of fascism in contrast with the promises of a better land in the USSR's Jewish Autonomous Region. This time the couple had three sons whose futures they must place above their own: Isaiah, known as a gifted artist with plans to enroll at the University of Iowa; Gabriel, with a record of straight A's at Woodrow Wilson Junior High; and George, once the star of Central High, now an outspoken Communist with an arrest record.

It is possible that the Kovals made their decision to leave a few weeks after George's arrest when, according to county records filed on September 19, 1931, they sold a piece of property they owned in downtown Sioux City. Several months later, in 1932, there was another real estate transaction, this one for their house on Virginia Street: a warranty deed that transferred the ownership of the house to one of Abram's sisters, Goldie Gurshtel, for one dollar. Then, on May 13, 1932, at the US District Court in Sioux City, Abram Koval applied for "an instant passport," which he received the very next day. Passport #499861 was a family passport, which meant that it was officially filed under Abram's name only. On the application, he wrote that he intended to depart from the United States on "approximately June 1, 1932" "for travel to England, Poland, and Russia for the purpose of employment." The identifying witness on the form was Goldie Gurshtel, and the applicant was described as follows: "49 [years old]; 5 feet 9 inches tall; dark brown hair, graying; brown eyes; occupation, carpenter, 619½ Virginia Street, Sioux City, Iowa."

Abram's decision to leave Russia in 1910 had come partly from his trust and confidence that America would be a better, kinder, freer place to live than czarist Russia. Now he was leaving that place of dreams, though still a believer in a better world—a belief that now ironically motivated his departure.

The shortest route between America and Birobidzhan in the Soviet Far East was from the Pacific coast, and in 1932 shipping companies such as the Japanese NYK Line were offering special rates in IKOR publication ads for passengers leaving from San Francisco to "Travel to Biro-Bidjan, USSR." Competing IKOR ads featured a North Atlantic course leaving from New York City, one on the "fast-service" Hamburg-America Line and another on the Cunard Line, which noted in its ad that it was endorsed by IKOR.

The Kovals, whose trip was arranged by Intourist, the official Soviet travel bureau, took the transatlantic run, leaving in the first week of June from New York's Pier 54 on the RMS *Majestic*, then the largest ship in the world. After a stop in Southampton, England, they arrived in Hamburg, and on the sixteenth of June they boarded another ship heading to a port on the Baltic Coast. From there they had planned to visit Ethel and Abram's hometown, Telekhany, but because Abram developed a severe rash, they were blocked from entering Poland, which was where Telekhany was now located. Their next stop would be Moscow, and by early July the Koval family would arrive at Birobidzhan, five thousand miles east of Moscow.

It had been twenty-two years since Abram Koval had stepped off the train from Galveston in Sioux City. And though he would never return to America, his son George would.

PART II

THE DECEPTION

The people who bind themselves to systems are those who are unable to encompass the whole truth and try to catch it by the tail; a system is like the tail of truth, but truth is like a lizard; it leaves its tail in your fingers and runs away knowing full well that it will grow a new one in a twinkling.

—Ivan Turgenev,
from an 1856 letter

CHAPTER FOUR

"THE BUSINESS TRIP"

*N*ailebn, or "New Life," was the title of IKOR's official publication. Issued monthly out of New York, in English and Yiddish, it featured essays, poetry, fiction, satire, photos, and letters—all covering life in the Jewish Autonomous Region of the Soviet Far East. Each month one page was devoted to letters sent by Birobidzhan settlers to relatives and friends in America. In the June 1935 issue, the page featured only one, quite lengthy, missive introduced to readers as follows: "A letter from a young man who was born and raised in Sioux City, Iowa, and migrated with his parents to Biro Bidjan [*sic*] in 1932. He is at present in Moscow, where he was sent from Biro Bidjan to study."

The letter was dated April 24, 1935, and began with an apology for not writing sooner. It then moved into high praise for Russia: "I want so much to give over to you what a wonderful country this is: what a great race are the 'BOLSHEVIKS.'" And more: "Sometimes when I am reading or only sitting and thinking about the Soviet Union a great feeling of love and pride fills my heart for the country. . . . When one reads Lenin and sees how clearly he thought, how well he knew capitalism, how well he saw all the possible factors in the fights; how he knew when to act and what to do, how he led, fought against the slightest deviation, it seems impossible that a person could be so great. . . . And now the victory is won, Comrades. Now no one doubts. All who dominated before, cannot find words of praise now. There is still much, much to do, Comrades. But the hardest is behind us. WE are going ahead with tremendous strides. . . . Our mills, factories, mines, every day give more and more production. We've Won!!!"

This was George Koval at age twenty-one. His letter went on to describe his chemistry studies at the D. Mendeleev Institute of Chemical Technology in Moscow and his lodging at "Student City" in one of the eight six-story apartment buildings housing five thousand students, three to a room. At the school, he wrote, the popular slogan was that a Soviet engineer "must be the best engineer in the world," and thus he studied day and night "almost without sleep." Because his grades were "excellent," the Soviet government was treating him well by paying for his education and even for a vacation in the Caucasus, in July after his last exam. Soon there would be the May Day celebrations in Moscow, he wrote: "If the weather will be good, one can be crazy from joy."

If his new life was as upbeat as his letter, such a spirit had come at a big price after his first years in the Soviet Union in Birobidzhan. For the gulf between the Spartan reality of life in Birobidzhan in the 1930s and the idealistic visions of its dedicated pioneers, such as the Kovals, was as expansive as Russia itself. The first group of colonists, 654 in total, had settled in 1928 followed by increasing numbers, with the highest being 14,000 or so arrivals in 1932. There was hope that there would be as many as 25,000 newcomers in 1933. But because of the long, severe winters; the inadequate, unheated housing, best described as "barracks"; the shoddy roads; and the sparse food, more settlers left that year than arrived. Tired of the hardships, they returned to their capitalist countries. The theory of "work first and whether or not you are fed and clothed is not important" did not inspire the many thousands who departed. Some even began to believe early rumors about Birobidzhan. These were stories they had discounted, adamantly, as anti-Soviet propaganda: like the one about the Soviet government recruiting thousands of Jews to live along the Russian-Manchurian border to help protect the USSR from a Japanese invasion and strengthen its foothold in the Far East.

In 1934, massive famines across the USSR forced substantial numbers of settlers to leave the Jewish Autonomous Region, where food was already scarce. And by the end of 1935, only 14,000 Jewish residents remained, some living on collective farms and some in the region's capital, the town of Birobidzhan. "Not every settler who has come to this province is constituted of pioneering stock," wrote New York journalist Paul Novick, after a two-month visit to the Jewish Autonomous Region in the summer of 1936. "In fact, during the first years after it was opened to immigration, many were unable to surmount the material hardships and so returned. After the province has a few more years of development, there will be a different story, but today there is no place [in Birobidzhan] for the seeker of a ready-made paradise."

When later interviewed about his view of the region's future, Novick, who lived in the Bronx and was the associate editor of *Freiheit*, a New York Jewish newspaper, said, "Housing and roads must be developed. You must bear in mind that many sections of the Jewish Autonomous Province are still dense forests and swamps and that the province is still practically unsettled." He talked about the Jewish settlers he had met, including the two families from the United States living on the collective called IKOR Kolkhoz—one being "the Kovals, from Sioux City, Iowa."

IKOR Kolkhoz was one of the best in the province, Novick said, and "Koval is one of the province's outstanding men, honored not only as a good farmer but also as a member of the plenum of his district soviet. Two of his sons are studying to be chemists at the Mendeleev Institute in Moscow. A third [Isaiah], on the farm with him, is one of the known outstanding Stakhanovites of all the Jewish collectives. Koval has a comfortable home, his own garden, grain from last year, a cow and other domestic animals."

The Stakhanovites were members of a movement to increase worker productivity, named after Aleksei Stakhanov, a coal miner who made the cover of *Time* magazine in December 1935 for reportedly setting a new record of mining 227 tons of coal during a single shift. In a 1935 article in the *Moscow News*, Isaiah was referred to as "Koval junior" and attention was drawn to his skills as an artist. When the young Stakhanovite wasn't driving a tractor or fishing he was busy sketching and drawing. "The entire commune takes pride in this budding artist," the article said.

In the summer of 1936, Abram Koval's sister and husband, Goldie and Harry Gurshtel, ventured from Sioux City to Moscow. Before taking the sixteen-day train trip from Moscow to the Soviet Far East to visit the Kovals at IKOR Kolkhoz, they spent ten days in the Soviet capital, where they often met with George, who told them stories about the first years in Birobidzhan. He had stayed for two years, he said, partly to help his father but also to improve his Russian language skills. He talked about his "great difficulty" in learning Russian, largely because he didn't roll his "r's" enough, he said, and his "ch" was without the softness of true Russian. He told them stories about the torturous period of the Kovals' early months there, saying that "only the fanatically dedicated," those with a strong utopian vision, could or would adjust to the hard work. It had been a push into the unknown, he said, especially living in one of two big barracks, each housing at least 150 people. Hunger, endless rain and mud, and the demands for constant work made it a time of challenges as he labored at the collective's lumber mill and then worked as a mechanic repairing farm machinery, and finally as a locksmith.

Mostly, though, George talked about his academic coursework at the highly respected Mendeleev Institute, named after Dmitri Mendeleev, the Russian chemist known for inventing the periodic classification of chemical elements. George was able to enroll partly because of a prize he won in Birobidzhan for his dedicated labor at the mill; he used the funds to travel to Moscow and, while there, he took an exam at the institute and was quickly accepted. The local newspaper in Birobidzhan told the story of his move to Moscow in an article with the headline "Achiever Koval." It was in the autumn of 1934 that he had enrolled to earn a chemistry degree, which he believed he could complete by 1938 or 1939.

George also introduced the Gurshtels to Lyudmila Ivanova, a classmate at Mendeleev who went by "Mila"—and was his fiancée. Mila was a slender young woman with short light brown hair, about five feet four inches tall and, like George, very studious and bright. Born on June 25, 1912, Mila was exactly eighteen months older than George. She was christened in 1919 at a Russian Orthodox Christian church and her family, the Ivanovs, had been part of the aristocracy of imperial Russia. Mila's grandfather was one of the founders of a candy factory in Moscow that was quite prosperous and best known for its chocolate, renowned, in fact, as a favored chocolate of the czar and his family. And her father had served in the czar's imperial army for nearly four years before joining the Red Army in 1918. Mila entered Mendeleev in 1934, the same year she was given full membership in Komsomol, the Communist Party for Youth.

In October 1936, Mila and George were married in a small ceremony at the Moscow home of a mutual friend from Mendeleev. Her mother and George's younger brother Gabriel, also a student at Mendeleev, attended. George then moved from his dormitory room to live with Mila, her mother, and eleven others in apartment #1 at #14 Bolshaia Ordynka, the spacious home once owned by Mila's grandfather. After the revolution, it had been divided into several communal dwellings. The goal for the newlyweds was to complete their course studies at Mendeleev by 1939, at which time George would apply for graduate school while Mila would secure a post, preferably at a chemical company in Moscow.

That was the plan. But for a man and a woman to start a life together in the Soviet Union during the autumn of 1936 must have been tantamount to birds taking flight in a storm. They married shortly after the beginning of what would be known as Stalin's Great Purge: the brutal years when millions of Russians died from executions or forced labor in the camps of Siberia. The exact number of deaths is unknown, though by most accounts, during Stalin's years in power, eighteen to twenty million people were sent to the camps, or gulags, and nearly six million of those men, women, and children died from overwork, starvation, exposure, or diseases. In the years 1937 and 1938 alone, executions were in the range of 950,000 to 1.2 million: among them, government officials, Red Army commanders, counterrevolutionaries, and Stalin's political opponents, some from the past and some from potential opposition groups. To Stalin, any criticism of his policies was a direct threat to his power.

Considering Stalin's propaganda campaign to block the truth from ordinary citizens, Mila and George were likely unaware of the extent of the purges. So focused were they on their studies and goals and so dedicated to defending their society, no matter what the cost might be, they may have shut their eyes to what was happening around them. But whatever their beliefs, the purges in the Red Army—11 out of 13 army commanders, 57 of the 85 corps commanders, 110 out of 195 division commanders, and countless numbers of spies—would have an immense impact on their lives, soon sweeping aside any personal plans with the force of an avalanche.

By 1938 the treachery of informing on neighbors had become part of Soviet culture: to avoid the gulag, to get a job, or even to acquire more space in a cramped apartment by alerting police to reasons for arresting fellow tenants. At some point in late 1938 or early 1939, George received a typewritten note from an anonymous sender telling him that someone in the couple's apartment had reported information to government authorities about them—details that could put them at risk. The note read: "My dear friend, Zhora [nickname for George]. In your apartment, there lives one who has many ties with police and investigative organs. With her talkative tongue, she tells people who you are, what you do and where you came from. You are former landowners and you own a typewriter. You frequently host evenings with unknown people. Be careful. Burn this letter."

The tenant with the "talkative tongue" was a woman who, along with her husband and three-year-old son, lived with George and the Ivanovs and all the others in apartment #1 at #14 Bolshaia Ordynka. She was pregnant and due in early 1939 and thus it was possible, even probable, that she had attacked Mila and George to instigate their arrest, thus improving the living space for her expanding family.

But for Mila and George the danger in drawing the attention of authorities went far beyond the ownership of a typewriter. There was the fact that Mila's father had not only been a landowning aristocrat, but also an officer in the czar's imperial army. Worse still, when he did enlist in the Red Army after the revolution he served in a high command position under Leon Trotsky, the Communist Party leader who was the founder and former head of the Red Army and whom Stalin had exiled from the Soviet Union in 1929. In Stalin's view, Trotsky was the archenemy of the Soviet state.

Also threatening was the fact that George and Mila had not reported to government authorities that a cousin of Mila's was married to an Austrian who had recently returned to his country of birth. Though moving to Austria was not a crime, the cousin did not report her husband's emigration and thus was arrested for her silence. And Mila and George did not send an account to the government about any part of the drama—not the defection of the cousin's husband or her arrest. For this, the newlyweds received government reprimands, which were filed in their records. This was not in their favor, nor was the fact that this cousin's parents had been expelled from Moscow in 1927 or 1928 for engaging in "gold speculation work," so said the records.

On their side, however, were a few positive factors that could please the Soviet government rather than set off an alarm, including the fact that George was an excellent candidate for Soviet intelligence work. He could fill one of the many vacancies caused by the recent Red Army purges. By 1939 nearly half of the Soviet Union's military intelligence corps had been liquidated or sent to Siberia, including spies in America who were forced to return to Russia.

Whether it was because of a Red Army hunt for replacement spies, or because of the fellow tenant's wicked alert to the secret police, by May 1939 officials in Red Army intelligence had to have known about George Koval: a young student of chemistry soon to graduate with high accolades from Russia's esteemed Mendeleev Institute, who could be quickly trained for espionage work in America. He was fluent in English, without a hint of a Russian accent, and deeply familiar with American culture. His unique array of skills could eliminate at least half of the training time for a spy. And so it was that by the late spring of 1939 a process had begun to bring George into Soviet military intelligence, the GRU (Glavnoe Razvedyvatelnoe Upravlenie, Main Intelligence Department).

In mid-May, a Mendeleev official asked George to attend a meeting in a building where the Central Committee of the Communist Party of the Soviet Union was known to work. As he would recall years later, "I was told to go to a room where there were a hundred people just like me who were graduates or soon to be graduates of Moscow schools of higher technological education. We filled out forms and we were interviewed and we did not understand why we were doing this. Someone did tell us the [GRU] was going to turn ordinary engineers into extraordinary spies."

On May 26, 1939, the director of Mendeleev and the secretary of the Communist Party Committee at Mendeleev received an "urgent" request from the GRU asking "to send characteristics regarding student George Koval." It was signed by the deputy chair of military intelligence. The school quickly put together a report, dated May 28, and sent it to the GRU the next day. It included such details as the Koval family's 1932 arrival from America, George's place of birth, and the following: "He is soon finishing Mendeleev in nonorganic materials. He is an excellent student. Conscientious. A member of Komsomol [the Young Communist organization]. He is developed politically. He participates actively in community work and he is the best professional organizer of his student class. He was chair of the trade union student bureau. Before the institute [Mendeleev] he worked at a collective farm as a shop engineer or project engineer. He has relatives abroad but no contact with them since 1937."

Soon thereafter George was instructed by a Mendeleev official to go to a particular address right away. As he would recall later, "Why and who was inviting me wasn't indicated and, of course, I didn't ask. I came to the address, the door opened when I pushed the button, and I was issued a pass to see a commissar. The interview seemed to be more of an interrogation than an interview. He had my 'case' on his table, a folder with my filled-out questionnaire and my biography. After listening to my story, he was terse. 'I think you'll do,' he said. That was all. Then we went down a long corridor and into another office where a man with diamond stickpins on his lapel was sitting. Must have been a head of intelligence boss. Meeting with him changed my life drastically." Though there was no direct reference to espionage in that conversation, nor any offer, the decision to recruit George into military intelligence was likely made that day. "I was twenty-six, energetic, and obedient. I was what they wanted," he would say later.

During the summer of 1939 George met with members of the GRU on several occasions, and he discussed the possible opportunity of committing to military intelligence with Mila. But there were still no papers signed or final deals made; he was repeatedly told to "stand by." He was also informed that if he agreed to proceed with what they were calling his "business trip" to America, at some point Mila would be sent to join him.

From George's point of view, working for Red Army intelligence was a way to protect Mila and her mother from retribution for allegations against them. In the past three years George had witnessed the consequences for people who did not appear to be loyal to Stalin. Joining the GRU and committing to "the business trip" would give his family a higher level of security. And if he were to die, Mila would be the recipient of a GRU widow's pension, which could secure her future.

Also, George had a patriotic loyalty to his country. He wanted to trust the Communist Party and be part of its quest. In the autobiography required for his GRU file, in October 1939, he wrote: "I believe that the [Communist] Party is wise and it will work out all untruthful accusations if you don't omit things and if you are honest." Translation: I will believe in you if you do the same for me.

But Mila saw it as a dangerous proposition. She didn't trust Soviet officials, and she did not want her husband to be so tightly bound to a system that she believed could suffocate or betray its followers at any moment. She assured George that she could make enough money for family support while he was in school. And because he would be a graduate student soon, he would not be drafted by the Red Army. From her perspective, there was simply no reason for him to do this. Many years later, George would say, "I knew that Mila did not want me to go, but I had to."

On June 29, George graduated from Mendeleev with honors, earning a degree in engineering with a specialty in the technology of nonorganic substances. By August 8, he had taken a job in

Moscow in the Laboratory of Rare Gases at the All-Union Electric Technical Institute, a post he planned to keep only until he could begin graduate school at Mendeleev. Throughout August he studied for the school entry exams, while Mila was assigned to work for the People's Commissariat of the Chemical Industry of the USSR in Moscow as a chemist at the main lab of the Stalin Chemical Factory.

By the end of August, there had not been any official requests or notices for George's placement in Red Army intelligence; and without an ironclad offer, there seemed to be no need for him to change his plans. Thus, on September 1, 1939, he submitted his graduate school application. But on that same day, at 4:45 a.m., 1.5 million German troops invaded Poland while German bombers hit Polish airfields and German warships attacked Polish naval forces in the Baltic Sea. Within two days, Britain, Australia, New Zealand, India, and France had declared war on Germany. And the week before Hitler's invasion, a nonaggression pact between Nazi Germany and the Soviet Union had been signed in Moscow by the foreign ministers representing each nation, respectively, Joachim von Ribbentrop and Vyacheslav Molotov.

After the Ribbentrop-Molotov Pact, the Nazi bombing of Poland, and the beginning of a second world war, the Soviet Union's laws for conscription changed. Until then, eighteen-to-twenty-year-olds were drafted with the exception of students, scientists, teachers in rural areas, and migrants, including the communal dwellers in Birobidzhan. Male students were required to enroll in classes for military training, which George had already completed at Mendeleev. His plan had been to fulfill his military duty to the USSR by using those class credits to serve in the reserve corps while he attended graduate school. That would have worked, until September 1. Now there was no escape from war.

Adding to the personal suspense in the life of the young couple, George's acceptance notice to graduate school arrived. Classes would begin in early November. Around the same time, he received an order from the Red Army to fill out a lengthy form, including a detailed biography. Between then and his induction date, on October 25, he was officially informed that he would be working for the GRU, something he surely expected would happen. His low military rank, as a private, was chosen to allow him to easily disappear from Moscow without notice and to relocate for his new schooling, as a Soviet spy. Exactly where he was trained is unknown, though there was a school built "in the woods outside of Moscow" in the 1930s that was known to employ veteran spies as teachers for new Soviet intelligence recruits.

His assigned mission in America for Soviet military intelligence was to investigate the latest research in chemical weapons at American laboratories. He was told "to recruit sources of information about the chemistry used in the military, especially in the area of new types of poisonous substances, about bacteriological weapons in possession of the US Army, and to memorize a list of American labs, companies, and factories connected to mass production of chemical weapons." His approved code name was "Delmar"—referred in some documents as "Agent D." Why Delmar? In later years, there would be many theories. But if George had chosen it himself, the reason could have been a popular novelist from his teen years, Viña Delmar, whose parents had been renowned vaudeville players in the Yiddish theater—and thus was likely known in the Sioux City Yiddish community of George's youth.

By December 1939 his training had begun. It ended by late summer 1940. Before leaving the USSR, George was informed that his "business trip" in America would last no more than two years and, as he was told earlier, Mila would be sent to join him. But in a time of war there was no guarantee that such pledges could be kept, as they both must have known. In September, Mila would receive a written message about her husband being on a military train passing through Moscow at a particular time the following day. She went to the station, waited for the train, and boarded it upon arrival. "They just saw each other and visited for a short while," a friend later said. "It was her last chance to be with him." She couldn't have known that it would be eight years before they would meet again.

George Koval's first ocean voyage had been in 1932 from America's heartland to the Soviet Far East. There was no record of his departure on the ship out of New York because the Koval family passport was registered in his father's name. Now he was returning to America, with a false passport, and so there would be no US Customs record of George Koval from Iowa either leaving, entering, or reentering America. It was as if nothing had changed. But that wasn't true, for in 1932 George had been a passionate idealist infatuated with Communism and now he was a trained military intelligence officer locked into an inescapable commitment to the Soviet Union to betray America.

CHAPTER FIVE

UNDERCOVER IN THE BRONX

One September night in 1940, somewhere in the East China Sea, mountainous waves were tossing a small cargo ship on which George Koval was en route from Vladivostok, a port in the far southeast corner of the Soviet Union, to San Francisco. "We almost got into the center of a cyclone," he wrote in a letter to Mila. "The rocking was huge. And all books and furniture were falling on us as we fell off our beds." Crossing 4,554 nautical miles, the trip would take more than three weeks, adding to Koval's six-day, 5,772-mile train journey from Moscow to Vladivostok.

During the calm days "when the winds were a total delight," Koval wrote that he played chess or dominoes with the ship's captain and read stories to the captain's nine-year-old daughter, who called him "Uncle Grisha." Bonding with the captain's family on such a long passage would prove essential when the ship docked in America. Though he carried a fake passport, Koval planned to help unload the cargo and then slip away, possibly to a meeting place in the San Francisco Bay area where he would be given whatever was needed for his continuing travels.

Because it was a cargo ship, the customs patrol didn't process entry papers for crew members returning in a quick turnaround to Vladivostok. Still, US officials conducted a seemingly thorough inspection of the ship, during which Koval hid in a storage bench in the captain's quarters. Sitting on top were the captain, his wife, and his daughter. The English-speaking inspectors asked to see identification documents for the captain and his family, a process that apparently took longer than the little girl could tolerate. And so she looked up at her mother and asked, in Russian: "Will Uncle Grisha have to stay under the couch much longer?" The mother smiled, said nothing, and continued to hold her daughter's hand while her husband focused on the officials. The calm response of the mother and father, plus the fact that the inspectors likely knew little, if any, Russian or were simply paying no attention to a little girl's exchange with her mother, saved the day for the Soviet spy. Soon Koval was boarding a train to New York City.

For at least a month after his arrival, he used a false name and lived in an apartment on Fort Washington Avenue in northern Manhattan. Then on January 2, 1941, he filed his US selective service registration, using his real name, thus establishing that Iowa's George Koval was now a resident of New York City. The day before, he had moved to an apartment on Cannon Place, a quiet street in Kingsbridge Heights in the Bronx. This was a neighborhood of narrow curvy streets and steep inclines so high that sometimes concrete stairways with dozens of steps linked a street at the base to another at the top. A large building set into a hill with stairs along one side could have two different addresses, one for the street at the bottom and another for the street around the corner at the top—which was true of Koval's new home.

Shortly after he settled into the Cannon Place apartment, he moved to an address on Giles Place, which happened to be in the same building, part of a complex called the Sholem Aleichem

Houses. His residence was in one of the fifteen five-story apartment buildings built in 1927 with subsidies from members of the Workmen's Circle. Started by East European Yiddish-speaking Jews, this was the same association whose western division Abram Koval had directed during George's childhood. Driven by utopian collective visions, the New York members wanted to move out of the lamentable ghetto life of the Lower East Side, and thus raised the money to build cooperative housing in the Bronx. It was a community devoted to preserving Yiddish literature, art, music, and theater—and specifically dedicated to the renowned Yiddish writer and Bronx resident Sholem Aleichem.

For Koval to be placed in such a Yiddish oasis must have cushioned the initial jolt of his return to America to a new life. He grew up in a family that embraced Yiddish culture. In high school, he had acted in a play written by Sholem Aleichem. And his Giles Place landlady, Tillie Silver, not only lived in the same building but also had the same surname as one of his Sioux City uncles—though no relation. Above all, she was connected to the network of contacts now controlling the twists and turns of Koval's double life as a spy. Tillie's brother, Benjamin Loseff, a jeweler in lower Manhattan, sometimes conducted business with Benjamin William Lassen, the GRU officer overseeing Koval's espionage operations—his handler. Loseff, whose store opened on Nassau Street in late 1938, was one of the hidden sources of funds for Lassen, whose network of spies had begun to operate at around the same time. The Loseffs were also cousins of Lassen's wife.

Koval would never be exposed to the many members of Lassen's intricate setup of agents, couriers, bankers, retailers, travel agents, scientists, professors, diplomats, and relatives. Trained to follow strict rules, Koval didn't associate with other spies—except for his handler. And Lassen's connections in the Soviet espionage realm pointed to a strong possibility that Koval may have been operating in a cell structure modeled after underground revolutionary groups in czarist Russia. This meant, as one historian has noted, that it had an "agent group leader" and that "each member knew little or nothing about his network, possibly only the leader. Only the leader knew all the members."

Though he likely never met the other Soviet spies living in the Bronx, Koval must have known that Lassen lived on Creston Avenue, not far from the Giles Place/Cannon Place building, and that Tillie Silver was somehow tied to Lassen—a situation that bolstered Koval's security as well as the efficiency of his work in this new secretive life in which nothing was what it appeared to be. Not the landlady. Not the cover shops. Nor the handler, whose original surname was Lassoff, not Lassen, and whose life was a mystery to many.

By the time Koval had moved to the Bronx, Lassen's main cover was Raven Electric Co., an electrical supply shop on West Twenty-Third Street, half a block west of Broadway. According to former Raven employees, their boss spent a good deal of time collecting cash that seemed to have nothing to do with Raven's daily trade. Besides the Nassau Street jeweler, there was an export business on Madison Avenue and there were at least seven banks in Manhattan where Lassen held accounts and visited regularly. Lassen's compensation from Moscow was paid through one of them, the Broadway Savings Bank, at 5 Park Place.

With his rimless glasses and expressionless face, Lassen, a man of medium height, about five feet seven, seemed quite ordinary. His thin brown hair showed specks of gray at an early age, and by the time Koval met him the graying around the temples was a solid feature, as was the diamond stickpin he always wore on his tie or lapel. What made him blend into a gathering of strangers and yet stand out among acquaintances was the fact that he rarely smiled. By most accounts, he exuded an aura of skepticism and caution. A former colleague would describe Lassen as "very private and discreet," a man with whom few wanted to spend time "due to some unknown fear of him. Maybe it was just his silence. He looked hard at people. Said so little."

Lassen, as Lassoff, was born on April 6, 1882, in a Ukrainian town on the outskirts of Kiev, possibly in the same area where Sholem Aleichem had written about the brutal pogroms in October 1905. It was shortly after that, very early in 1906, when Lassoff came to America to live with relatives in Brooklyn, New York. His Jewish parents could have been among the casualties of the czarist mobs that only three months before had proclaimed in Kiev "all Russia's troubles stem from the Jews and socialists."

Within the next few years, Lassoff enrolled at Ohio Northern University to study electrical engineering. There he became a member of the Society of Engineers and the Adelphian Literary Society, as well as an organizer launching the school's 1912 entry into the American Institute of Electrical Engineers, the national organization for the electrical profession. Clearly a club enthusiast, Lassoff was also on the school's executive committee for organizing the Socialist Study Club, a chapter of the national Inter-Collegiate Socialist Society. In March 1912, an Ohio newspaper announced the new "flourishing chapter" and its goal to "make an intelligent study of socialism pro and con." The plans of its student leaders, including "B. Lassoff," were to bring in renowned speakers from nationwide organizations. That spring, Lassoff graduated from ONU, soon to enroll at the Massachusetts Institute of Technology for a master's degree in electrical engineering.

Living in Boston during his MIT coursework, Lassoff met Gertrude Kaufman, whom he tried to persuade to move with him to Russia after the 1917 October Revolution. Though Gertrude was born in Russia too, in 1891, the revolution did not inspire her to return. She had become a US citizen in 1914 and was intent on studying in America to become a doctor, as one of her brothers had successfully done. Though she refused to leave America, she did agree to move to Brooklyn after their September 1918 marriage. At that time, Lassoff was working for the firm Stone & Webster, best known then for operating streetcar systems in cities across the US. But soon the Lassoffs would move to Oakland Place in the Bronx, and he would start a new job as a "junior electrical engineer" for New York City's Public Service Commission district.

By 1920, Lassoff was not only an active member of the American Institute of Electrical Engineers, but he had also joined the Communist Party of the USA (CPUSA). Contacts in one or both organizations must have opened the door to his next job, which was a project to expand the electrification of the vast nation of Russia. This meant designing a network of electrical lines for industry transportation. To do that required analyzing waterpower sources, selecting sites for building electric stations and transmission lines, and evaluating the prospective consumption of electricity in various locations. The information Lassoff collected was sent to the State Committee of Electrification of Russia in Moscow and, in the US, to Charles P. Steinmetz, General Electric's star engineer, renowned for his development of alternating electric current.

Steinmetz, a devout socialist who believed in the potential progress instigated by the Russian Revolution, was impressed with the work coming out of the Russia electrification project. In late 1922, he published an article about it in *Electrical World* magazine. Whether or not Steinmetz and Lassoff ever met isn't known, but Lassoff's work on the project gained recognition at GE through Steinmetz. And soon he was given a consulting job to introduce American-made electric machinery to Russia, mainly for GE. By early 1924, he won the tug-of-war with Gertrude over Russia, for the Lassoffs moved to Moscow.

Perhaps the rigid immigration laws laid out that year or the frequent news stories about the Ku Klux Klan persuaded Gertrude that living in Russia might be easier for a Jewish couple than staying in America, where anti-Semitism seemed to be spreading. For the next three years, Gertrude studied medicine in Moscow, while her husband continued to work as a scout for GE. During the same time, he was hired as an expert on hydroelectric power stations for a Russian government trust. And what came out of all that experience was an opportunity in 1927 for Lassoff to be appointed to a managerial position at ARCOS Ltd., the All-Russian Co-operative Society in London.

ARCOS was the purchasing and selling agent of the Soviet trade delegation in England, and Lassoff was put in charge of its electrical manufacturing department. As such, he provided British companies with information about trade prospects in the Soviet Union and he started a new branch of work: supplying Soviet industries with technical details about British products. The Lassoffs would live in London for two years, until Benjamin was sent to New York in 1929 to be a Soviet buyer at the ARCOS branch in America. The branch was known as Amtorg, short for Amerikanskaya Torgovlya (American Trade).

In 1929, Amtorg, located at 261 Fifth Avenue, was a quasi-embassy for the Soviet Union, which had not yet been recognized as a nation by the US. As such, it served as the USSR's single purchaser in America. Companies wanting to do business with the Soviet Union negotiated their contracts through Amtorg, effectively establishing their own diplomatic relations, though warned by the State Department that they were operating "at their own risk." General Electric, Ford, International Harvester, DuPont, and more than a hundred other American companies, seeking to sell products to Russia, shared massive amounts of detailed industrial information with Amtorg's representatives. What the Americans didn't know was that by the late 1920s, Amtorg's employee list included members of Red Army intelligence who were using Amtorg as a cover. And, by some accounts, this was the start of the phrase "going on a business trip" as a euphemism for the work of Soviet spies coming to America.

These were fast-moving times for the Lassoffs. In 1929 Benjamin was an active member of the Central Committee of the Communist Party, and evidence suggests he was one of the framers of an underground operation tying the CPUSA to Soviet intelligence agents. That was the year too that Gertrude and Benjamin had their first and only child, Seymour. Then, on September 7, 1931, in Bronx County, New York, Benjamin William Lassoff legally changed his surname to Lassen, as did Seymour and Gertrude. Shortly before establishing this new identity, Lassoff dropped out of the Communist Party. Gertrude had never joined; and the new Benjamin William Lassen would never be a member, though his loyalties never changed with his name.

About six months after the name change, the Lassens began to tell their friends in America that soon Benjamin would be operating an import-export leather business, largely focused on markets abroad, and that the family would be spending a good deal of time away from the US. The truth was they were moving to Warsaw, and soon thereafter Benjamin was recruited into Red Army intelligence—a GRU spy with the code name "Faraday," after the renowned nineteenth-century British electrical pioneer, Michael Faraday. At that time, on his American passport, Lassen listed his legal address as 9 Commodore Road in Worcester, Massachusetts, the home of Gertrude's brother, a highly respected doctor. And while living in Warsaw, he continued to use the brother's address to renew his American passport twice, for trips to various European nations and to England, in 1934 and 1936.

Lassen must have been gold to the GRU. He was an experienced electrical engineer with strong ties to American companies, including GE, and he worked with Amtorg. He was fluent in Russian, English, French, German, Polish, and Ukrainian. And he was an American citizen. On his prized American passport, he even had an address in an upscale neighborhood near Boston, Massachusetts. And what all of that meant was that Lassen could easily travel anywhere the GRU wanted him to go—to recruit, to infiltrate, to organize, to gather information.

In the 1930s, establishing a legal address while living other places seemed to be in vogue among his peers. When the Lassens returned to America in 1937, they lived in a Washington Heights apartment, as he began his GRU assignment in the "Fourth Section of Red Army Military Intelligence, under cover at Amtorg." Then, by the time he was establishing a network as "Chief Illegal Resident Agent of the 4th Section," they had moved to Creston Avenue in the Bronx—all the time using Gertrude's brother's Commodore Road address.

What is known about Lassen's work for the GRU in America is that he was ordered to organize networks and to establish places in New York City—"conspiratorial headquarters" as one report described them—where he could safely meet with network members and conduct sessions with newly arriving spies. His main work, however, was to operate the networks, to be "a cell leader" who transmitted funds from Russian sources to those working for Soviet intelligence and who assigned spies to jobs at cover shops in various cities nationwide, though mostly in New York.

For example, there was the Midland Export Corporation, which had opened on Madison Avenue between Forty-Third and Forty-Fourth Streets in 1939. It was owned by Michael W. Burd. Russian-born Burd and Lassen had known each other since the 1920s when both were members of the CPUSA. Though Lassen dropped his party membership in the early 1930s, Burd continued his own until 1940, around the time that Midland had become a busy shop. It was there that Burd, as he would later disclose, received money "from Russian sources" and sent it to Soviet agents in Latin America and Mexico. Burd also ran the American Merchandising Co., which would share the 347 Madison Avenue address with Midland for a number of years before changing its address to 20 West Twenty-Third Street, home to Raven Electric.

A few months after Burd opened his shop, Lassen incorporated Raven Electric, on January 17, 1940. For the first year of operation, it was located on Broadway near the corner of Twenty-Eighth Street in a small two-story commercial rental. Then by early 1941, when Koval would begin his work at Raven as a so-called store clerk, Lassen had moved the business to a five-story building at 20 West Twenty-Third, two blocks from an office Lassen used on West Twenty-Fifth Street, and half a block from the intersection of Fifth Avenue and Broadway at Twenty-Third Street. Conveniently, at that very junction, only five minutes from the front door of Raven Electric, was Madison Square Park where Lassen was known to make occasional midday visits. One building overlooking the park was the famed triangular structure known as the Flatiron Building, which housed, on its seventh floor, World Tourists, Inc. By some accounts, Lassen's first "conspiratorial headquarters" was located on the seventh story of the Flatiron Building.

World Tourists opened in 1927, appearing to be a business under contract with Intourist, which was the official Soviet travel bureau. It made its money from commissions for selling Intourist services, which included travel to and from, and within, the Soviet Union, plus lodging and some assistance with customs requirements, such as appropriate documentation for passports. Most, if not all, of the American businessmen Amtorg encouraged to visit the Soviet Union used World Tourists—and so did the stream of Soviet tradesmen coming to America to tour US industry. Thus, the fits and starts of American-Russian commerce largely depended on World Tourists, as did Communist Party members and Soviet intelligence agents needing false passports for their "business trips" to the US.

American passports were hugely treasured because of their credibility with most international border authorities. And, at that time, they were as easy to fabricate as slipping on a costume mask. The staff at World Tourists rarely, if ever, questioned the facts on documents given to them by CPUSA travelers or by Soviet spies. And yet some facts were clearly fiction, having been derived from the death records of children in the genealogical section of the New York Public Library. With a list of such birth dates, certificates could easily be obtained and false witnesses would swear to passport officials that they knew the person using the name of the dead child. Unknowingly, customs workers approved hundreds of such false passports in the 1930s.

To be sure, World Tourists and its fraudulent passport expertise moved forward smoothly for a number of years, eased in part by the atmosphere surrounding it. During the 1930s, Soviet espionage in the US expanded considerably, with little effort to detect or expose it. The FBI had barely three hundred agents in 1933, largely untrained in counterintelligence activities. Criminal investigations were their expertise and their domestic security focus was on fascist paramilitary groups such as the Silver Legion of America, known as the Silver Shirts, an underground organization based in North Carolina and modeled after Hitler's Brownshirts. As the decade unfolded, the threats of German, Japanese, and Italian espionage would claim higher priorities than any concerns about potential invasive Soviet spies. As one scholar wrote about the mid-1930s, "the Justice Department had little interest in prosecuting Soviet espionage, and the popular press paid scant attention."

Though anti-Communism would never vanish in America, it had diminished somewhat by 1933 when the US recognized the Union of Soviet Socialist Republics as a nation with diplomatic rights. Soon Soviet embassies and consulates would open throughout the US. And logically as the fear of Communism dwindled in the 1930s, Soviet power grew. More Americans than ever before surmised that what was happening in the Soviet Union—effectively an experiment in collectivism, socialism, and communalism—could be the wave of the future. Conditions in Depression-ravaged 1930s America swayed people away from capitalism and into the grip of Communist ideology, making the decade the glory years for membership in the Communist Party—swelling to sixty-six thousand at its apex in January 1939.

Most party members in America were not spies. And those who weren't sometimes facilitated the work of those who were by serving as couriers or intermediaries in underground networks. With the CPUSA serving as an espionage device as well as a political party, Soviet intelligence was not alone in its work in America. The secret underground "was not, in fact, a single apparatus, but several networks," as one historian wrote. Some networks were focused on American politics to bend DC bureaucrats in favor of the interests of the Soviet Union. Others were ordered to gather military and industrial secrets, such as chemical weapons research. From each of those focal points, networks were linked to Soviet intelligence through conduits such as Lassen and Jacob Golos, a cofounder of the CPUSA. Golos, who was known for his spy recruiting skills, was a principal stockholder of World Tourists. Its undercover owner was the CPUSA.

Lassen and Golos had known each other since the 1919 launch of the CPUSA, and they both had worked at Amtorg. The two spies were known to meet occasionally at the World Tourists office. To be sure, by one account, Lassen "had a habit of dropping by Golos's office," on the seventh floor of the Flatiron Building.

In late 1938, Lassen had one of his meetings with Golos, which may have been among their last encounters at World Tourists. For soon after Nazi Germany and the Soviet Union signed their alliance in August 1939, the US government widened its list of potential threats of espionage to include businesses and activities tied to the Soviet Union, Hitler's new ally. This helped to direct suspicion straight to the CPUSA. In October, its head, Earl Browder, was arrested for the fraudulent use of passports. A string of indictments and charges against Golos and World Tourists followed. In early 1940 Golos was fined $500 and given a suspended jail sentence after pleading guilty to failing to register as the agent of a foreign power, the USSR.

Though World Tourists would continue to operate as a travel agency, the seventh floor of the Flatiron building became too hot to remain a gathering place for spies. Thus, Golos and the CPUSA opened a new cover business called the U.S. Service and Shipping Corp. at 212 Fifth Avenue—a convenient location for all involved. The building was situated at the corner of Fifth and West Twenty-Sixth Street, a few steps from one of Lassen's favorite spots, Madison Square Park, and on the same block as Amtorg. And, in the spy business, where coincidences rarely exist, early 1940 was when Lassen established Raven Electric nearby. Lassen would use the fourth floor of the Raven building for nighttime meetings, possibly establishing a new location for his assigned "conspiratorial headquarters." There would be no more accounts of Lassen meeting at World Tourists after 1940.

During the months of setting up his new business, Lassen contacted colleagues in the passport business in San Francisco—a move that could have included arrangements for Koval's discreet new identity during his initial months back in the US, though there is no proof of that. Evidence does show, however, that in late 1940, shortly after Koval's arrival, Lassen posted an ad in a New York newspaper offering his services and those of a "colleague" as machine designers for weapons production. That "colleague" could easily have been Koval, still using his false identity. A job broker who answered the ad and interviewed both Lassen and the "colleague" said later that the two men were quite open about their passion for "weapons design work and their belief that the best companies for them would be the ones with government contracts." But the broker didn't ask them back. "Their experience did not seem deep enough," he later said.

Koval apparently never found a job using his false name. Soon after re-establishing his identity as George Koval on his draft registration and beginning his job at Raven Electric, he enrolled in the University Extension program at Columbia University for coursework in chemistry. This was a decision that could have been solely based on Koval's passion for science, especially chemistry. After all, he was a graduate of a world-renowned scientific institute, with honors and a degree in chemical engineering, after which he had worked for several months at the All-Union Electric Technical Institute's Laboratory of Rare Gases in Moscow.

Whenever Koval faced the challenges of transitions, he went back to school. Perhaps it was a distraction from the risks and insecurities of an edgy life. For him, school could have been a return to the familiar in the midst of the unknown. He did it after moving with his family to the Soviet Union; and now after his arrival in the Bronx, he was taking classes again—something he would do two more times while in America.

However, this time, considering the reasons for his "business trip," the Columbia enrollment might have been his handler's idea. For this was a move that appeared to be less about the lure of taking classes, especially at an Ivy League school, and more about the school's illustrious 1941 faculty in the departments of physics and chemistry.

CHAPTER SIX

GENERAL CHEMISTRY

Columbia's General Chemistry classes in its University Extension program for adult education met from 6:45 to 9:50 p.m. on Tuesdays and Fridays in Havemeyer Hall. Havemeyer was near other science buildings, such as Pupin Hall, home to the Physics Department. Each week, the class began with a lecture in the grand multilevel theater on the third floor, followed by lab work on the fifth floor. It was team taught, and one of the professors happened to hold a reserve commission in the US War Department's Chemical Warfare Service division—possible inspiration for Koval not only to listen to lectures but also to meet the instructors and get to know as many as he could. By the time of Koval's enrollment in 1941, Columbia had become a magnet for some of the most highly regarded physicists and chemists in the world—some destined to play stellar roles in the upcoming production of the first atomic bomb.

In January 1939, Enrico Fermi, the 1938 Nobel Prize winner in Physics, and his wife fled fascist Italy and came to America where he joined Columbia's Department of Physics faculty. Later that month, on January 25, at the Men's Faculty Club, on campus, Fermi dined with a colleague, associate professor John Dunning, at which time they discussed recent experiments made by German physicists in Berlin in late 1938 based on a discovery by an Austrian scientist, Lise Meitner: when a uranium atom is bombarded by neutrons, it splits, releasing energy and producing more neutrons in a process called "fission." That night in the basement of Pupin Hall, Dunning, who had already published two dozen papers about neutrons, gathered with four other professors—Herbert Anderson, Eugene Booth, G. Norris Glasoe, and Francis Slack—to conduct the first experiment in the US to measure the energy released from fission.

Housed at Pupin was a machine called a cyclotron, an atom smasher, which Dunning and his adept team had built in 1936 in the Pupin basement, five years after the cyclotron was invented by Ernest O. Lawrence at the University of California at Berkeley. Using the Columbia cyclotron, on that January night in 1939, Dunning and his colleagues bombarded a thin plate covered with uranium oxide. If, during the fission process, the uranium emitted more neutrons than it absorbed, then green lines would appear on a screen, indicating the release of energy. "Enormous kicks," Dunning called the many green lines that did indeed appear.

There would be more experiments, more discoveries, and more geniuses at Pupin Hall that year, all monumental in their future significance. Fermi and a colleague would confirm that "each fission produced an average of two neutrons." This proved that the released neutrons could repeat the performance, which would cause a chain reaction. As Fermi would later write, "If fission released enough neutrons, a chain reaction was nearly unstoppable; too few, and it was unstartable." This process required a massive amount of uranium-235, which was the refined form of uranium ore, known as enriched uranium. U-235 had to be separated from the more abundant uranium-238. Only 1 percent of natural uranium consists of U-235. One method for separating the U-235 was called gaseous diffusion, which became the main focus of Professor Dunning's research, beginning in 1939.

Fermi and Dunning were at the forefront of atomic physics, as were their colleagues, including Eugene Wigner, known for introducing quantum mechanics into the US; Budapest-born American physicist Edward Teller; Eugene Booth, an expert in gaseous diffusion research; and Leo Szilard, a Hungarian American physicist. Since the early 1930s Szilard had envisioned finding an element that when split by neutrons would emit two nuclei, keeping one, releasing the other and in a large mass initiating and sustaining a chain reaction. Soon he would collaborate with Fermi on the design for a machine to do exactly that—a nuclear reactor.

Such dedicated research depended on a use for the massive quantities of energy that would be generated. One pound of U-235 contains as much energy as 15 tons of TNT. In January 1939, on the morning after the release of the "enormous kicks," Dunning sat in his Pupin Hall office and wrote in his notebook, "Believe we have observed a new phenomenon of far-reaching consequence."

In March that year, on the same day that Hitler annexed Czechoslovakia, George Pegram, the chair of Columbia's Department of Physics and the dean of Graduate Faculties, called the assistant secretary of the navy to arrange for Fermi to meet with him and to hand-deliver a letter from Pegram. The letter informed the US government about the significance of the pioneer experiments at Columbia. Pegram wrote that a uranium chain reaction would "liberate a million times as much energy per pound as any known explosive."

But this information aroused little interest in Washington. About three months later, in July, Szilard, Teller, and Wigner, perhaps motivated by such apparent indifference, visited Albert Einstein at his Long Island cottage to ask him if he would be willing to sign a letter written by Szilard, to President Roosevelt about the recent research in atomic energy at Columbia, about its potential, both good and bad, and about the unnerving possibility of such a powerful explosive being developed in Germany. Einstein, who was then at the Institute for Advanced Study, signed the letter on August 2. It read: "Some recent work by E. Fermi and L. Szilard, which has been communicated to me in manuscript, leads me to expect that the element uranium may be turned into a new and important source of energy in the immediate future. Certain aspects of the situation which has arisen seem to call for watchfulness and, if necessary, quick action on the part of the Administration. . . . In view of the situation you may think it desirable to have more permanent contact maintained between the Administration and the group of physicists working on chain reactions in America."

President Roosevelt received the letter on October 11, and after reading it he reportedly said, "This requires action." Ten days later the newly formed Advisory Committee on Uranium met for the first time. In 1940, it would become part of the government's National Defense Research Committee, whose members included Dean Pegram as well as the chair of Columbia's Chemistry Department, Harold Urey. Soon, out of the US Department of the Navy's budget, the federal government offered the first-ever funding for atomic energy research: $6,000 to Columbia University. This meant that the unofficial beginning of the project to build an atomic bomb had occurred at Columbia—a project soon to evolve into the US Army Corps of Engineers's Manhattan Engineering District, first located at 270 Broadway in Manhattan and later known as the Manhattan Project.

In April 1940, Columbia research into the vast potential power of enriched uranium was the focus of an article in *Physical Review*, the official publication for American physicists, highly respected by scientists worldwide. It caught the eye of a watchful reporter at the *New York Times* who, on page 1 of the newspaper's May 5 edition, delivered the news and its significance in laymen's language, with the headline "Vast Power Source in Atomic Energy Opened by Science." The article began: "A natural substance found abundantly in many parts of the earth, now separated for the first time in pure form, has been found in pioneer experiments at the Physics Department of Columbia University to be capable of yielding such energy that one pound of it is equal in power output to 5,000,000 pounds of coal or 3,000,000 pounds of gasoline, it became known yesterday."

The article explained the challenge of extracting purified uranium—U-235—from the U-238 isotope and disclosed that physicists at Columbia had done this by using the university's cyclotron. The *Times* also referred to *Physical Review* several times, including a mention of the work of scientists at the research labs of General Electric Company, who were sharing their findings with Columbia. The GE scientists had even set up a machine to separate "a relatively large sample of U235, which they sent to the Columbia physicists for experimental tests."

The word was out. This was big news. Even the popular magazine *Collier's* was telling America's general readers about the latest findings in physics. The *Times* described this event as the ushering in of "the long dreamed of age of atomic power, and therefore, as one of the greatest, if not the greatest, discovery in modern science." The *Times* also warned that despite the contagious enthusiasm, many physicists and chemists were reluctant to discuss the experiments outside their own scientific communities, largely because of the potential impact of the discoveries on the outcome of the European war.

And though there must have been pledges of professional secrecy, especially at Columbia's Pupin Hall, there were no official rules yet for censoring conversations about the progress of the experiments and the findings, as there would be once the government's Manhattan Project was established. And there in Columbia's adult education program was George Koval, capable of understanding the languages of physics and chemistry. Whatever technical detail or hopeful hypothesis he may have heard, as he walked between lectures and labs at Havemeyer, or sat on a bench in the small park between Havemeyer and Pupin, or took a coffee break with fellow students, instructors, or their assistants at one of the nearby cafes on Broadway, he could easily comprehend.

For Koval, enrollment at Columbia was part of his job as a spy, following the Soviet model for student spies specializing in science, which had started at MIT in the 1930s. The science spy model established a logical, effective strategy for acquiring the latest research in America's most highly regarded laboratories and for recruiting fellow scientists. Red Army–trained spies would enroll at the school, becoming physics or chemistry majors, join student clubs and professional societies, and meet lecturers and scholars in their assigned espionage fields. It was a proven way to connect to the inner scientific circles of America as "the science community acted as a club; once you were on the inside it was easy to build a network, you just needed the right introductions."

There were numerous examples, such as Semyon Semenov, who in 1937 joined the NKVD, the Soviet secret security agency— forerunner to the KGB—and then enrolled at MIT, graduating in 1940. He then worked undercover as an engineer at Amtorg while specializing in scientific espionage. There was also Stanislav Shumovsky, who, credited with acquiring extensive US aviation secrets, had launched his quest in the classrooms of MIT while earning undergraduate and graduate degrees. He also worked at Amtorg, beginning in 1936. And there was Gaik Ovakimian, whom Lassen knew from Amtorg and who, after the consulates opened in 1933, was assigned to be head of NKVD intelligence in New York.

Later known as the "puppet master," Ovakimian boosted the science spy networks in America in multiple ways: as an early architect of the student models, as Shumovsky's trainer for recruiting scientists, and as the designer of an efficient espionage cell structure. As a conduit between sources with scientific information and Moscow's intelligence headquarters, he was instrumental in shaping the new concept of a spy who focused only on science. In 1938, four men who had recently arrived in America from the Soviet Union, with their families, met with Ovakimian at Amtorg to hear what their goals must be while at MIT: first to perfect their English language and second "to network as broadly as possible in the scientific community with both students and teaching staff." By the time Koval arrived at Columbia in 1941, Soviet intelligence favored the scientific communities at MIT and Columbia.

Lassen had to have read the May 1940 *New York Times* article about Columbia, or perhaps he was informed about the latest discoveries from his contacts there or at MIT. Thus, Koval, before enrolling, likely knew about the activities in Pupin Hall. And though his face may have beamed with the curiosity of any eager student, the lessons of general chemistry were not what he was seeking. His mission on the Columbia campus was to get to know the chairman of his department, who worked closely with the chairman of the Department of Physics, to learn about the breakthrough science surrounding him, and to fulfill his Red Army intelligence assignment to learn all that he could about American research in chemical weaponry. He especially wanted to know about one of Columbia's gifted chemistry instructors, Clarence Hiskey.

Only one year older than Koval, Hiskey was a tall, slender man who wore glasses with light brown tortoiseshell frames. With his thick, red hair and his loud, overbearing personality, he was hard to miss. A sloppy dresser, he often wore the same shirt and trousers for days in a row, and he was a heavy drinker for whom discretion was sometimes a challenge, sober or not. But he was also considered to be an outstanding chemist, which is how he and Koval found common ground. In 1939, Hiskey earned his chemistry doctorate from the University of Wisconsin. That year he was also inducted into the army's reserve commission in the Chemical Warfare Service, which, established in 1918, focused on the research and development of chemical munitions that might be necessary or useful in the war. Before arriving at Columbia, he had taught chemistry for more than a year at the University of Tennessee in Knoxville.

Hiskey would have learned quickly that Koval shared his passionate interest in cutting-edge chemistry. And there was other common ground that Koval must have known about. Hiskey had been closely tied to the Communist Party since his college days at the University of Wisconsin—though in later years he would deny ever having joined the party. Member or not, Hiskey, as well as his wife, frequently engaged with Communist Party members in New York, though that was hardly an uncommon occurrence in America at that time. The talk of the day on American college campuses was about fascism and the impact of appeasing Hitler, and professors like Hiskey, among many others at Columbia then, were quite open about siding with socialists and Communists against the forces of Hitler and Mussolini. This was a time when fear and hope were driving the fight to destroy fascism—not Communism.

It's unlikely that Koval would have discussed Communism with Hiskey. He was more interested in the expertise of Columbia's professors of physics and chemistry, as well as in the potential significance of their recent experiments. Perhaps they even talked about the gaseous diffusion method of separating U-235 from U-238.

How lucky for Hiskey to get a university appointment at a place like Columbia and for Koval to be taking a course or two in chemistry during such a remarkable time at Columbia. And soon there would be one more fortunate individual in this scenario, a dedicated Communist who worked with Lassen. His name was Arthur Alexandrovich Adams, code name "Achilles." And, as documents confirm, he "worked under and received his directions and payments through 'Faraday'"—that is, Lassen—as did Koval, who likely assisted in bringing together Hiskey and Adams for the first time. That meeting would prove to be a landmark moment in the history of atomic bomb espionage.

Like Lassen, Adams had been recruited by Soviet military intelligence in the early 1930s in Moscow. By some accounts, however, despite the timing of his official GRU recruitment, Adams had been serving Soviet intelligence from a base in America since the immediate aftermath of the Russian Revolution. From 1919 to 1921, he worked at the Soviet Russian Information Bureau in Manhattan, the unofficial embassy run by Ludwig Martens, funded by the Soviet government, and located on two floors of the World's Tower building on West Fortieth Street. The work of the staff focused largely on exchanging letters and conducting interviews with representatives of major US companies eager to do business with the new Russia, considered to be, as one journalist described it then, American capital's "greatest market in the future." Because of anti-Bolshevik hysteria and intelligence reports about spies planted from day one at the doorstep of the bureau—typically referred to as the Martens Mission—the US government shut it down in 1921, an order that forced Adams to depart for Moscow. By then he had bonded with a bright, feisty American woman, Dorothy Keen, who had worked with him at the mission since its inception in 1919. Later labeled by US agents as "an ardent Communist," Keen too left for Moscow, in August, on the SS *Adriatic*.

For the next seven or so years, Adams held leadership posts in the Soviet auto and aviation industries, while Keen "for a time after her arrival in Soviet Russia was a secretary to Lenin." Later, she worked as a translator and gave private English lessons. Then in the late 1920s Adams became a representative of Amtorg, and back to America he and Keen went, soon to marry, in November 1932. Adams's assignment at Amtorg was to place orders of US products for the Soviet armaments industry, a job that required exploring America's latest developments in areas such as radio engineering and military chemistry. And evidence suggests that it was at Amtorg that Adams first became acquainted with Benjamin Lassen—then still Lassoff—though logic suggests they likely met in New York at the time of the founding of the CPUSA in 1919. From the start they had a lot in common, especially as devoted Communists who would cross paths for many years.

Adams's trips back and forth between New York and Moscow were a quintessential spy drama, especially in the 1930s. But, as an "old Bolshevik" who had first met Lenin before the 1917 revolution, Adams had a past that could easily be used against him during the reign of Stalin, including at one point a working relationship with Trotsky. It was not surprising that he would be accused of being a Trotskyist conspiring against Stalin and thus be called back to Moscow from New York in the summer of 1937. After hiring an attorney to argue his case to prove his loyalty to Stalin and to the Soviet Union, including his years of espionage work in America, Adams was cleared in late 1937. But slipping back into America was more difficult than expected.

The plan arranged by comrades in New York had been for Adams to reenter the US through Canada. The first attempt was in December 1937, devised by Sam Novick, who was listed on Adams's visa application as the owner of the Wholesale Radio Service Co. on Sixth Avenue. In a letter to the State Department, Novick stated that Adams had worked for him in Canada for ten years, and now he needed Adams's assistance in America. But the letter, later revealed as filled with "false statements on Adams' behalf," failed in its mission to justify Adams's return to America.

Next, Jacob Aronoff, an attorney known to work for the CPUSA, swiftly formed a company called Technological Laboratories, which in its corporate filing, on May 9, 1938, listed Adams as president/treasurer and Aronoff as secretary. Adams filled out his visa form as the president of Technological Laboratories, with Aronoff as his support. Then Aronoff opened an account at the Corn Exchange Bank and Trust Company in Manhattan in the name of the company and deposited $4,000 with the name Arthur Adams as treasurer. In Canada, Adams received a letter on May 14 to a Toronto address showing the details of the account.

That worked. Adams returned to New York on May 17, 1938. His wife stayed in Moscow where she would work as secretary to *New York Times* correspondent Harold Denny while Adams lived in Manhattan using two businesses as covers: Novick's Electronic Corporation of America, on Sixth Avenue (same address as Wholesale Radio Service) and a nearby record company, Keynote Recordings Inc.

The meeting between Adams and Hiskey that Koval likely set up happened in September 1941 at a record store called The Music Room, on West Forty-Fourth Street between Broadway and Seventh Avenue. It was owned by Eric Bernay, who also had started the small, independent company Keynote Recordings, in 1940. Keynote's early releases were records of songs from the Spanish Civil War and music from the Soviet Union, such as performances by the Red Army Chorus. From 1936 to 1938, Bernay was a member of the Communist Party and the advertising manager for *The New Masses*, the Party's official organ. Bernay's business office for Keynote was at 522 Fifth Avenue, on the corner of Forty-Fourth Street and Fifth, only a few blocks from the record store and right across the street from Jacob Aronoff's law office at 525 Fifth. Among other businesses in the neighborhood closely connected were Michael Burd's import-export cover shop, only a block away from the Keynote office; Sam Novick's Electronics Corporation of America, on Broadway, just a block from The Music Room; and a jewelry shop, two blocks away from the record store, whose owner, Victoria Stone, worked closely with Adams and Jacob Golos.

And so it was that Adams and Hiskey met one September afternoon in a small area at the front of The Music Room. The tall, young Hiskey with his bushy red hair and the shorter, middle-age Adams, balding, with spectacles, walking with a slight limp separately perused the merchandise. Soon they would engage in a conversation about "labor issues and about Spanish questions," as one document would later disclose, referring to the Spanish Civil War. Then the chat moved on to Hitler's invasion of the Soviet Union a few months before, on June 22, breaking the German-Soviet alliance. Three million German soldiers, in 150 divisions with three thousand tanks, had attacked Russia in Operation Barbarossa. Any pro-Communist belief or rhetoric was now an acceptable part of the mosaic of American politics and could easily slip into conversations, especially between two men who had long saluted Communism as a solution. Later, Hiskey would tell a friend that it was at that first meeting that Adams recruited him into Soviet espionage. His code name would be "Ramsey."

Whether planned or coincidental, such a meeting in September 1941 would not have been among the concerns of America's counterintelligence agents, who were focused on tracking spies from Japan, Italy, and Germany—not the Soviet Union. No one was following Adams or Hiskey. And though someday both would be in the spotlight of fierce surveillance, on the day their bond began they were unnoticed. To a bystander their meeting would have seemed as commonplace and insignificant as any chat in an aisle of any record store in Manhattan.

But in the web of spies that included Adams, Lassen, and Koval, the tie to Hiskey was brimming with incalculable value. Hiskey was soon to resign from his teaching post at Columbia to begin highly specialized work at Columbia's newly established Substitute Alloy Material Laboratory. The tireless quest of SAM, as it was called, would involve perfecting gaseous diffusion as the solution for separating U-235 from U-238. Hiskey would be able to convey to Adams the progress of this research. And there was one more relevant detail:

Hiskey got the job at SAM despite a 1942 US Army intelligence report warning Columbia's Chemistry Department chair, Harold Urey, to look more closely at him.

The army saw the brilliant young chemist as a risk because they listed him as an active Communist. Urey, highly respected in his field, having won the Nobel Prize in Chemistry in 1934, listened to the caveat and gave Hiskey a stern word of caution about the importance of being discreet. Then he brought Hiskey on board. Such a decision was an early sign that in the task at hand to develop an atomic weapon, political persuasion would be less important to the esteemed scientists and administrators of the Manhattan Project than the much needed scientific expertise.

By spring semester 1942, Koval was no longer enrolling in chemistry classes at Columbia, perhaps, as some evidence shows, because he believed he would be returning to Russia relatively soon. America's entering the war in December 1941 and the Soviet Union's becoming an official ally could have spurred a sudden reevaluation in Moscow of Koval's American "business trip"—especially after he was registered as eligible to be drafted on February 12, 1942. Wouldn't the GRU want him to return?

As his Raven Electric boss, Lassen applied for Koval's first deferment in April 1942 using the "occupational, essential to the war effort" employee exemption as a reason. Koval had been recently promoted to the post of company manager and also placed on the board of directors at Raven, which had acquired numerous war contracts, including ones with the US Army Corps of Engineers and the US War Department. Thus, on paper, he appeared to be a director at a patriotic enterprise boosting the war effort. It was not surprising that Lassen's application was approved.

Simultaneous to that approval Mila received a letter from her husband, implying he would be returning home soon. By then Mila was living in Ufa, a large industrial town over a thousand miles east

of Moscow but west of the Ural Mountains. For both Mila and her
mother, the forces of unwanted change had escalated dramatically
in the aftermath of Hitler's June 1941 attack on the Soviet Union. In
October that year, likely because of Koval's work in the GRU, the
two Ivanova women received what was labeled "special treatment"
when they were evacuated out of Moscow to Ufa. There they were
given a room in an apartment unit and Mila was sent to work at
a chemical factory that made explosives from the residuals of oil
processing. It was the textbook definition of a toxic workplace. And
because of the hard work and the harsh 1941 winter, Mila was hospi-
talized for a respiratory condition from which she apparently would
never fully recover. Nor would she escape the long-range impact
on her nervous system from the factory's toxicity, later blamed for
her inability to have children.

In an undated letter to Koval, likely written in January 1942,
Mila expressed her fears about recent wartime events and described
some details of the winter thus far and her illness. Koval may have
received it by late February or early March, for the letters couriered
to and from New York and Moscow and Ufa often took two months
or more. It may have taken until late April for Mila to receive his
response. She did pencil "April 27" at the top of his one-page letter,
a missive that appeared to have been written in haste:

> Dear! I have exactly five minutes in which I must write a letter. It's
> a very short time, but the most important can be said very quickly
> and the rest doesn't matter. I often think about all of you and every-
> thing you are going through. I would very much like to be there
> with you, Mila, but you know that in these times, you can only be
> where you have to be. And this unfortunately is not decided by our
> desire. We must not complain and do not become more angry. You
> scared me with your letter. You are probably tired and working hard.
> I beg you to take care of yourself, for me, if not for you. Time has

gone. I'm healthy, energetic and very busy. I miss home, but we'll tell each other everything when we see each other again. Goodbye for now. Kisses until we meet shortly. See you soon. Yours, George Thank TV [the initials of Mila's mother] for the letters. Big thank you and greetings to the parents. George.

There was no mention of his draft notice, though he may have wanted to not worry her. Or perhaps he thought the draft would result in an earlier than planned return to the Soviet Union, which was why he wrote that he would see her "shortly" and "soon." Of what use could Koval be to Red Army intelligence if he were to be fighting for the Americans in Europe? After investing so much time and money in their science spy, hearing about his conscription could have sounded an alert to bring him home—that is, unless the GRU had learned something in 1942 or early 1943 that could have eased such concerns.

On July 20, 1942, Lassen sent one of his underlings, William A. Rose, to the Selective Service Local Board 126 in the Bronx to request an extension of Koval's deferment. The second delay was approved. Then, on November 30 Rose traveled to Albany, New York, to seek yet more extra time. But that would be the last of such requests by Lassen and his assistant Rose to postpone Koval's departure, possibly because no more deferments could be granted. Soon, in the spring of 1943, the so-called occupational exemption indeed would be dropped. But there was also the possibility that Lassen no longer needed to fret about whether Koval could be helpful to the Soviet cause while in the US Army.

Every two weeks from August 18, 1942, to late April 1943, Raven Electric paid Rose a considerable amount to travel to various destinations in the US, such as Chicago, DC, and Boston. Then on December 5, 1942, he added Knoxville, Tennessee, to his travels. He returned to Knoxville on January 27, 1943. But Raven had no contracts with businesses in or near Knoxville.

Though there is no confirming documentation, it is possible that Lassen's quests for Koval's deferments may have been part of a plan for Koval's "business trip." Perhaps William Rose on his trips that year—especially to Knoxville—learned something relevant to Koval's GRU assignment of probing America's chemical weapons.

In mid-June 1942 President Roosevelt had received a report from the director of the Office of Scientific Research and Development, Vannevar Bush, and James B. Conant, chairman of the National Defense Research Committee, about the results of a study focused on the "consequences, challenges, hoped for results" of what was soon to become the Manhattan Engineering District. This was America's highly secretive military initiative to weaponize nuclear energy and build an atomic bomb. Three months later, on September 17, General Leslie Groves of the US Army Corps of Engineers was put in charge of the project. On September 19, he approved a government directive for the acquisition of 56,200 acres of land in eastern Tennessee, twenty miles west of Knoxville, near the small town of Clinton in the foothills of the Appalachian Mountains. In late fall 1942, on that land, code name "Site X," construction began on what would be called Oak Ridge. It would house 75,000 workers and vast factories to produce the fuels for the atomic bomb. On the day before the land was acquired, tons of uranium were taken out of storage at Staten Island—1,250 tons of uranium ore stored in 2,006 steel drums—and shipped to Tennessee.

On February 4, 1943, Koval was inducted into the army at his Bronx draft board, filling out a form that included such details as his chemistry coursework at Columbia in 1941. This was information that could prove to be important if he wanted the army to know that he had a science background. After all, he could not mention that his degree in chemistry came from the Mendeleev Institute in Moscow.

CHAPTER SEVEN

LIES AND TIES

Rose Stephenson and Marian Greenberg met in a jail cell in Newark, New Jersey, in early 1943, and driven by that unsettling mix of desperation and creativity that poverty will induce, they devised a scheme for making money in Manhattan. Though their plot was hardly original, they nonetheless worked for days sketching out every detail.

The plan went like this: Together they would approach a man on the street—their choice would be West Forty-Fourth Street between Broadway and Seventh Avenue—and ask him to join them at a nearby bar. After at least one drink, Marian would excuse herself and leave Rose with their "date." She would then walk briskly to an apartment that she and Rose had rented just for that night's job and hide outside, close enough to see Rose and the gentleman enter the building. Rose would leave the apartment door unlocked and begin seducing the man in the living room or kitchen, where he would take his clothes off before she moved their romance into the bedroom. And while Rose proceeded to seduce him, Marian would enter the apartment to steal his wallet, money, and valuables. She would then leave the apartment and knock on the door from the hall saying that she was the landlady and had a special delivery letter for Rose. This would compel Rose to dart out of the bedroom, leaving the naked man behind. She and Marian would then rush out of the building as quickly as two foxes in a hunt. Their hope was to do this twice a week, always in a different apartment, never in a hotel, and to alternate roles as the robber and the lover. After their release from the Essex County jail, they put their conspiracy into motion. It's unknown how often they did it because there are records only for the time when they were caught.

One evening between eleven and midnight in March 1943, on one of those rainy nights in Manhattan when the downpour is so heavy that the water pools on the sidewalks and people take shelter in doorways of apartment buildings and retail shops, a man of medium height who weighed about two hundred pounds stood at the entry of Whelan Drug Store on West Forty-Fourth Street. Nearly bald with graying hair around the temples and a mustache, he was wearing a brown suit and a gray Oxford coat with slightly frayed sleeves. For the young schemers, the man stood out because of his tie, which showed off a diamond stickpin—a detail they could not miss as it sparkled slightly from the glow of a storefront light. And he had no umbrella, which gave them a reason to make his acquaintance.

They took him to a nearby bar where all three had drinks and talked about who knows what, until Marian announced that she had to go home. She then walked swiftly in the rain or took a cab to an apartment somewhere on West Sixty-First Street. And because of the weather, she entered the rented room and hid in a closet. Soon, Rose and her prey took a cab to the apartment, where he left his trousers on a kitchen chair. Then, Rose faced a double challenge: how to remove the diamond stickpin from his tie while entertaining him. In the midst of that quandary, Marian suddenly emerged from the closet, ripped the wallet out of a rear pocket of his trousers, and snatched a small package wrapped in tissue paper out of the other. As planned, she left the apartment, only to return seconds later to knock on the door, beckoning her partner, who excused herself from the bedroom and then raced out of the building with Marian.

In the dark of a secluded doorway a few blocks away, the two women sorted through their victim's wallet and found eleven dollars, which they split. Rose was disappointed she couldn't nab the diamond stickpin. Then, in their usual anxious rush to end a caper, Marian kept the wallet and the package as they made a plan to meet a few days later. But that never happened, largely because of what Marian found in the package wrapped in tissue paper.

As Marian would later tell the police, she returned to her apartment on Seventh Avenue and unwrapped the small package, peeling off the layers of tissue and finding one hundred neatly folded $100 bills. She then grabbed the worn leather wallet and spilled its contents onto the floor, looking at every detail as quickly as she could. What she saw were about two dozen little pieces of tissue paper with typewritten letters "from the English alphabet in unnatural sequence." And as she unfolded those, out rolled a Social Security card, a draft registration card, and a business card for Raven Electric with the name of one "Benjamin Lassen."

Soon thereafter Marian and her boyfriend spent about $4,000: he, on a Cadillac convertible coupé for $1,500, and she, on clothes and jewelry for about the same. Another thousand was split between her two roommates, who had been watching when she had emptied the package, as a safeguard against any betrayals.

Out of the remaining $5,000, only a thousand would ever be documented and that was because Marian had used it to try bribing an undercover cop who was on to the two-person robbery ring of Marian and Rose.

Much ensued in the days ahead, including the cops locating and questioning Lassen, who assured them that at no time had he ever been robbed of $10,000! He did say that "around March 1, 1943, he had lost his wallet at Stewarts Restaurant in New York, though he had not called anyone's attention to it because he knew there was only about ten dollars in it, at the most. But he had no time to be bothered with it." In truth, Lassen had shirked his duties to his Soviet bosses for several hours, during which he had lost what must have been funds to be distributed to spies in his network.

When Marian was interrogated, she described the strips of tissue with the different configurations of letters as "strange, like something a spy would have," as one newspaper article quoted her. But nothing came of that. In those months of 1943, Americans were focusing on news about American tanks defeating the Germans in Tunisia, about the RAF bombing the Ruhr Valley in Germany, and about the start of shoe rations in America—not on a prostitute's suspicions about a Soviet spy on West Forty-Fourth Street.

By the time of Lassen's "roll," Raven Electric was well established in the five-story building on West Twenty-Third Street. The electrical retail business, supplying a wide range of industrial and residential light fixtures, parts, and services, was conducted on the first floor with most of the inventory stored in the basement. On the second floor was a photography studio owned and operated by one of Lassen's nephews; Lassen was a silent partner. The third floor was leased to a silkscreen designer who seemed to have no connection to Lassen or to any of his business partners, unlike the fifth floor, which was rented out to a company partly owned by Lassen's Michael Burd.

The fourth floor was puzzling. The door to the main room was always locked, and though Lassen told his counter clerks that he used the entire fourth floor for storage, the silkscreen artist would later say that it sounded as though meetings were held there. On several occasions, he heard multiple footsteps across the ceiling of his studio where he would sometimes work late into the night. But only once did he ask Lassen about it. He was told "somewhat harshly" that he must have imagined it and perhaps he shouldn't work so hard, so late.

Lassen typically described Raven as a General Electric franchise. But the inventory at the start of the business was quite low, valued at around $10,000, during a period when far more, perhaps $35,000, was the required minimum to launch a GE franchise. Some of his employees believed he must have a strong tie to GE, making the requirements looser for him, perhaps. And though he did sell lamps provided by GE on consignment, the shop's inventory rarely, if ever, exceeded $20,000. Interestingly, as a former employee would later recall, "[Lassen] often just sold items at cost or at some unprofitable figure and he didn't seem to care." Lassen's longtime accountant observed that "he [Lassen] did not do business in the American way, that is, for profit. He sold merchandise for less than he paid for it." Then there was the man who played cards with Lassen for years at a restaurant on the corner of Sixth Avenue and Twenty-Third Street, only a block from Raven. He said that Lassen tried to act like "an ordinary shop owner, just a manager of an electric shop, but he was secretive: about his money and just the way he ran his business and about most things. He was always gone, out of the shop doing something and I couldn't understand how he could have so much money, which he did, I know, when he did not sell at a profit."

One day a Raven store clerk visited Lassen at his office at 11 West Twenty-Fifth Street and saw a copy of the *New York Herald Tribune* under the pad on his desk. While the clerk was waiting, he pulled the paper out to read and discovered a copy of the *Daily Worker*, the paper of the Communist Party, rolled up inside. Another time, at Lassen's office, when the same clerk was returning some keys and arrived a bit early, Lassen was reading the same newspaper. That time Lassen dropped all pretenses and urged the clerk never to tell anyone about what he had just seen. The clerk said later, "I hadn't any reason to open his secrets, whoever he really was. He told me he came from Russia and I heard him talk in Russian with two regular visitors to the shop. So that part was true. I know that."

What else was true, his clerks and his agents would likely never know. He avoided questions, sometimes even pretending he hadn't heard a word. But then what could he say about the late-night meetings conducted on the fourth floor, or his many hours spent away from the shop, or his order to send one of his workers to Knoxville, Tennessee, at least twice between December 1942 and February 1943?

In the months after Koval began his stint in the US Army, Lassen, through his many contacts, could have learned about the plans for a highly secretive atomic project, or at least enough to know that someone with Koval's scientific expertise might find his way to one of the project's research and production sites. Lassen's superiors in Moscow knew that American scientists were focusing on making a nuclear weapon. Soviet physicists were aware of this in part, because of the April 1940 article in the *Physical Review* about what was happening at Columbia's Pupin Hall. In June 1940 the same magazine had published a report by two associates of the Soviet nuclear physicist Igor Kurchatov announcing they "had observed rare spontaneous fissioning in uranium." When there was no response in the US to that announcement, the silence "convinced the Russians that there must be a big secret project under way in the United States."

In late 1940, NKVD station chiefs in the US, Britain, and Germany received orders from Lavrentiy Beria, head of Soviet secret police, to compile "evidence on possible work on the creation of atomic weapons." As early as August 1941, details of British atomic research were sent to Soviet intelligence in Moscow from the British physicist Klaus Fuchs. In the spring of 1942, Beria sent a memo to Stalin about atomic bomb research in which he noted, "In a number of capitalist countries . . . research has been launched into the utilization of the nuclear energy of uranium for military purposes. . . .

In designing the bomb, its core should consist of two halves, whose sum total should exceed the critical mass."

Stalin then ordered his foreign minister, Vyacheslav Molotov, to evaluate what the Soviet Union must do to catch up, and by October 1942 Molotov had commanded "the resumption of pre-war investigations of radioactive elements." On November 27, scientist Kurchatov sent a report to Molotov concluding that work on the creation of an atomic weapon in the Soviet Union was "significantly behind" that in the West. In December, Molotov dispatched the Soviet intelligence expert on foreign atomic research, Leonid Kvasnikov, to New York City "to pursue all leads about the atomic bomb." The Soviet code name for the nuclear bomb espionage in the US became "Operation Enormoz."

Delayed by wartime transit complications, Kvasnikov arrived three months later and set up an office on the fourth floor of the Soviet consulate in Manhattan. This was also the Soviet base for spies in New York. As such, it housed the office of GRU chief in New York, Pavel Mikhailov, the Soviet vice consul: real name Melkishev and code name "Moliere." Tied to both Adams and Lassen, Mikhailov could have enlisted Lassen to send his assets to hunt for details about America's plan to build a nuclear weapon. Also, before Kvasnikov arrived, one of the Soviets' most accomplished scientific and technical spies, the MIT graduate Semyon Semenov, had learned about Enrico Fermi's December 2, 1942, nuclear chain reaction at the University of Chicago. By late January 1943, intelligence headquarters in Moscow had received his report about the Americans' monumental step toward the making of an atomic bomb.

To be sure, toward the end of January 1943, as one scholar noted, "Stalin's government openly asked the U.S. Lend-Lease Administration to send 10 kilograms of uranium metal and 100 kilograms of uranium oxide and uranium nitrate to Moscow." General Groves, wanting to appear calm, even disinterested, approved the sending of the uranium oxide and uranium nitrate, knowing that the requested amount would not be helpful in producing a weapon. Both had limited applications, unlike the uranium metal, which could have been very useful in the making of nuclear fuel—and which he didn't allow to be sent.

In February 1943 Molotov appointed Kurchatov to direct a Soviet uranium project. And in March, Kurchatov wrote to Molotov about atomic information he had recently received from Gaik Ovakimian, saying that documents that had been sent to him had "an inestimable value to our country and Soviet science. . . . The documents contain vital markers for our research, allowing us to bypass many highly labour-intensive phases of development and uncover new scientific and technical ways of resolving issues." By the summer of 1943, it was "indisputable that the Soviets had glimpsed the outlines of the Manhattan Project," American historians Joseph Albright and Marcia Kunstel later wrote.

While news about the Manhattan Project could have reached Lassen through his Moscow connections, he also had ties to informed government sources in Washington. One connection was through the War Production Board (WPB), the US agency established in January 1942, which Soviet espionage code-named "Depot." The WPB directed the nation's production of weapons and military supplies, assuring that factories making everything from machine guns to tanks to parachutes had the materials they needed. Certain WPB divisions would be closely involved in allocating supplies for the Manhattan Project, such as the uranium controlled by the Miscellaneous Minerals Division. Among the WPB's tasks was to balance the demands of the nuclear project with the needs of programs providing munitions for the battlefronts.

WPB board members included prestigious leaders of industry and government such as the president of General Electric; the secretaries of War, Navy, and Agriculture; and the chair of the Board of Economic Warfare (BEW), who was US vice president Henry A. Wallace. Serving on the BEW in 1942 was economist Nathan Gregory Silvermaster, code name "Pal," who had begun reporting information to the Soviets through Lassen's associate Jacob Golos, among others, in 1940. According to sixty-one deciphered cables sent between the US and Moscow, Silvermaster, who was running a ring of Soviet spies, delivered "huge quantities of War Production Board data on weapons." In addition, the assistant to the BEW chair, Frank Coe, code name "Peak," was tied to Silvermaster.

Lassen had other valuable sources in 1942 besides his connections to the WPB. The principal contractor for the massive construction of Site X, Oak Ridge, which began on the Sunday before Thanksgiving in 1942, was Stone & Webster, the Boston-based engineering firm. Lassen, then still Lassoff, had worked in its New York office years earlier. He had enduring ties to MIT scientists, some of whom were involved in research tied to the war effort. And there was Arthur Adams, whose connection to the nuclear chemist Clarence Hiskey must have been invaluable to Lassen.

In 1942, a year after Adams and Hiskey first met, Hiskey had begun his atomic energy work at the Substitute Alloy Material Laboratory, or SAM, at Columbia, Then in September 1943, he was transferred to the Metallurgical Lab at the University of Chicago, where only nine months before Fermi had successfully built the world's first nuclear reactor. Later it would be known that from the start of his appointment in Chicago, Hiskey was meeting with Adams—five or six times—handing over documents about atomic research from the Met Lab and also about Site X (Oak Ridge).

Whoever informed Lassen about Site X may never be known. It's irrefutable, however, that his contacts were vast and that Adams was well-connected to parts of the project's research core. Lassen had to have known about Oak Ridge in 1943, at the latest. And in 1944 he also must have been told about the loss of Adams as a useful player. For in April that year, federal agents raided Adams's room at the Peter Cooper Hotel in New York, finding "sophisticated camera equipment, materials for constructing microdots, and notes on experiments being conducted at the atomic bomb laboratories at Oak Ridge, Tennessee." By April 27, Hiskey was drafted and sent to northern Alaska. And in July that year, Hoover ordered the beginning of the daily surveillance of Arthur Adams.

It was Lieutenant Colonel John Lansdale Jr., head of the Manhattan Project's security, who first directed the FBI to Adams, reporting that "Adams is known to be a contact of various scientists employed on the project, particularly in the metallurgical laboratory of the University of Chicago." Lansdale's view of such a discovery, however, was that "it would be most undesirable for Adams to be permitted to leave the United States for the Soviet Union with the information that he has undoubtedly been able to obtain concerning the DSM [Manhattan Project]." Thus, Lansdale made it clear that the army "did not wish to have Adams prosecuted at this time on the basis of his espionage activity concerning the [Manhattan Project] inasmuch as such prosecution would bring the Project out into the open."

Adams was likely unaware of his unofficial immunity status, especially because he had to have known he was being tailed daily—and nightly—after the government had whisked Hiskey out of Chicago. From then on, Adams was locked into a cat-and-mouse game with the Feds that would limit his effectiveness. But by the time that began, whatever Adams had learned from Hiskey had to have reached Lassen, either directly or through their mutual contact, Mikhailov, at the Soviet consulate in Manhattan. And that information had to have been part of the reason that on August 11, 1944, Soviet spy George Koval would report to duty for his new US Army assignment in the Special Engineer Detachment at Oak Ridge. It was not a matter of luck.

CHAPTER EIGHT

THE MAN IN THE JEEP

George Koval had a hidden talent for designing tapestries finely woven with truths, half-truths, and blatant lies, especially regarding his life story. His security file at Oak Ridge was filled with the proof of that. From it, his superiors could learn that his mother and father were born near Pinsk in "about 1888" and "about 1885," respectively. Both were Jewish: he, a carpenter, and she, a housewife. And both were dead: the father dying in 1933 and the mother in 1934, in Sioux City, Iowa, Koval's place of birth. The truth, both were still alive. They could also learn a few true details such as Koval's membership in the National Honor Society in high school and his attending the University of Iowa. But then there were more big lies, such as his working for three years from 1933 to 1936 at the Square Deal Clothing Company on Fourth Street in Sioux City, run by his uncle Harry Gurshtel, and living in New York City on West Seventy-Second Street beginning in 1936.

The file stated that he had started work at Raven Electric Co. in 1939, when in truth that was the year he had graduated from the Mendeleev Institute in Moscow, and had begun his military intelligence training somewhere on the outskirts of Moscow. Also, tucked into the file was his army registration form, which noted his 1941 enrollment in the Chemistry Department at Columbia University "to obtain a bachelor of science degree" perhaps the most useful of all his half-truths.

The most important fact regarding the file, however, may have been that there were no obstacles to his advancement in the US military, thanks to his detours from the full truth. Here was an all-American guy who had graduated from high school in Iowa at age fifteen; who studied chemistry at an Ivy League university; and who appeared to delay his Selective Service duty for two years because of sheer dedication to a company with government contracts supporting the US war effort. As his deferment forms had stated, he was Raven's "key man."

No one at Oak Ridge in 1944 must have thoroughly checked or analyzed the forms. But there appeared to be no reason to do so, especially considering Koval's quite impressive record in the US Army since his 1943 induction.

On July 20, 1943, after several months in training at Fort Dix in New Jersey, Koval was sent for three weeks to The Citadel military college in Charleston, South Carolina. There he was tested and evaluated to determine his assignment going forward. The Army General Classification Test, designed to identify technical skills and assess intelligence levels, was used to match the aptitudes of recruits with the needs of the military. Koval scored 152, more than twenty points higher than an above average score. That score helped to place him in the Army Specialized Training Program, ASTP. Beginning in December 1942, the ASTP was a wartime program sending skilled draftees to universities and colleges nationwide for advanced technical and scientific training. Its main purpose was to fill the mounting demand for scientists, mathematicians, and engineers in wartime projects—such as the creation of an atomic weapon. To be accepted, a soldier had to complete basic military training, score 115 or more on the Army General Classification Test, and successfully move through a series of interviews with Army officers.

Thus on August 20, 1943, Corporal Koval of Company A, 101st Engineer Battalion, reported to duty in the ASTP unit at City College of New York at 137th Street and Broadway, along with thirty-nine of his colleagues from The Citadel. For the next twelve months, he would take courses in electrical engineering and become what classmates later described as "a model student." One CCNY classmate, Arnold Kramish, would someday note, "There was no better man than George. He was superb at any job he had."

At that time, CCNY was known for its keenly progressive faculty and student body. For Koval that was common ground, which may have fostered an unexpected sense of security, in turn inspiring him to land a few long-lasting friends—such as Herbert J. "Herbie" Sandberg and Kramish. From his selected electrical engineering classes to the required military ones, such as the course on advanced camouflage techniques, Sandberg and Kramish were steady classmates. But soon he would enter what, for a Soviet spy, must have seemed like enemy territory. He was chosen to be part of the elite First Provisional Special Engineer Detachment and soon assigned to Oak Ridge. Referred to as "the SEDs," these were GIs with technical and scientific backgrounds, from skilled mechanics and machinists to electrical engineers and chemists, selected to handle essential jobs in the making of a nuclear weapon, and often assigned to work as assistants to the Manhattan Project's senior scientists.

The SED had started in early summer 1943 for the purpose of allowing scientists and technicians already at the Project to remain there after being inducted into the army. During the next year, as Project sites expanded and plants developed, the hunt for scientific skills in the ranks of the military became urgent. Soon the quest for scientists had spread to colleges and universities, and to the groups of highly desirable ASTP members.

Koval was well respected at CCNY, especially among the top instructors in the Electrical Engineering Department, some of whom Koval would list as references on future forms and applications. They likely did not know, however, that one of their star students was a Soviet spy trained by the Red Army. And how Koval got into the SED would never be fully explained. Perhaps Lassen's legion of spies devised a masterful plot to fix Koval's SED placement, or Koval was exactly what the government had been seeking for the Manhattan Project.

Eleven of Koval's CCNY colleagues in the ASTP were chosen for the SED, and most of them would later say they had no memory of any selection process. This meant, as one selected classmate noted, if such a design had existed, it must have been "extremely secretive." Another ASTP classmate who didn't make it to the SED later said he was totally unaware of anyone at CCNY being assigned to an atomic bomb site, though in retrospect it seemed quite logical "in view of the highly technical training we had, as if we were being prepared for such a thing."

Others would have hazy memories of an adjutant officer in their program who was responsible for "the discharge of assignments" and likely had some knowledge about Koval's lucky draw. But that adjutant officer would later say he knew nothing about a selection process. Besides, he had "no knowledge of an ASTP class member ever having been assigned to Oak Ridge," adding that if that had happened, such action "would have been so top secret that in all probability it would have resulted from specific orders emanating from somewhere in Washington, D.C."

Yet another of Koval's ASTP colleagues was sure that the "Commanding Officer of Units" knew all about the questionable process. That was Colonel Raymond P. Cook, who denied any such knowledge. However, choosing Koval, he said, "could have been the result of a preconceived plan if [Koval] had colluded with a faculty member at CCNY" or if he had a tie to a "highly placed member of the Armed Forces or someone in the War Department" or if he knew "someone with such a tie." Further, the colonel noted that "a goodly number" of the faculty members at CCNY during and prior to 1944 had performed some assignment in connection with the Manhattan Project. Thus, it was possible, according to Colonel Cook, that Koval's acceptance into the ASTP and his subsequent assignment from that program to the SED "could have resulted from the influence of a well-informed member of the faculty at CCNY who knew [Koval's] skills would be welcomed at Oak Ridge."

Ironically, the most helpful suggestion in later years regarding efforts to solve the mystery of how Koval ended up at Oak Ridge might have come from the former SED member who, when asked about the selection process, simply recited a jingle, "We were special GIs. The chosen few. Selected for knowledge and high IQ."

The reality was that no matter how well connected Koval's comrades and controllers might have been to seats of power in wartime Washington or how astute were the inner machinations of the Soviets' espionage networks within America, or even how much the Soviets must have known about Site X by 1944, Koval would still have been high on the list of potential SED recruits at CCNY—a top choice among his classmates. If others were selected, he would be too.

Unless the lies and half-truths in his records had been discovered, he simply could not have been rejected. He was a star in a group that was hugely wanted and needed in 1944 wartime America. Despite the US-based grid of Soviet spies at that time, there was likely no need for a Byzantine plot to assure that Koval was in the right place at the right time. That had already happened when the GRU sent him to America to work as a science spy with a handler who had vast contacts, enough to be informed about a military weapons project that would welcome Koval's expertise. He was an excellent choice for the scientific drama that he became a part of. That was the lucky act—not a chance landing of a spy at one of the Manhattan Project sites.

On August 15, 1944, Koval was fingerprinted as "a mathematician" at Oak Ridge and registered on the National Defense Fingerprint Chart. By then, the plan for the Manhattan Project was to build two bombs. One, code name "Little Boy," would use enriched uranium as its fuel: neutrons striking a uranium nucleus, releasing energy as well as more neutrons which in turn split into more nuclei and so on, causing an explosive nuclear chain reaction. The second, code name "Fat Man," used plutonium surrounded by conventional explosives that are detonated to create a critical mass of plutonium, leading to the atomic explosion. Plutonium, which occurs naturally in tiny trace amounts in uranium ores, was first produced synthetically in 1941 in a cyclotron at the University of California, Berkeley.

To design, build, and fuel the two bombs, research and production took place at more than thirty sites in the US, Canada, and the United Kingdom. As one scientist would later write, it consisted of "a formidable array of factories and laboratories—as large as the entire automobile industry of the United States at that date." There were three primary locations. Los Alamos, New Mexico, code name "Site Y," was where the bombs were designed and assembled. At Site X, Oak Ridge, also called the Clinton Engineer Works, enriched uranium was produced in the purity and quantity needed for the Little Boy bomb; a pilot graphite reactor manufactured plutonium for Fat Man, the implosion bomb; and the element bismuth was irradiated to produce the polonium essential to the neutron-generated triggers, or initiators, which started the fission chain reaction for each of the bombs. The Hanford, Washington, Site W on the Columbia River was dedicated to the full-scale manufacture of plutonium in nuclear reactors for which the Oak Ridge X-10 reactor was the model. Hanford also, like Oak Ridge, irradiated bismuth for synthesizing the polonium. The enriched uranium and the plutonium were sent to Los Alamos and the irradiated bismuth went to plants in Dayton, Ohio, where polonium was produced and purified and then transported to Los Alamos, to be used in the initiators.

At Oak Ridge there were three main plants by the time Koval arrived. On the western edge of the site was "K-25," code name for the factory that used the novel gaseous diffusion process, perfected at Columbia's SAM Laboratory, to enrich uranium, that is, to separate the easily fissile uranium-235 from uranium-238, which is more abundant but far less capable of fission. Opening in the autumn of 1943, this 44-acre building employed fourteen thousand or more workers. The facility was the world's largest building under one roof.

On 825 acres in the central southeastern part of the Tennessee site was the Y-12 plant, where twenty-four thousand men and women worked and where the electromagnetic method was used for the uranium separation. This process forced the uranium through a magnetic field causing the lighter U-235 atoms to spin away from the heavier U-238. The method used what were referred to as electromagnetic racetracks, built by the Stone & Webster Engineering Co.

Ten miles from Y-12 was the X-10 facility, which was run by the University of Chicago's Met Lab. X-10 converted uranium-238 to plutonium-239. It was the smallest of the factories, with its 1,500 or so scientists and technicians, plus about 100 SED soldiers. But its significance was immense because its graphite reactor became the model for the much larger plutonium plants at Hanford. And it was at X-10 that the element bismuth was bombarded with neutrons, or irradiated, to manufacture polonium. Bismuth, a brittle metal known since ancient times, looks like tin or lead, and when irradiated, bismuth-209 becomes bismuth-210, which swiftly, in five days, decays into polonium-210.

By some accounts, Koval spent more time at X-10 than anywhere else on the site, though his work gave him access to all the facilities. With other SEDs, he became part of a technically skilled scientific group at the Health Physics Department, which had started in December 1942 in the aftermath of the University of Chicago's nuclear chain reaction. By the time he was assigned to Oak Ridge, the potential health hazards for everyone involved in the making of an atomic bomb had demanded new types of duties, such as measuring workers' radiation tolerance, shielding exposure levels, inventing the monitoring instruments, and conducting chemistry lab tests. As the health physics profession's founder K. Z. Morgan would later write, the health physicists "instituted remote handling of radioactive material, controlled access to 'hot' areas and use of protective clothing, and devised decontamination procedures for all those inadvertently exposed."

Dr. Morgan, who was based at Oak Ridge, would later comment that Koval's work was about "mathematical problems in connection with radiation detection and measurement of instruments," adding that such work required routine "access to confidential and secret information." Most, if not all, information pertaining to health physics during Koval's tenure at Oak Ridge was classified. Also, because Koval spent a good deal of his time surveying the radiation at the X-10 facility, and because his focus was on mathematical problems, he "would have been given access to the highly classified information," said Dr. Morgan.

Health physicists had to learn the basic chemical properties of all the radioactive materials they were monitoring. They were asked to be present whenever repair work was done on any equipment at the plants, and no shipment could leave the site without the approval of the Health Physics Department. Also the health physicists conducted routine surveys of all offices and labs, as they checked for signs of contamination. On the "Job Break-Down Sheet" for training new arrivals in the health physics section at Oak Ridge, there were lists of duties such as "determine where hazard exists, decide on protective measures, report salient events to management, at all places in jurisdiction." Three important steps for the health physics workers were always noted in their training materials: "Know all operations in your area. Be alert to changes. Make thorough surveys."

At such a covert operation where most jobs were strictly compartmentalized to prevent workers from seeing the larger purpose of their work, a post like Koval's was unique. Not only did he have access to multiple buildings, but he also worked with high-level scientists on the project—and he had top-secret clearance. Though a very small number of people were aware of the full project operations, the scientific personnel, especially in health physics, were regularly updated about the goals at each of the plants. As one of Koval's coworkers would later say, "A person in his position would have known a lot, like the fact that uranium-235 was being processed at Oak Ridge and that it was being shipped from there, that the activity at Oak Ridge was connected with the development of an atom bomb; all members of our group were so informed."

Because of Koval's obligation to visit the plants as part of his work routine, the army equipped him with a jeep. And so it was that in the autumn of 1944, a Red Army spy was driving his US Army jeep daily across a swath of land in Tennessee at a crucial location in America's top-secret military project. At the close of each day, he drove to the area of huts and barracks where SED soldiers lived and where, for the sake of camouflage, they shared the same living quarters and cafeteria with the military police, the MPs.

It would seem that the expertise of a spy could be measured in part by the level of the enemy's security at the assigned locale. At Oak Ridge, for example, as early as February 1943 when the construction of plants was still in progress, there were armed guards called "Safety Forces" to protect the secret site from accidental travelers or curious intruders. They worked at each of the seven entry gates, four of which provided access to the administrative offices and to the workers' community, and three to the "prohibited" factory areas. There were also mounted patrols that cantered routinely along the banks of the Clinch River, watching for interlopers. And there were barbed-wire fences at strategic points surrounding the site.

During the next two years, the security forces would expand to 4,900 civilian guards, 740 military policemen, and more than 400 in a civilian police force. By then, there was also an intricate system of coded badges required to be worn by every resident and visitor, each susceptible to being stopped for security ID checks. By the time Koval had arrived in 1944, there was a new sort of security established, the Intelligence and Security Division, claiming to be "the primary unit for assuring secrecy throughout the Manhattan Project."

While General Groves agreed only to minimal FBI involvement in Project security matters, the Army Corps of Engineers had its own intelligence corps of uniformed and civilian agents headquartered at Oak Ridge. And, for the cause of keeping the Project a secret, they could be called to duty anywhere in the world. For example, when an ex-employee broke out in a skin rash in South America and expressed concern that it may have been caused by a "queer ray" at Oak Ridge, the story quickly reached the American embassy and an agent at Oak Ridge was sent to investigate the situation and to nullify the "queer-ray" hypothesis. The stories abounded. Even a minister in the nearby Tennessee town of Maryville was sought for questioning, after referring to an atom in a sermon.

What must have most concerned Koval was the close monitoring of both military and civilian personnel by carefully placed resident spies, men and women recruited by the Intelligence and Security Division. It worked like this: an intelligence officer would call a resident worker to his office and remind him or her about the importance of the Oak Ridge work to the war effort. The officer would explain why tight security was imperative and why any suspicious behavior or loose talk must be reported. Once accepting the duties of being an unofficial intelligence operative, the workers were told to send the information they uncovered in the form of "chatty" letters addressed to a fake company with the name Acme Credit Corp., in Knoxville.

By some accounts, a substantial number of men and women at Oak Ridge worked as local spies for the Project in 1944 and 1945. Residents were told that even the phone book was classified and could not be taken off the site. Binoculars, telescopes, firearms, and cameras required registration. The banner across the top of the newspaper, the *Oak Ridge Journal*, warned that the published stories were "Not to be Taken From the Area." And there were the signs and billboards reminding people of the high security ambiance, such as "What you see here, What you do here, What you hear here, When you leave here, Let it stay here."

The Project's official *Security Manual* contained advice about identifying "individuals whose background indicates that they may possess affinity for a foreign government, as indicated by 1) visits to a foreign country, 2) a relative who resides in or owes allegiance to a foreign country, and 3) service in the Army of a foreign country." The manual urged readers to watch for "individuals having membership in organizations known to have been enemy sponsored or otherwise subversive or committed to the violent overthrow of the Government of the United States, or to adherence to the interest of any foreign power to the detriment of the interest of the United States."

Other instructions in the manual included what to do with "restricted documents," which must be torn to shreds or burned or otherwise destroyed "by an authorized employee so as to render them useless." There were also the rules for the disposal of waste: "Classified waste, including all work sheets, drafts, carbon paper, stenographic notes, imperfect copies, stencils, etc., shall be torn into small pieces and safeguarded until burned under the supervision of a trusted employee who has been properly cleared to handle classified information." Warnings and instructions seemed endless.

Like his fellow residents and SED colleagues, Koval used the permitted time away from his job as constructively as possible, sometimes to advance his on-campus work as a health physicist, thus impressing supervisors and peers. For example, he researched and wrote a scientific article entitled "Determination of Particulate Air-Borne Long-Lived Activity," which was released to fellow scientists, in manuscript form, on June 22, 1945. In the paper, he alerted health physicists to the fact that a correction must be made in the process for evaluating levels of radioactivity in contaminated air. What had not been considered in such tests, he wrote, "was the presence in the collected sample of active materials found in the atmosphere due to the natural radon and thoron content of the air." As he explained, radon and thoron were colorless, odorless radioactive gases emitted from the uranium present in the Earth's crust.

It was a short, highly technical article, with many equations, footnotes, and graphs, that immediately was classified "Secret." It was his second impressive piece of scientific research that year. In January, his expertise gained attention in an article about the pros and cons of recent advancements in the methods and machines used to collect dust for analyzing levels of radioactivity. Koval was one of two scientists at Oak Ridge labs recognized for uncovering a number of safety concerns regarding dust sampling techniques, such as the toxicity of the radioactive dust being "higher than that of materials for which the [instruments] were designed to detect."

Koval's scientific expertise and industrious nature must have indeed impressed his Oak Ridge supervisors. But evidence suggests that he used at least one allotted leave from Oak Ridge to equally impress his Soviet bosses. According to a GRU historian, Koval, while assigned to Oak Ridge, met with "Faraday" to deliver details about the layout of the Oak Ridge site, its "three main sectors"—K-25, Y-12, and X-10—its purpose of producing uranium-235 and plutonium-239, and its job to send the enriched material "by military plane to laboratories in Los Alamos." Koval also reported observations from his work at X-10. And confirming that such a meeting may have occurred on one of his leaves is the fact that Koval and an Oak Ridge colleague, Duane M. Weise, took a weeklong furlough to New York City in late May or early June 1945. Weise later recalled that while he visited his family in New Jersey, "George just disappeared into New York. He never discussed the details of his week. But we were used to holding secrets, being discreet. That was the way it was at Oak Ridge."

Shortly before Koval's trip with Weise or quickly after their return from New York, Koval was told that he would be transferred to a new post, joining the team of health physicists and SEDs at facilities in Dayton, Ohio, dedicated to the production and purification of the rare and dangerous element polonium. By then, there were thirty-four SEDs stationed at the labs in Dayton run by Monsanto Chemical Co., which was known in Moscow by the code name "Firm K." After his arrival, Koval would sign an affidavit certifying that part of his duty as a member of the US Army assigned to a top-secret project was to secure all classified information that came to his attention.

CHAPTER NINE

THE PLAYHOUSE SECRET

The motives for crafting secrets have never changed—whether to protect, betray, or empower. Nor has the fact that the longer a secret is buried, the greater the chances its role in history may never be recognized. Such was the case of what happened in Dayton, Ohio, in a hidden room in the mansion of the Manhattan Project, a secret within *the* secret and one that would remain unknown for many decades, much like its on-site Soviet spy.

Though renowned as the home of Wilbur and Orville Wright and the birthplace of aviation, Dayton, was rarely, if ever, acknowledged for its long line of visionaries and their dozens of life-changing inventions. In 1900 there had been more patents per capita in Dayton, Ohio, than in any other city in the nation. It was America's start-up capital for the first half of the twentieth century. And it was a well-established military air base. By 1944, Wright Field and Patterson Field, soon to merge, had expanded from 2,500 military and civilian workers at the start of the war to more than 50,000. And between 1941 and 1944, Wright Field grew from 40 buildings to over 300, while managing more than 800 major war-related projects such as refining plane engines and building the air force's first jet. Citywide there were at least 60 war-production industries employing 115,000 people.

So it was that Dayton's legacy of groundbreaking inventions and its high-level military projects, in combination with its low-keyed image and its relative obscurity internationally, made it a smart fit in the risky, secretive project of inventing a US weapon fueled by nuclear energy. The assignment at the Dayton site was the production and purification of polonium, code name "Postum." And the challenges were staggering. There had never been enough polonium produced even to see it, much less to provide the necessary quantity to fuel the initiators for the atomic bombs. From the start of the Project's polonium tasks, Dayton chemist Dr. Charles Allen Thomas was in charge.

An inventor with nearly a hundred patents by the early 1940s, Thomas was renowned in scientific circles and bore a reputation of boundless energy. His biographer described him as "a visionary with pioneering ability to predict new directions for science." With a master's degree in chemistry from MIT, Thomas had years of experience codirecting the largest chemical consulting lab in America, which was based in Dayton. By the time he was contacted by the leaders of the Manhattan Project, he was the director of the Central Research Department at Monsanto Chemical Company. He was also the deputy chief of Roosevelt's National Defense Research Committee (NDRC).

It was in May 1943 that Harvard's president, James B. Conant, who was also the NDRC chief, and General Groves met with Thomas in Washington, DC, to unveil their plans to build what they hoped would be the world's first atomic bomb and to discuss the project's probabilities as well as their concerns. They wanted Thomas to be codirector with physicist J. Robert Oppenheimer at the Los Alamos Laboratory, taking on the charge of overseeing and coordinating the project's chemistry at all sites. He was much needed, they told him, because "the amount of chemistry in the project had been under-estimated." To do this, however, Thomas would have to live in Los Alamos, and so Groves and Conant flew him there for two days to tour the operations and to meet Oppenheimer, the University of California at Berkeley professor of physics who was the Project's chief scientist.

Not wanting to move his family away from Dayton or to abandon his responsibilities at Monsanto, which included overseeing the com-pany's war contracts, Thomas declined to take the job. In response, Conant and Groves would offer it again—this time with the base in Dayton. While directing the Manhattan Project chemistry at all sites, Thomas would also be in charge of the polonium production at Day-ton plants. He accepted the post and on May 24, 1943, the contract with Monsanto Chemical Company for the Project's research and development of polonium, run by Thomas, launched what would be known as the Dayton Project. And in the quest to hide the work of such a secretive mission, Oppenheimer suggested that Thomas's work should not be officially tied to the Manhattan Project.

From the start, this would be a feverish operation, replete with a pack of skeptics voicing loud doubts about the possibility of pro-ducing enough polonium in time to make a difference in the war. But Thomas was an optimist. Like Oppenheimer, Groves, Conant, and all the risk-takers committed to the Manhattan Project, he was determined to turn uncertainties into realities. His job began in July.

A month earlier Oppenheimer had written a letter to Groves explaining the crucial role of polonium as the neutron generator in the detonation of the bomb. How vital Dayton's polonium labs would be to the success of the bomb was best described later by one of Thomas's technicians, who said simply: "No trigger, no bomb." Polonium was a key part of the trigger, or initiator—code name "Urchin"—which was, as one scholar described it, "the minuscule innermost component of the bombs." Whether using uranium or plutonium, the bomb had to incorporate a neutron-producing mechanism—the initiator—that would release the neutrons at exactly the right moment to ignite the chain reaction. If the neutrons were discharged too soon, the explosion would fall below the designated yield—and, if too late, the bomb might not explode at all. A mix of polonium and beryllium—two elements that produce neutrons when in contact with each other—could meet the challenge. In the plutonium bomb, implosion would force the alpha particles out of the polonium to strike the beryllium, releasing the neutrons to begin the chain reaction. And in the uranium bomb, a conventional gun-powder charge would cause the polonium and beryllium to make contact.

Beryllium, contained in the mineral beryl and gemstones such as emeralds and aquamarines, is a steel-gray stable metal found in the Earth's crust and in volcanic rocks. Its crucial feature in the delicate timing of initiating the detonation of the bomb was that it is both a neutron moderator and multiplier. After being bombarded by polonium alpha particles, it has the capability of slowing down the speed of released neutrons by absorbing an alpha particle and emitting a neutron. Polonium, on the other hand, with its "high alpha activity," lacks any such stability.

Discovered by Marie Curie in 1898 and named for Poland, her homeland, polonium is one of the most toxic substances known. Particles emitted by polonium can damage organic tissue if inhaled or ingested, and the scientists and technicians in Dayton would eventually be working with the largest amounts of polonium ever produced. Silvery with a soft-as-cream-cheese look, polonium, one of the rarest elements, was very difficult to produce. By 1943, in fact, no weighable quantities of the pure element had ever been isolated. As Major General Kenneth Nichols, deputy to General Groves, later said, the polonium was "a very difficult assignment, not only because it had never been seen before, but also because of the radiation involved." Each initiator used about 50 curies of polonium, a curie being the basic unit measuring the intensity of radioactivity.

Because the production of polonium was still experimental, two different techniques were being tried. Synthesizing the polonium by irradiating bismuth was believed from the start to be the best way to make relatively large quantities of the element. But in 1943 the bismuth method was still at an early stage, at both Oak Ridge and Hanford. Thus, Dayton was at first assigned an alternative method, and that was to extract the polonium from lead dioxide residues, in which the polonium occurs naturally.

Taken from Canadian and African uranium ores at a radium refinery in Port Hope, Ontario, in Canada, lead dioxide residues were shipped in truckloads to Dayton: 70,000 pounds between November 1943 and May 1945. However, only 0.2 or 0.3 milligrams of polonium could be produced from six metric tons of the Port Hope lead dioxide. (There are 2,204.6 pounds in a metric ton.) So in late spring 1945 Dayton discontinued this process and began to use only the bombarded, irradiated bismuth sent from Hanford and Oak Ridge.

By June 1945 when Koval arrived in Dayton, there were several buildings dedicated to the polonium processing, all tucked into residential and commercial neighborhoods, bringing the phrase "hidden in plain sight" to its fullest meaning. From the start, finding enough lab space and staff housing in Dayton had been challenging. This was, after all, a time when war projects were consuming much of the city's commercial property. The National Cash Register Company had even stopped work in two of its factory buildings to loan the space to another highly secretive government quest: employing nearly five hundred people to decrypt the German codes.

There had been no time to build new research laboratories in Dayton and rental space was at a premium. Thus, in the autumn of 1943, personnel recruiting and preliminary planning for the polonium project took place at Monsanto's Central Research Department in a building referred to as Unit I, southwest of downtown Dayton. Unit II was a leased warehouse on East Third Street, in an industrial district. And demonstrating the desperation in finding adequate space, Unit III was a vacant three-and-a-half story building splattered with broken windows and missing a staircase between the second and third floors. It had once housed a theological seminary, and more recently the local Board of Education had used it for storage. Unit III was extensively renovated to become a chemical research laboratory with one floor dedicated to health physics experiments and a special laundry for decontaminating workers' clothing. The "campus" of Unit III quickly expanded to a dozen or more smaller buildings nearby.

But as the magnitude of the polonium processing unfolded, it quickly outgrew the capacity of Dayton's three units. In less than a year, two hundred technicians, physicists, chemists, and lab assistants had been brought to the Dayton Project from at least seven states. By the start of 1944, there were no buildings of adequate size in Dayton that could be occupied as swiftly as the project demanded. So in February that year, Thomas took over "the only suitable structure in Dayton ready for immediate use," an artful, Italianate building known as the Runnymede Playhouse, isolated on a heavily wooded, winding road in the most upscale part of the Dayton suburb of Oakwood.

Thomas's Playhouse would resolve two major problems: finding large enough space for the main polonium lab and, at the same time, securing living quarters for the expanding workforce. To be sure, staffers could rent rooms in the neighboring mansions, some with as many as sixteen rooms. The Playhouse was a private recreational facility built in 1927 as part of the estate of a prominent Dayton family, the Talbotts. It had been the setting for Thomas's marriage to Margaret Talbott in 1928. And it was Margaret who agreed to lease the building to the government, to be used for "a film laboratory for the US Army Signal Corps," as described in public documents.

As part of the lease, the government was legally required after the project was complete to restore the building to what it had once been—a pledge that, due to radiation contamination concerns, would not be kept.

The palatial two-story Playhouse—one of the two units where Koval would work—provided some of the most unusual facilities ever to be part of a scientific laboratory: an indoor tennis court under a corrugated glass roof, a squash court, changing rooms with Italian marble showers, card rooms, a spacious lounge with a two-story stone fireplace, a playhouse stage with two tiers of balconies on each side of ample seating, two greenhouses (one on each end), and an outdoor swimming pool. In recent years, the Playhouse had been used largely for community theater performances, charity benefits, music recitals, and annual dinners of all sorts. But beginning in March 1944, it became Unit IV, enveloped in barbed-wire-topped fences, twenty-four-hour floodlights, heavy power lines, and armed guards (forty-three in all), some patrolling the site while others watched from two guardhouses. All that remained of the original interior were the balconies (sealed off and used as radiation-counting labs), the corrugated glass roof, and the greenhouses, one turned into a loading dock.

Any large shipments of materials were delivered first downtown to Unit III in unmarked commercial trucks, and then, in an effort to limit public attention, the loads were shuttled in parts in small vehicles to Unit IV. If neighbors questioned guards or peeked through fences, they were told that this was a Signal Corps facility—just as the documents on file stated.

But the biggest threat was not public exposure of the project. Rather, it was the radiation from the processing. Polonium is the most radioactive element. It is 250,000 times more toxic than hydrogen cyanide gas, known for its use as a chemical weapon. Aware of the hazards, Thomas, in the spring of 1944, established a new subdivision in the Dayton Project's medical unit to monitor and test the levels of radioactivity in the labs. Because so little was known at that time about radiation's impact on people or animals, the methods of detecting radioactivity in the human body were discovered as the project itself evolved, as was the case at each of the Project sites. Unit III set up its own clinical lab in February 1945, drawing in part on the expertise at other sites, including Koval's experience with the radiation issues at the X-10 reactor in Oak Ridge.

When he transferred to Dayton from Oak Ridge, Koval joined a new health physics group. As a site inspector he was required to oversee employee radiation testing and to examine each of the units for potential dangers. This gave him access to all Dayton Project facilities. Though his official assignment was "Survey Unit #3," one of his monthly reports showed "Routine surveys consisting of thirty or more spot checks and six air samples *in each lab* every day." Beyond any doubt, Koval was trusted, based on his eleven successful months at Oak Ridge; his recently published research; his June 23, 1945, security oath; and his record of loyalty and hard work.

To be sure, life for Koval in Dayton appears to have been all about work. His responsibilities required a six-day workweek and often ten-hour days. His roommate, John Bradley, was an SED colleague from Oak Ridge assigned to Dayton at the same time as Koval. Bradley was a general supervisor based in Unit IV, and he and Koval would be the coauthors of a special report about potential contamination in the area surrounding Unit III. As roommates, they first shared a small dwelling in a boardinghouse on Main Street, and later moved to more spacious quarters in a nineteenth-century white-frame home with a sweeping veranda on Grand Avenue, near Dayton's art institute.

Dayton was not like Oak Ridge or Hanford or Los Alamos, which were sites isolated from populated areas. In Dayton, the top-secret units were located in the grid of a metropolitan area, making the lifestyle rules for workers quite restrictive. No military uniforms were allowed. Conversations about work were forbidden at public venues. And no army jeeps were allotted to technicians. This was not a problem for Koval because Dayton's buses and trolleys were close enough to his labs and lodging that he could function easily without his own vehicle. And his social life in Dayton was minimal. Later, Bradley would comment that Koval had no friends outside of the workplace.

He did, however, have a girlfriend, as had often been the case since his "business trip" began. Surely, he must have been taught that the best cover for a spy in the US was to look as apple-pie American as possible. And courting a pretty young lady could help in the crafting of such an image. There was also the possibility that he chose women based on what information he could gain from their observations or connections. For example, in Dayton, the charm on his arm was twenty-two-year-old Janet Fisher who, with her sister Marge, worked at Unit IV, the Playhouse, during the summer of 1945.

The sisters lived at home with their parents in an old Dayton neighborhood about a quarter of a mile from Bradley and Koval's apartment. Koval was known to spend Sunday evenings at the Fishers' playing bridge, after an early dinner. But his usual social charm did not beguile Janet's parents. Years later, Janet's mother would say that she wasn't fond of Koval because she was bothered that he wouldn't talk about his family. No matter how many ways she approached the topic, he always averted it. This, she told her daughter, wasn't normal. It seemed even suspicious, though she was unaware of any reason for such an instinct; he simply made her uncomfortable.

By June 1945, when Koval and Bradley arrived in Dayton, the fact that polonium could be obtained more easily and in greater quantities by using the bismuth process had been established. The irradiated bismuth at Oak Ridge and Hanford was shipped regularly to Dayton for the extraction and purification of the polonium. The polonium was then transported in trucks to Los Alamos, where the initiators were assembled.

By then too, plans for testing the first nuclear bomb were in place, having begun, with optimism and determination, more than a year before. The code name for the test was "Trinity." The chosen site was in the Jornada del Muerto desert in southwestern New Mexico. The test weapon would be a plutonium-based implosion-type bomb, code name "Gadget." Whether Koval knew of the plan is unknown, but the tension in Dayton to ship enough polonium to Los Alamos in time for the test, scheduled for July 4, would have been hard to miss, especially for a health physicist.

The importance of the polonium labs in Dayton was never clearer. On March 15, Oppenheimer had fully committed to using the beryllium-polonium initiators, and the "most promising" design for the initiator had been selected on May 1. Then, as one historian put it, "only a full-scale test culminating in a chain reaction could prove definitively that the design worked." Soon Oppenheimer's previous request for monthly shipments of the purified polonium from Dayton changed to weekly, and the total amount per month would increase from 10 curies to 500 curies, code name "cases." It took five days for the irradiated bismuth at X-10 to be cooled and transported to Dayton, and ten days for the material to do the same from Hanford. Adding twenty-five days for the polonium extraction and purification processes, it would take one month to ship the fuel to Los Alamos.

In June there were daily communications between Dayton and Los Alamos, as "quantities and delivery dates were set and then changed," showing "the immense importance of the polonium and the pressure on scientists in Dayton," as Thomas's biographer noted. "Some deadlines were so close that an employee would be sent to talk with the courier and to keep him occupied while the final touches were put on the packages," wrote a Dayton Project historian.

The July 4 "fishing trip," as Trinity was referred to in several official exchanges, was delayed by nearly two weeks, largely due to problems regarding the implosion lenses for the bomb. The new date would "not be before July 13 and would likely be July 23," wrote Oppenheimer in mid-June. Then, on July 16, at the Alamogordo Bombing and Gunnery Range in New Mexico, Gadget was detonated at 5:29 a.m. About 425 people were present, including Oppenheimer and Thomas. And despite knowing every detail of the bomb's composition and the struggles of building it, the scientists among the observers that day would try for months to describe their shock at what they saw. Oppenheimer would later say, "We knew the world would not be the same. A few people laughed, a few people cried. Most people were silent. I remembered the line from the Hindu scripture, the Bhagavad Gita: Vishnu is trying to persuade the Prince that he should do his duty and to impress him he takes on his multi-armed form and says, 'Now I am become Death, the destroyer of worlds.' I suppose we all thought that, one way or another."

The day after the test, Thomas wrote a letter to his mother, telling her, "It will take some time for the people of the world to know of this demonstration, and even after they know about it, to fully realize what it means." But for security reasons, Thomas's letter would not be mailed until late August, several weeks after the bombs were dropped on Japan. For security too, a fake story was released to calm the anxious curiosity of people living in outlying areas of the test who had seen the startling bright light or had heard the unidentifiable sounds. The story was that a considerable amount of "pyrotechnics" had exploded on the nearby Alamogordo Air Base early that morning.

Two weeks later on August 2, on an island 1,500 miles from the mainland of Japan, the uranium bomb, Little Boy, was assembled and readied to be dropped on Hiroshima. Delayed by a typhoon, the bomb was detonated on August 6, killing an estimated 135,000 people. President Harry S. Truman made his announcement that day: "The battle of the laboratories held fateful risks for us as well as the battles of the air, land, and sea, and we have now won the battle of the laboratories as we have won the other battles." A Dayton newspaper headline was: "Allies Win Great Scientific Race, U.S. Drops New Atomic Bomb on Japs." And the attempt to bury what had happened in Dayton, to sustain that wartime secrecy, began that day, as one Dayton article noted: "The atomic bomb is news to military personnel at Wright and Patterson Fields, they said this morning. There has been no testing of the bomb here whatsoever, a survey showed. The Monsanto Chemical company's Dayton plant also denied any knowledge of the bomb's development."

The plutonium bomb, Fat Man, was dropped on Nagasaki on August 9, killing 70,000 people. Six days later, the Japanese surrendered. And on that day, General Groves wrote a letter to the head of Monsanto saying that what had happened at the Dayton labs had to remain a secret, despite the success of the bombs and the celebration of the surrender. "A detailed description of your efforts must still remain undisclosed because of security requirements," he wrote, "but I want you to know that Dr. C. A. Thomas and his associates made a major contribution to our success. Dr. Thomas personally coordinated a very important phase of the chemical research pertaining to the project; he also completed vital research and solved the production problems of extreme complexity without which the Atomic Bomb could never have been."

The scientists achieved their atomic feat and the Allies won the war, but soon after Nagasaki and before the Japanese surrender, Truman authorized the release of an unexpected report, one that would stir the long-standing debate of national security versus the public's right to know. The report, issued by the US Army, soon to be published by Princeton University Press, was entitled *Atomic Energy for Military Purposes: The Official Report on the Development of the*

Atomic Bomb under the Auspices of the United States Government, 1940–1945, known henceforth as the Smyth Report.

On Saturday, August 11, the War Department's Bureau of Public Relations informed radio commentators that they could broadcast news of the report after 9 p.m. that night, and newspapers that they could publish it in Sunday morning editions, on the twelfth. Written by Henry DeWolf Smyth, chairman of the Physics Department at Princeton, and under the direction of General Leslie Groves, this report was, as its foreword described, "the story of the development of the atomic bomb" written for the general public. "Laymen with even elementary scientific knowledge will understand the report in general; scientists in any field will find it easy reading."

However, its publication shocked many Americans, especially atomic scientists, many of whom were "dumfounded [*sic*]," so claimed the *Bulletin of the Atomic Scientists*. David E. Lilienthal, the head of the Tennessee Valley Authority, who would soon be the chair of the new Atomic Energy Commission, told a Senate committee that the report was a "principal breach of security." General Groves responded, publicly, in a *Saturday Evening Post* piece as follows: "It might have been possible to keep the entire project quiet in a totalitarian state, but certainly not in the United States of America, where freedom of the press is one of our basic concepts. To have disclosed no information whatever would have been to misjudge entirely the temper of the American people and the Congress of the United States. No government official can ever refuse to tell the U.S. congress what he has done with $2 billion of public money. And, of course, many, if not all, legislators have always held—and quite properly so—to the principle that they were entitled to know anything that they felt it was necessary for them to know in order to fulfill their responsibilities to the electorate."

In other words, the information in the Smyth Report would eventually find its way to the American public, so why not have control over its release? Groves also assured America that the report did not give away any useful secrets to potential enemies. Addressing the growing fears of the Soviet Union he wrote, "We started to build almost all our plants while research was still in progress to determine just how those plants should be designed. We had a task comparable to manufacturing the world's largest steeple clock with the precision and delicacy of a lady's fine wrist watch. Russia just isn't technologically equipped to duplicate this."

And in the preface Smyth wrote, "Secrecy requirements have affected both the detailed content and general emphasis so that many interesting developments have been omitted." Groves backed that up by saying that the goal of the report was quite simply "enough secrecy for safety, enough information for sound discussion."

So it was that the Smyth Report told only the physics of the bomb story. No metallurgy or chemistry. No mention of polonium. It described the development of the production sites of Oak Ridge, Los Alamos, and Hanford, but nothing about Dayton.

Whatever the intentions or motives in issuing the report, it became the authority on the chronology and major players of the Manhattan Project. And the circulation was vast, including a Russian translation. Proof of its wide readership at the time of its release would be found in the pages of Aleksandr Solzhenitsyn's *The Gulag Archipelago*. At a prison while being transferred between gulags, he was asked by a fellow inmate to deliver a report as part of the requirement for being accepted to what was called the Scientific and Technical Society of Cell 75. The inmate happened to be a renowned Russian biologist who was an expert on the biological effects of radiation. So what report could Solzhenitsyn deliver to most impress him?

"Right then I remembered that in camp I had recently held in my hands for two nights the Smyth Report, the official report of the United States Defense Department on the first atom bomb, which had been brought in from outside. The book had been published that spring. . . . After the rations were issued, the Scientific and Technical Society of Cell 75, consisting of ten or so people, assembled at the left window and I made my report and was accepted into the society."

In Dayton, in the months following the end of the war and the Smyth Report, the work with polonium continued and the responsibilities of Thomas and his staff began to expand. Plans were made for the construction of a bigger polonium production plant, run by Monsanto, as all US polonium manufacturing would soon be centered at Monsanto. And the making of the initiators would be moved from Los Alamos to Dayton, which had to sustain its secrecy.

Such a plan was likely the reason that Koval and Bradley had been transferred from Oak Ridge in late June 1945. More polonium production obviously would raise the radiation dangers and thus increase the demand for such experienced health physicists to establish routines and design programs. The number of facilities would grow from four units to seven, scattered across Dayton. And as Monsanto became *the* U.S. manufacturer of polonium and of the bomb initiators, it would also acquire government contracts to research future military uses of polonium and peacetime applications of atomic energy. Its growth would continue, especially after the seven units were replaced by a 178-acre site twelve miles southwest of Dayton, which included an underground structure protected against biological and chemical warfare. The former units were then stripped, refurbished, and returned to their owners—except for the Runnymede Playhouse.

Unit IV, a hub for the polonium processing, would be totally dismantled. Even the cobblestones in the driveway were torn out and seven feet of dirt unearthed from beneath the building. Trucks were loaded with jagged strips of peeled-off wood, large slabs of Italian marble, and countless numbers of boxes filled with corrugated glass. All the pieces of the Runnymede Playhouse were then transported, with stones and dirt, in hundreds of truckloads to Oak Ridge to be buried.

What was accomplished at Unit IV during the war would not be revealed for more than a decade after Hiroshima and Nagasaki, and then only to an audience of scientists in a nearly four-hundred-page, highly technical report issued by the US Atomic Energy Commission. Thirteen years later, Monsanto would publish a twenty-page pamphlet, with photos, geared to the public and entitled "The Dayton Project." According to Thomas's biographer, he never talked about his wartime work with friends, fellow workers, or even family members. And although he received recognition as a top-drawer scientist on several occasions during those nearly twenty-five years of sustained secrecy, the crucial polonium project in Dayton was rarely known.

The layers and years of secrecy not only caused Dayton's recognition in the Manhattan Project to be long delayed but also assisted its resident spy's undetected status. In the small, isolated community of experts at Units III and IV, Koval was noticed only for his scientific expertise. He had even gained enough respect to be invited as part of a group of "respected specialists" to travel to Hiroshima and Nagasaki in September 1945. These were individuals sent by the army, the navy, and the Manhattan Project to study the impact of the atomic bombs—among them, radiation experts. At first, Koval accepted the honor. But according to one Russian scholar, he backed out at the last minute.

Around the same time, someone at Monsanto, likely Thomas, offered Koval a job that would allow him to continue his work as a health physicist after his demobilization from the army. It paid well and presented opportunities for professional advancement—plus, from his viewpoint and that of his handler, there would be priceless contacts for retrieving the latest information on nuclear research. But he declined the offer, perhaps recalling that when the ice is thin, it's best to walk fast.

CHAPTER TEN

SPYCRAFT

On February 12, 1946, at Camp Atterbury, Indiana, the U.S. Army discharged George Koval and awarded him three military honors: the Good Conduct Medal, the World War II Victory Medal, and the American Theater Service Ribbon. His Army Separation Qualification Record disclosed he had spent one year studying organic chemistry at Columbia University, had worked as a purchasing agent at Raven Electric for four years, and had been an "engineering aide" on the "Manhattan Engineering Project" during the war. At his exit interview, conducted by a commanding officer of the Special Engineer Detachment, Koval, like all enlisted personnel who had served on the Manhattan Project, agreed to the contents of a document entitled "Safeguarding Information."

The document included this: "After relief from assignment to the Manhattan District, you will not make any unauthorized disclosure of any classified information concerning this district to anyone regardless of status, grade, or rank, under the penalties provided by the Articles of War and the Statutes of the United States. Any violations will be viewed as serious." Then there was a list of qualifications for information considered to be high security, such as "the characteristics of the bomb, information which will reveal defensive tactics which may be employed against the weapon or its effects, and information on research methods, results, or plans."

The very next day, on February 13, 1946, part of the secrets that Koval had delivered to a courier, or his handler, months before was beginning to circulate at Soviet intelligence quarters in Moscow. This was the second section of a bundle of information from Koval that had arrived sometime in December 1945 at "Department S," which coordinated the incoming atomic bomb intelligence from abroad.

"Department S" was directed by Lieutenant General Pavel Sudoplatov, and its purpose was to improve the efficiency of gathering outside information to assist the Soviet atomic bomb project. Among other things, the department was responsible for making sure that Soviet scientists received all intelligence reports in Russian, not English. Beginning operations in February 1944, "Department S" became the destination for atomic espionage data sent from both NKGB and GRU intelligence agents abroad. And that meant that in America, NKGB and GRU atomic spies would at times work through common couriers and transports, despite their usual divisive competition.

The NKGB, previously the NKVD and later the KGB, was part of a succession of Soviet secret police and internal intelligence agencies, which during the war made organizational and functional changes, including the addition of foreign intelligence work—usually the territory of the GRU, or Red Army intelligence. Fiercely independent of internal intelligence officials, the GRU was the primary foreign intelligence service and, as such, it had been the Soviet leadership's main source of intelligence in America during the 1920s and 1930s. The GRU operated "*rezidenturas*"—"legal" spies in Soviet embassies and consulates, and "illegal" ones in cover shops and government agencies. And it had a long-running program to recruit "illegal" spies, those who worked without diplomatic cover and lived on their own for years in foreign countries. In the 1940s, however, the NKGB gained power over the GRU in America, though the GRU kept its footing.

Both the NKGB and the GRU assigned officers to track progress on America's atomic bomb project, and more. There were dozens of Soviet intelligence officers stationed at Soviet consulates or working undercover during the war. As one GRU scholar wrote, "The intelligence department of the Red Army had well-placed sleeper agents in wartime America whose goals were to collect technical information for military purposes." The Soviets also recruited a large number of Americans in military and diplomatic posts to work as couriers and informants in the Soviet espionage networks. Unlike Koval, these were "walk-ins," meaning they were spies "by impulse and sympathetic leaning rather than rigorous training." Exactly how many individuals in America had a covert relationship with Soviet intelligence will likely never be known, though decrypted cables sent between the US and Moscow during the war would later reveal the identities of 349 individuals.

Also unknown is the number of reports with atomic information sent by Delmar or Agent D. to Moscow from the time of Koval's enlistment in February 1943 to his discharge three years later. Offering a hint of the extent was a letter written in June 1944 by a GRU official sent to the Soviets at the New York *rezidentura* condemning the disappointing amount of useful materials acquired since the beginning of Operation Enormoz. The letter complained that the New York network's "direction remains unsatisfactory, and to cite our frequent reminder, other than Agent D., we don't have anything." A Russian scholar would later note in his interpretation of the letter that "The Moscow leadership was valuing Agent D. as one who was a direct participant in the performance of the nuclear program."

While at Oak Ridge, Koval gave reports to "Faraday," a fact that matches the memory of Duane Weise about their trip together to New York in late May or early June of 1945. But Koval also met with a contact identified as "Clyde" at least once while at the Oak Ridge site. "Clyde" could have been another code name used by Lassen, or by someone working for Lassen, such as his assistant William Rose, whose name did appear twice on the Oak Ridge visitor records in the spring of 1945. And Koval may have used a February 1945 leave to meet Clyde outside of Oak Ridge, as one account claims. Whoever Clyde may have been, Koval delivered details to him about the Oak Ridge site, including the monthly volume production of plutonium at X-10.

Then, in late November or early December of 1945, Koval delivered to Faraday facts about the polonium lab work in Dayton: "giving firsthand access to the research carried out on polonium." That information was in a report signed on December 22, 1945, by Major V. E. Khlopov, the "head of the first directorate of main intelligence at general headquarters" in Moscow. It was then sent to Sudoplatov at "Department S." And it read: "The polonium is sent to the state of New Mexico, where it is used for the creation of nuclear bombs. Polonium is produced from bismuth. On November 1, 1945, the plant volume of polonium produced was 300 curies per month, but that amount has now been raised to 500. A brief description of the process of polonium production will be sent to you soon." The February 13, 1946, report forwarded to Sudoplatov from Khlopov outlined the process of manufacturing polonium "that we received from a reliable source." That was Delmar.

Koval's accounts made it to Moscow through Lassen's link to the GRU officer, Pavel Mikhailov, at the Soviets' New York consulate, which sometimes used cables, the fastest method, or postal packages or letters, which took at least ten days to reach Moscow and were sent to false addresses as covers for Soviet intelligence. According to one

GRU historian, diplomatic pouches out of the Soviet embassy in DC were often used. And any reports going out before August 1945 could have been tucked into diplomatic suitcases sent on planes with war materials from the US to the Soviet Union as part of the Lend-Lease agreement. Roosevelt's Lend-Lease program, approved by Congress in early November 1941, gave billions of dollars in military aid to anti-Hitler allies, allowing them to purchase, on credit, airplanes, weapons, tanks, steel, even combat boots. And for the Soviet Union, which received more than 17 million tons of supplies racking up a bill of nearly $11 billion, it provided a potential conduit for intelligence shipments carried by the Lend-Lease planes loaded at the massive air force base in Great Falls, Montana, destination USSR. The last Lend-Lease shipment to the Soviet Union was in August 1945.

The content of Koval's December 1945 and February 1946 reports showed in part why his handler and others were vexed by his decision to turn down the job offer at Monsanto in Dayton, a post with access to classified information. The potential for what he could learn at Monsanto in the years ahead was likely a heart-throbbing vision to the GRU. For instance, by the end of 1946, all equipment and designs for the manufacture of atomic bomb triggers would be moved to Dayton, where Monsanto "personnel would obtain full information from Los Alamos and from equipment manufacturers" about how to make the initiator. For the GRU, the position would have been ideal: an astute scientist fluent in English, well respected at Monsanto, and now adept at espionage as he entered the sixth year of his "business trip" to America.

But Koval's seasoned instincts must have warned him to decline the offer. The Monsanto security check would dig deeper into his past as a new employee than perhaps the recent forays into his files as a member of the elite SED, especially after being part of the Army Specialized Training Program at CCNY. Any in-depth background check would turn up Koval's vulnerabilities. All it would take was the discovery of one lie in his records, one tie to someone in the wartime web of Soviet spies in the US, whether NKGB or GRU, or one family member in the Soviet Union—just one clue to his hidden identity.

Having grown up in America, Koval had a history of relationships and activities that could have popped up at any moment. He could casually run into a former classmate from Sioux City or the University of Iowa, someone who would know that he and his family had moved to Russia in 1932. Then there was the fact that although his name was not on the family passport, it certainly could be found in official files, such as those regarding the Iowa State Convention of the Communist Party held in Chicago in mid-August 1930, which Koval attended as Iowa's delegate of the Young Communist League. The convention report was filed in Des Moines at the Iowa Communist Party headquarters. Of more concern, a detailed account of the convention had been filed at the Chicago headquarters of the American Vigilant Intelligence Federation, the vigorous anti-Communist organization loaded with informers covering such events and listing the names of every participant. The AVI forwarded its report to the local branch of the FBI, which in turn sent it to Hoover, as he instructed them to do in the 1920s. The AVI document was also published in a congressional report in October 1930.

Another damaging public record—one that the FBI would eventually discover—was his September 1931 arrest file at the Woodbury County Sheriff's Office in Sioux City. This revealed that he was arrested for acts committed as an ardent member of the Unemployed Councils, set up by the Communist Party's Trade Union Unity League. The story about Koval's arrest that made the front page of the *Sioux City Journal* noted his charges as allegedly inciting a "raid" at a government office.

Then there was the lengthy letter he wrote in 1935 to his relatives and friends in the US about his life in Russia and his love for the Soviet Union, published in IKOR's official publication, *Nailebn*, or

"New Life." "What a great race are the 'BOLSHEVIKS!'" he wrote. Also appearing in the magazine's July 1932 issue was the Koval family passport photo. And there was the 1936 article about New York editor and writer Paul Novick's two months at the Jewish Autonomous Region in the summer that year, including details about "the Kovals of Sioux City, Iowa."

All these records could be found if there was a reason to look, such as the discovery of just one false statement on an official document during a security check of Koval's files at Oak Ridge or Dayton. And, in post–World War II America, the winds had changed direction and were blowing hard. During the war, a Soviet spy suspected of atomic bomb espionage might be followed and reported, but not arrested or prosecuted. Such action would have exposed the secret of the bomb project, particularly if the suspect was a spy with scientific expertise. By September 1945, none of that mattered anymore and a spy like Koval had a choice: stand on the cliff expecting to be pushed and hope for a safe landing, or make a well-timed plan to cautiously escape.

In the aftermath of the war, the nation's fears had shifted from Japan and Germany to the Soviet Union. America's wartime ally was no longer needed, and thus Communist Russia was slammed back into its prewar status as the declared enemy of America—with renewed, inflamed passion. No longer was Mother Russia a friend.

Helping to bolster anti-communist views was the House Un-American Activities Committee (HUAC), formed in 1938, and once headed by Martin Dies Jr., the Democratic congressman from Texas who in 1940 said, "God gave us America and the Marxists shall not take it away." HUAC's initial quest, as an investigative committee of the US House of Representatives, was to expose both the fascist and communist groups that posed a threat to American security by allegedly infiltrating schools, government, even Hollywood. Its legacy, however, would be its unrelenting pursuits to uncover and uproot Communist espionage.

In 1944, Dies retired and John Rankin, a Democratic congressman from Mississippi, became the new HUAC chair. With a reputation as an ardent anti-Semite and a hardcore racist, Rankin disseminated the theory that communism was a Jewish plot. Hence, he used Red-baiting as a strategy to investigate what he claimed was the Jewish conspiracy behind the American liberals and the New Deal. In the aftermath of the war, HUAC, under Rankin's leadership, became a standing committee, soon to enter its fiery heyday.

But in addition to congressional Red-baiting and risky public records, what must have stirred Koval's caution enough for him to reject the Dayton job were the Soviet defections and detections that occurred in late 1945 and early 1946—potentially inching closer to Koval.

CHAPTER ELEVEN

DEFECTIONS AND DETECTIONS

As a cipher clerk at the Soviet embassy in Ottawa, Canada, and a GRU intelligence officer, Igor Gouzenko had access to the secret communications of the GRU and NKGB between Canada and the Soviet consulates and embassies in Britain and the US. He was even able to open the safe in the embassy's cipher room, which contained such documents as officer dossiers and coded telegrams. Cipher clerks were the background players in the espionage world where spies were the featured performers. But in early September 1945, Gouzenko captured the limelight, bringing fame to his cryptic trade when he left his office never to return again, stuffing in his shirt 109 top-secret Soviet cables and more than a hundred documents outing Soviet spies in Canada, Britain, and the US, including some connected with atomic bomb espionage. It was "a dazzling cache of stolen GRU documents," as one scholar later described the feat.

In the days ahead, Gouzenko sought asylum for himself, his wife, and their fifteen-month-old son, as he gave the bulging contents of his theft to the Royal Canadian Mounted Police. After the RCMP informed the FBI, J. Edgar Hoover, on September 12, sent an urgent message to President Truman about the defector and his claims, one of which was that Stalin had made "the obtaining of complete information regarding the atomic bomb the Number One Project of Soviet espionage."

Because of Soviet mole Kim Philby, who was chief of British counterintelligence, the Soviets knew almost immediately about the defection. "For the Russians, the defection was nothing short of a disaster, calling for a thorough reexamination of their intelligence operations," a scholar later wrote. Lavrentiy Beria, by then Stalin's deputy premier, his "first lieutenant," would soon send a cable to every *rezidentura* abroad, warning that "G.'s defection has caused great damage to our country and has, in particular, very greatly complicated our work in the American countries." Instructions would soon be sent, he wrote, regarding ways to improve all agent networks and rules to tighten security. "The work must be organized so that each member of the staff and agent can have no knowledge of our work beyond what directly relates to the task he is carrying out."

There was reason for panic, as Gouzenko had exposed Canadian and American spy networks and ignited a firestorm of counterintelligence searches for Communist spies on both sides of the border. Spies with whom Koval had ties were among those affected, such as Arthur Adams who, among other things, had once obtained a false Canadian passport through Sam Carr, head of the Canadian Communist party and one of the Soviet agents exposed by Gouzenko. Passport secrets were indeed among those the cipher clerk uncovered, showing the ways such fraud was devised.

Gouzenko unveiled numerous stars on the Soviet stage of spies, including an unnamed assistant to the US assistant secretary of state—later identified as Alger Hiss. He also outed Fred Rose, a member of the Canadian parliament. Considered to be one of the most important Soviet agents in Canada, Rose was the head of the GRU's Montreal group of spies. As such he was connected to

Pavel Mikhailov at the Soviet consulate in Manhattan, linking Rose indirectly to Arthur Adams, Benjamin Lassen, and thus to Koval. When Rose was elected to the Canadian House of Commons in 1943, Mikhailov cabled Moscow, "Fred, our man in Lesovia [code for Canada] has been elected to the Lesovian parliament."

Fred Rose, like Adams, Lassen, and Jacob Golos once had worked at Amtorg in New York. Both Golos and Lassen, through Mikhailov or World Tourists, had used Rose to obtain Canadian travel documents for agents they assisted. One of Rose's spy duties was to help "with bogus documentation for Soviet illegals seeking entry into the USA and beyond."

Whether Koval had ever met any of these people other than Lassen is unknown. But in the months ahead, Fred Rose's organizational ties in both the Canadian and American spy networks would begin to surface, often in front-page news stories on both sides of the border. Hoover would send an urgent memo to his bureau chiefs announcing that the Gouzenko case must be their "no. 1 project" and that every resource should be used "to run down *all* angles very promptly." It was in the midst of such exposures that Koval was offered the job at Monsanto in Dayton.

Like an aftershock to the Gouzenko earthquake, a few months later, another spy defected, this time an American by the name of Elizabeth Bentley, who had been the deputy and lover of Jacob Golos. After his death in 1943, Bentley took over two Golos networks of Communist informants: both headed by economists, one on the War Production Board and the other on the Board of Economic Warfare. Both men had ties to individuals known to Lassen. Though she likely did not know Koval, Bentley must have known Lassen because of his long-lasting ties to Golos and because Golos leased an apartment in the same building where Lassen maintained his principal office. The details she released would not be widely known to the public until the summer of 1948, but on November 6, 1945, when she walked into the FBI's New York bureau and began to spill the names and operations of dozens of Soviet spies she had known for the previous seven years, Bentley would further shake the trembling foundation of Soviet espionage in the US. Her interviews, which filled a 115-page single-space dossier, revealed the details of a vast infiltration of Soviet spies in America, especially during the war years. The Bentley defection was quickly known in Moscow.

The next strike against the spy networks connected indirectly or directly to Koval came within days of Bentley's last November meeting at the FBI's New York bureau. That was a four-part series about Soviet espionage in America published in the *New York Journal-American*, a widely circulated and highly conservative newspaper owned by William Randolph Hearst. The writer, Howard Rushmore, was a former editor at the *Daily Worker*, the CPUSA official organ, and a former party member. He was expelled from both in 1939 when he refused to write an unfavorable review of the film *Gone With the Wind*—a task ordered by the Communist Party, so claimed Rushmore. At the *Journal-American*, Rushmore specialized in anti-Communist articles, and his boss at the paper was a former FBI agent effectively serving as a conduit to the Feds—thus, a grand source for a rich assortment of incriminating details about Soviet spies in the US. He was also the newspaper's connection to Hoover, who was a master at using the press for his own purposes. In the case of Rushmore's series, Hoover wanted to humiliate President Truman into taking a harder stand against Soviet spies. Arthur Adams was the focus of the first article of the series, on December 3, 1945.

Using the fictional name "Alfred Adamson," Rushmore introduced an alleged Soviet agent under investigation by the FBI, who used a job at a music company located on Fifth Avenue as his cover work. The firm was owned by the same person who ran a small music store on West Forty-Fourth Street and who paid "Adamson" $75 a week. That person was clearly Eric Bernay, at whose store, The Music

Room, Adams had first met Clarence Hiskey years before. Rushmore claimed that "Adamson" had once received atomic bomb secrets from a scientist based in Chicago and that he had carried a heavy case of documents on a ride in a black Plymouth sedan that bore the license plate of the Soviet consulate, a number registered under the name "Pavel Mikhailov." He also outlined how Adamson sent cables to his American wife in Moscow through the wife of a Manhattan doctor who practiced on the Upper West Side. He stressed that it had been two years since the FBI had discovered a package of papers filled with atomic bomb details in the spy's hotel room and that despite the mounds of information sent to the State Department proving Adamson's espionage crimes, there had been "no action on his arrest."

The point of the article was to shame the Truman administration for not apprehending Adams-Adamson. It was also a scare tactic. Rushmore reminded his readers: "The real name under which [Adamson] operates and the name of the hotel in which he is staying are known to the *Journal-American*." This was a warning to Adams and his associates: *Look at what we know. We're on your tail. We'll get you soon.*

It must have worked with Mikhailov. On December 13, the tall, slim vice consul with a blond pompadour was driven in a black sedan from the Soviet consulate in Manhattan to Jersey City, New Jersey, where he boarded the SS *Suvorov*, a Soviet vessel headed for Murmansk, Russia. What effect the series had on Adams or exactly when he had become aware of the round-the-clock attention he was getting from FBI agents is undocumented. However, certainly before the *Journal-American* series, his instincts as a well-seasoned spy must have been on high alert. Months after the Feds began tailing him in 1944, Hoover had ordered the tapping of his phone calls and the bugging of his room, #1103 at the Peter Cooper Hotel on East Thirty-Ninth Street. FBI agents were tracking his every move, even sitting behind him in movie theaters.

In late spring 1945, a gentleman visiting Adams in his hotel room informed him that as he entered the hotel he was photographed by men with cameras in the windows of a building across the street, and that he was then followed by two men who stood nearby as he stopped to straighten his tie. The visitor asked Adams if he knew about this. Adams told him he did, and that it was just "some trouble" having to do with his work in the recording business, at Keynote. Then Adams quickly changed the subject to the Met Lab in Chicago, where his guest had worked with Clarence Hiskey. Adams made clear without saying too much that he knew about the atomic bomb research in Chicago and he wanted to find out more. "Don't you feel that this thing you were working on belongs to humanity?" Adams asked. The man replied that he likely agreed with Adams, but with the qualification "only if the world were well ordered." Adams then began asking questions about the making of the bomb, with a polite and direct suggestion that his guest tell him what he should know. The guest, aware now that this must be some sort of recruitment, said "No, as long as the over-all policy for secrecy is in existence, I feel I must conform to that, even though I could be in disagreement with it." And then the conversation moved to the topic of the war, and the guest soon left. Clearly, Adams was unstoppable, or so it seemed.

In the aftermath of the *Journal-American* articles and Mikhailov's sudden departure, Hoover sent a memo to the New York bureau instructing it to summon Adams and interview him "for the purpose of eliciting his comments regarding the articles and particularly for the purpose of obtaining from him positive statements regarding his immigration and citizenship status. Since the departure of his Consulate contact, Mikhailov, Adams may be willing to discuss in detail his actual mission in the U.S. The interviewing agents should exercise extreme caution to conceal from Adams the extent of the Bureau's information concerning him and his cohorts since Adams may attempt to determine just what the Bureau does know."

That interview never happened. Instead an exchange took place between Adams and Special Agent Leonard Langen at a bus stop at East Fifty-Third and Madison, on January 12, 1946, at 9 p.m., during which Adams tried to do exactly what Hoover feared: manipulate an agent into revealing details about what the bureau knew while putting on an act. When Langen saw Adams running for a Madison Avenue bus that was extremely packed, knowing Adams's propensity for darting suddenly into a large crowd and disappearing, he moved to a position near Adams to be sure to board the bus with him—which he did. Then suddenly Adams jumped off the bus, as did the agent, as it pulled away, leaving him with the agent alone at the bus stop. And for the next hour and fifteen minutes, standing in the cold, they talked. Adams complained about the *Journal-American* article and vehemently denied that he was a Soviet espionage agent. He had never even been to Russia, he stressed. He said that he expected to remain in the US for the rest of his life and he was eager to become a US citizen as soon as he could gather the appropriate documents.

The last time any agents tracking Adams saw him was on January 23, 1946. At 1:30 p.m. that day, he visited Victoria Stone's jewelry store on Madison Avenue, carrying a small black bag and a cardboard box. Stone was one of Adams's intermediaries with Eric Bernay, Pavel Mikhailov, and others. He then walked to the New York Public Library on Forty-Second Street and Fifth Avenue, where he read a magazine about machinery. At 4:35 p.m. he returned to his office at Keynote Recordings, never to be seen again. Though agents watched the building and were told by a confidential informant that at 5:05 p.m. Adams was still in his office, the New York bureau couldn't find him. By 1 a.m. on the twenty-fourth, ten more agents were searching for him in Manhattan. Other field offices were notified. Immigration and customs personnel at all ports of departure from the US were placed on high alert. It was discovered that most of Adams's belongings at the Peter Cooper Hotel had been removed. The only evidence that he was still alive would be a postcard sent a few days later to Victoria Stone. Postmarked New York, New York, January 26, 7:30 a.m., it read, "Victoria Dearest: This is to let you know that everything is O.K. Regards to my friends and much love to you. A.A. January 25, 1946."

On February 16, the *Journal-American* ran a front-page story by Rushmore with the headline: "Red Atom Spy Eludes FBI as Canada Nabs 22; Ottawa Acts on Leak of Top Secrets." It began: "The ring leader of the international Soviet spy network, whose efforts to steal atomic bomb secrets were exposed in the *New York Journal-American* last December 3, fled in haste from his midtown hotel room three weeks ago, it was learned today. A man named in the *Journal-American* as Alfred Adamson is linked with the 22 persons now being questioned by Canadian officials on charges of giving secret atomic information to Russia." The article then discussed more details about "Adamson" and his ties to the Canadian spy ring, his mail-drop system of sending documents, and his link to the head of an electrical company who, the article said, "is now also under surveillance." It is unclear to whom the story referred.

Two weeks later, on March 5, the *New York Times* ran its first story about the Gouzenko defection. The *Times* had waited for the release of the official Canadian reports of the investigation into the "network of undercover agents organized and developed by members of the staff of the Soviet Embassy at Ottawa under direct instructions from Moscow." The first report made clear that information about the atomic bomb project was a high priority for the Soviet spies.

The second report on the investigation was scheduled to be released on the day in mid-March when Fred Rose was arrested at his home in Ottawa, after returning from the first session of the 1946 Canadian parliament. He was the first public official in the West to ever be charged with spying for the Soviet Union. Under a photo of Rose on the front page of the *Journal-American* was the caption "How Many of These Are in the U.S.?"

CHAPTER TWELVE

THE JOINER

By the time Koval had returned to New York in February 1946, anti-Communism seemed like an unstoppable blight. In early spring, as the media was spewing out more details about spies and stolen atomic secrets, the House Un-American Activities Committee was looking for leaks at Oak Ridge. This quest was partly triggered by a mid-March front-page article in the *Journal-American* about an employee at an Oak Ridge plant who was allegedly peddling information about "atomic developments" to spies in Arthur Adams's network. On March 24, Hoover sent a teletype memo from DC to the New York bureau, marked "urgent," with a reprint of the story. Around the same time, the US Army "ordered that all officers with 'subversive' views be moved out of positions of trust."

Koval must have known by then how smart he was to reject the job in Dayton, a post so closely tied to the military and to ongoing nuclear bomb research. He would seem to be safe from the recent defections as no direct line could be drawn between Gouzenko's list of names and himself. Also, while the outbreak had transpired, he was in the US Army—quite a cover. Still, he had indirect ties to the GRU Canadian network as well as to Adams, and he no longer had the shelter of his health physics post with the security clearance. The irony was that he had been safer from exposure during the war. Now, his plan must be to try to keep a low profile, request his return to Moscow and, while waiting for orders, avoid detection. Making the best of the challenges history was handing him, he applied for the US GI bill to return to CCNY for the completion of the degree in electrical engineering he had begun while in the Army Specialized Training Program.

For several months Koval lived in an apartment in Washington Heights. It may have been the same place on Fort Washington Avenue that Lassen had been using for temporary housing when he hosted new espionage recruits from abroad, where Koval had lived after his arrival in 1940. Then by summer he had moved back to the Bronx, this time to Valentine Avenue in a neighborhood with a different ambience from the Sholem Aleichem buildings. His new home was in a four-story apartment house on a busy street lined with parked cars, where no one, except perhaps the landlady, knew anything about anyone and where there were no direct ties to Lassen. There were no hints of communist idealism, no spy network, though the Lassens' apartment was only a four-minute walk away. And while the world continued to make its postwar adjustments and America turned up the volume on its Soviet fears, Koval soon settled into a routine at CCNY, his island surrounded by quicksand.

There is no firm evidence of Koval engaging in espionage in 1946. As one American scholar later wrote, "The Canadian disaster alone was enough to ice [Soviet] espionage operations in New York throughout most of 1946." The information he had previously supplied to "Department S" had been sent to Moscow by late 1945.

However, by 1946 Koval was adept enough at his craft to leave no traces. He appeared to dutifully follow the basic rules: Never socialize with members of the cell network. Never meet at the home of a courier or handler. Never connect with the Communist Party.

Never praise the Soviet Union or preach the Communist ideals. Always make contacts in public places, like parks or cafés. And one other piece of advice: Join clubs. To acquire useful contacts as well as the latest news in a spy's assigned field, he was urged to become an active club member. This was a lesson from the MIT science spy models and surely from Koval's espionage training, as well as from his handler's past experience—Lassoff, the club enthusiast. Be a joiner. Better yet, become the president of a club—which, by some accounts, is exactly what Koval did.

In 1946, around the time of Koval's return to school, the national honorary fraternity for electrical engineers, Eta Kappa Nu, opened a chapter at CCNY, under the faculty guidance of Henry Hanstein. Soon Koval would become committed to the new club and in the following year, he appeared to be running it. "He was extremely interested in fraternity affairs and we engaged in many conversations," Hanstein later recalled. That was not surprising considering that the two scientists shared a special interest in nuclear energy. In fact, a former colleague would later comment that, though Hanstein was not officially part of the Manhattan Project, "it is correct to say that he was one of the designers of the bomb." And in an October 1945 edition of the CCNY student newspaper, *The Campus*, Hanstein was on the "List of Faculty on Atom Bomb Project."

Hanstein, who was highly respected in the field of electrical engineering, had been a student of Enrico Fermi's during the early years of work on nuclear fission. He had earned his doctorate at Columbia in 1942, with a dissertation on the topic of Columbia's cyclotron. Koval could easily have met Hanstein at Columbia in 1941 or during his CCNY course studies in the Army Specialized Training Program, at which time Hanstein was teaching at CCNY.

Because CCNY's Eta Kappa Nu chapter had just begun, officially on February 16, 1946, Koval and Hanstein must have had meetings about program planning and the choice of lecturers. After all, item number six on the Eta Kappa Nu's twenty services list in its manual advised: "Plan and organize a lecture series of outside speakers on timely and provocative topics of importance to U.S. engineers." For Koval, such instruction could have echoed his Soviet intelligence training.

To be sure, Koval may have remained in touch with his handler. His Valentine Avenue landlady, Mrs. G. Gardner, later remarked about his "one regular visitor." She didn't know the man's name as she never met him, which did not surprise her as Koval "kept very much to himself." But she did observe that the visitor had thin gray hair, a short speckled beard, and a stocky build. He was likely in his sixties, about five feet seven. And, as she would later recall, he was a gentleman, always "cleanly dressed and nicely mannered." He also spoke with a foreign accent, which she thought might be French. This description fits Lassen, who by the late 1940s was in his sixties and was fluent in French, among his other languages.

Despite the espionage advice to avoid political activity, Koval did attend such an event in August 1947 in Old Westbury on Long Island. It was at the estate of Michael Whitney Straight, who was then the publisher of the *New Republic* magazine, owned by his family. The event's purpose was to rally support for former vice president Henry A. Wallace in his upcoming run in the 1948 presidential race. Wallace had been secretary of agriculture in President Roosevelt's first two terms of office and vice president in the third term. In that post, he worked on Roosevelt's Top Policy Group, which advised the president on the development of nuclear weapons, soon focusing on the production of the atomic bomb and evolving into the Manhattan Project. And in that role, Wallace, from late 1942, at least, had been privy to the project plans and reports, budgets, sites, and constructions. He was also a member of the War Production Board.

In Roosevelt's fourth term, Wallace was appointed US secretary of commerce, a post he continued to hold after the president's death in April 1945 for more than a year under Truman. But then in September 1946, Truman fired Wallace for giving a speech that proclaimed strong pro-Soviet views. After Wallace left the Truman administration, Michael Straight hired him to be editor of the *New Republic*. And in announcing the new post, the magazine published a front-page statement written by Wallace: "As editor of *The New Republic* I shall do everything I can to rouse the American people, the British people, the French people, the Russian people and in fact the liberally minded people of the whole world, to the need of stopping this dangerous armament race."

What drew Koval to Straight's home that day is unknown. Koval surely was aware that Wallace was born in Iowa, and Koval likely agreed with Wallace's views about the working class. As Wallace said at the Commodore Hotel in New York in May 1942: "I say that the century on which we are entering—the century which will come into being after this war—can be and must be the century of the common man."

And there was also Straight himself, with whom Koval shared knowledge of espionage and possible Soviet connections. In the 1930s, while a student at Cambridge, in England, Straight had worked with Soviet spies in a ring later known as "the Cambridge Five." In America in the 1940s, during the war, he developed a close association with an NKGB officer who was running two networks with ties to both Adams and Lassen.

Koval's motive for attending the Long Island lecture could also have been simply a need during his seventh year in America to quietly connect with like-minded people, especially in 1947, a time when those with left-leaning politics were so intensely under fire. Or he could have been following an espionage guideline of making contacts in public places.

Years later, a man who had attended the same gathering told an FBI agent inquiring about Koval that he remembered it as a political rally at an estate on Long Island and that he was surprised to see George Koval, his former colleague in health physics at Oak Ridge. The man and his wife had made the trip from Brookhaven National Laboratory, which was then under the authority of the Atomic Energy Commission, on Long Island, and his place of employment. With the quest to explore peaceful uses of atomic energy, Brookhaven had recently opened and it was building the first nuclear reactor in the US after the war. The man told the agent that the couple's visit to the event was "purely out of curiosity in the interest of seeing the estate," which they had been told was "quite fabulous." They knew nothing about a Henry Wallace rally scheduled for that day. Consequently, he and his wife, he stressed, had remained at the event for "only a short while."

However, he went on to say, he saw Koval standing alone in the crowd, with his hands in the pockets of his trousers, and looking very serious. And after Wallace's speech, the man tried to start up a conversation with Koval. "I sought him out merely to say 'hello' to him." But they exchanged few words, Koval saying only that he was "continuing engineering studies in New York City." That was all; the man was confident, he said, about his memory of the day. And he assured the FBI agent that he never again saw or spoke with his "friend from Oak Ridge." He said that twice.

Koval's classes at CCNY began in the first week of September that year, almost to the day of the second anniversary of Gouzenko's defection. By then, in 1947, ten defendants discovered through the 1945 exposure had been convicted and sentenced to prison, and sixteen others were either acquitted or awaiting appeals. Allan Nunn May, a British physicist who had sent small samples of uranium to Moscow and who was the first of Moscow's atomic bomb spies to be caught, was sentenced in May 1946 to ten years of hard labor at Wakefield Prison in West Yorkshire. It was May who had opened the Pandora's box about Soviet spies stealing atomic bomb secrets, jump-starting a hunt that would continue for at least the next decade. May expressed no regrets for what he had done. As his attorney told the court, "All scientific knowledge should become the property of all mankind."

But this was a view barely visible in the autumn of 1947, blocked as it was by rising waves of paranoia and burgeoning errors of hysteria. Months before, in May, HUAC had moved its guillotine to Hollywood, launching high-publicity testimonies to attack the alleged communist infiltration of the film industry. Even some of the most popular recent films came under brutal attack, such as the *Song of Russia*, a 1944 hit starring Robert Taylor that included scenes of wheat farmers dancing on collectives and dialogue about the US and Soviet Union being "two great countries brought together for this great fight for humanity" against Germany. But in October 1947, the author Ayn Rand testified that the film was a pro-Soviet propaganda piece, "a deliberate whitewash of the terrible reality of life under communism" in her native country.

Despite a petition signed by eighty stars, such as Gene Kelly, Humphrey Bogart, and Lauren Bacall, to denounce and block the committee's assault on political and personal privacy, at least forty studio executives, actors, writers, and directors were subpoenaed. Suddenly Hollywood was divided between what would be called "friendly" and "unfriendly" witnesses. The former consisted of those who would answer all questions asked by HUAC; it included famous players like Ronald Reagan, Walt Disney, Gary Cooper, and Robert Montgomery. Then there were the nineteen others—all men, mostly screenwriters, a few directors, and one actor—who claimed that the committee's pursuit was an unconstitutional and un-American invasion of privacy. Of those, eleven were called to testify, including Bertolt Brecht, the acclaimed German playwright who left the US on the day after his testimony, never returning.

The remaining ten, in the name of constitutional rights, took the First Amendment as their defense, refused to answer questions about their political and personal beliefs, and would not participate in "naming names." HUAC would not acknowledge their constitutional rights, and thus in the weeks ahead all ten would be held in contempt of Congress—the "Hollywood 10." And on October 27, *Time* magazine quoted the film director Sam Wood as saying, "If I have any doubt that they are [Communists], then I haven't any mind. I am convinced that these Hollywood Commies are agents of a foreign country. These Communists thump their chests and call themselves liberals, but if you drop their rompers you'll find a hammer & sickle on their rear ends."

But Hoover had been hunting for big game in the wrong field. In February 1948, a professionally trained officer of Red Army Intelligence, George Koval—also a demobilized US Army corporal—graduated, cum laude, from CCNY with a degree in electrical engineering. He ranked fourth in a class of 186 engineers and second in a class of 66 electrical engineers. Then on March 15, the US Department of State issued passport #170092 to George Koval—middle name Abramovich not used—which stated that he would need it to do business abroad for a New York–based company called Atlas Trading Corporation, for a duration of four to six months, during which he would visit France, Belgium, Switzerland, Sweden, and Poland. On the application form, he had indicated that he was an electrical engineer by profession and that his identifying witness was "Herbert J. Sandberg," whom Koval first met in September 1943 when they were both in the Army Specialized Training Program at CCNY. Sandberg, the form accurately noted, had known Koval "for a period of approximately five years."

Also in the application file was a letter addressed to the State Department's passport office on the stationery of "Atlas Trading Corp., 17 Battery Place, New York 4, New York." Dated March 8, 1948, it stated that "George Koval" would act as a representative for Atlas, an import-export firm, on a commission basis in Europe. The letter was signed by Pedro R. Rincones, who identified himself as the "President of Atlas."

But Atlas did business only in South America and never in Europe; it did not commission its sales representatives; and it had no record of an employee by the name of George Koval. Further, it was the owner of Atlas, Francisco Petrinovic, who ordered the company president, Rincones, to write the letter. A native of Yugoslavia, Petrinovic was a naturalized citizen of Chile where, by some accounts, he had been quite successful in the nitrate business. He lived in New York City during the war years, having close ties to Soviet diplomatic channels. Proof of that was a cable he sent in July 1944 to "Viktor," code name for Lieutenant General Pavel Mikhailovich Fitin, in Moscow. At the time of the cable, Fitin, who was credited with naming the Soviet atomic spy project Enormoz, was head of the NKGB's foreign intelligence. In the cable, Petrinovic wrote, "Refused permission; There is no chance leaving at the moment."

For Koval, it must have been a colossal relief to have secured a US passport, in readiness for his escape from America. When he would use it, he likely didn't know, as he continued his "business trip," now in its eighth year. And before the end of March, he would meet Jean Finkelstein, the charming sister of one of his fraternity brothers—perfect timing for a Soviet spy who in the months ahead would be surrounded by the suspicions and hysteria of mounting anti-Communism. As Koval's companion, Jean could be the ballast in what would turn out to be a volatile year for Soviet spies in the West—a time when differences of opinion could not be kept within reasonable bounds, when clues to the truth were blurred by fear, and when opportunists flourished in America, more than usual.

CHAPTER THIRTEEN

THE ESCAPE

From the point of view of his landlady, George Koval could be best described as an earnest student and a "true loner." Since his move to Valentine Avenue in 1946, Mrs. Gardner had observed his daily routine of leaving early each morning, returning several hours after dinner, and quietly walking up the four flights of stairs to his apartment. She assumed he would spend the rest of the evening doing all that good students do. The fact that he earned his CCNY degree in two years did not surprise her, largely because his studies were the center of his life—from her point of view, that is.

To Mrs. Gardner, Koval was a timid, remote man who appeared to be burdened by a sad past. This was likely because, as he told her, he had lost both parents at a very young age and was raised in an orphanage in Cleveland, Ohio. "He supposedly had one aunt who never took much interest in him," she later said, "and he appeared to be very poorly fixed financially."

However, when away from Valentine Avenue Koval was no melancholy introvert bordering on poverty. As one of his CCNY friends would later say, "He was very popular at school. Everybody liked

George." And because he was older than most of his classmates, he had "a moderating influence in virtually all forms of discussion." He also had a reputation for being "quite the ladies' man," as one of Jean Finkelstein's brothers later pointed out, adding, "Before he dated Jean, he would bring exotic looking, attractive, refugee-type women from Manhattan to parties. Always someone different."

Though his grades were consistently good and his class participation noteworthy, it was not uncommon for Koval to skip classes, or even occasionally to fall asleep in class as if he had been up all night. But this, like many things about him, easily slipped into the fabric of student life, almost unnoticed. A former classmate would later comment that he didn't think twice when he first saw Koval smoking a cigarette down to the last visible speck, pressing the stub to the point of burning both fingers. "I thought, not exactly the typical American way of doing it. More European or somewhere."

Another of his CCNY classmates described Koval as "a rather mysterious person." On the one hand, he was quite gregarious, but on the other "nobody knew much about him at all, very little about his background." And though he averted questions about himself, he did share his political views. "Koval was very conservative politically and he would let you know it. On one occasion when the American Youth for Democracy (AYD) gained control of the Student Council, Koval led a group of engineers in opposition to the tactics and policies of the AYD in the council," said the classmate. The AYD, formerly known as the Young Communist League, was an avid promoter of communism and actively involved in working-class struggles. It was on Hoover's hit list.

But whatever was even slightly enigmatic about Koval never scared away friends, of whom he seemed to have many. There were his classmates at CCNY; instructors at Columbia; fellow Eta Kappa Nu members; colleagues from the Manhattan Project, in both Dayton and Oak Ridge; and employees at the electrical supply shop in

Manhattan where he worked part-time. He even had a few tennis partners in Boston, where he went occasionally "on business," as he told Jean. Among his close friends, there was Herbie Sandberg, now a physics instructor at CCNY. Ten years younger than Koval, Sandberg may have been a protégé, especially considering that his political leanings matched those of Koval's secret life. Sandberg was a registered member of the American Labor Party and of the Teachers Union—both organizations suspected by Hoover in 1948 of being "Communist-led."

That year, 1948, Sandberg lived in a brownstone on West Ninety-Eighth Street, half a block west from Broadway, in a first-floor apartment with a wide bay window. Jean often accompanied Koval there for parties where she would meet graduate students and instructors from the physics, chemistry, and electrical engineering departments at both CCNY and Columbia. She would later describe them as "intellectuals who dressed and acted like Bohemians." From physicists, chemists, electrical suppliers, and travel agents to tennis players, academicians, bowling league members and more, the matrix of Koval's public life was far more expansive than Mrs. Gardner could have imagined or than Koval ever revealed.

It was the same about his work, which he rarely discussed, even with Jean. He told her only that he worked at an electrical supply company called Ace Electric, in the West Twenties in Manhattan. She never visited the place, never met any of his coworkers, and didn't even know exactly what his job was. She did know that it involved travel. He had explained to her that the "potential for foreign travel" connected with his job was increasing with time, though he never mentioned specific countries, what the work would entail, or when it might begin. The only job he ever talked much about was the one he had in the 1930s working at a radio station in New York. That was when he lived at 311 West Seventy-Second Street, he said. She didn't know that it was all untrue.

Born in Brooklyn, raised in the Bronx with three older brothers, Jean was a strong, street-smart young woman. Still, she admittedly never questioned the stories Koval told her. Besides, what he talked about most often was baseball. It wasn't the blossoming trees that made springtime in New York his favorite season: it was the return of his beloved sport. The 1948 season began in mid-April and from then on, partly because someone at his workplace apparently gave him tickets, he and Jean rarely missed a Yankees home game, especially during the team's nine-game winning streak that August.

During their nearly seven months together, Jean did not visit Koval's Valentine Avenue apartment, which was about two miles from where she lived with her parents on Morris Avenue in the Bronx. Later she would remember he was out of town only twice for any extended period. The first time was in late March, just after they had met, and he went to DC. He said he was meeting old friends there from the war years and they were planning to attend "an art show featuring paintings found by the US occupying forces of Germany and which were being exhibited in a museum somewhere in Washington." He was gone for several days.

Then in August, he left for a trip to the Midwest, for "business purposes," he told her. She wasn't sure where he went; possibly Kansas City, she said. The trip lasted about ten days, and when he returned he pulled a copy of his high school yearbook out of his duffle bag. When she asked if he had been to Sioux City, he said, no, but a friend had. And that was all that was said. That Jean was in love with a Soviet spy surely never occurred to her. If it had, then Koval's aura of discretion and occasional secrecy certainly would have made sense to her, especially in the summer of 1948 when HUAC was once again on the hunt for Soviet spies, with a sharp focus on the ones specializing in atomic bomb espionage.

In the months immediately following the 1947 "Hollywood Ten" indictments, HUAC had eased its blazing pursuits, coming under fire

Downtown Sioux City, Iowa, 1924. (*Courtesy of the Sioux City Public Museum*)

Ku Klux Klan members and float for October 11, 1924, parade in Sioux City, Iowa. The Koval family had settled there to escape Russian anti-Semitism. (*Swaim, Ginalie, "Images of the Ku Klux Klan in Iowa," The Palimpsest 76 [1995], from ir.uiowa.edu/palimpsest/vol76/iss2/5*)

George Koval with Interscholastic Debate Team at Central High School in Sioux City, 1929. (*Sioux City Central High School yearbook, 1929*)

The Koval family passport photo, 1932. Left to right: Abram, Ethel, George, Gabriel, Isaiah. This was the year that the Kovals emigrated to the USSR's new Jewish Autonomous Region.

George Koval in the 1930s.
(*Courtesy of Koval family archive*)

George Koval and wife,
Lyudmila Ivanova, ca. 1936.
(*Courtesy of Koval family archive*)

The Sholem Aleichem Houses in the Bronx, home to George Koval from 1941 to 1943. This housing community was founded in the 1920s to help preserve Yiddish culture. (*Matthew Kiernan/ Alamy Stock Photo*)

Benjamin Lassoff, later to change his name to Benjamin William Lassen. Lassen would be Koval's handler. (*Ohio Northern University yearbook, 1912, Ohio Northern University Archives, Heterick Memorial Library*)

20 West Twenty-Third St., Manhattan. Raven Electric, Benjamin Lassen's electrical supply shop. Raven was one of Lassen's main covers for Soviet intelligence operations. (*Municipal Archives, City of New York*)

George Koval at CCNY with fellow soldiers in the US Army Specialized Training Program, 1944. Koval is in the middle row, first on the right. Koval's friend Arnold Kramish is in the top row, third from right. (*Courtesy of Duane M. Weise [top row far right]*)

Manhattan Project Oak Ridge X-10 plant, where a graphite reactor produced plutonium and bismuth was irradiated for the production of polonium. Koval was stationed here from August 1944 to June 1945. (*US Department of Energy archives/Ed Westcott photo*)

The Runnymede Playhouse in the Oakwood suburb of Dayton, Ohio where polonium was produced and purified, then sent to Los Alamos and used with beryllium to fuel atomic bomb triggers. Koval transferred to this location from Oak Ridge in June 1945. (*National Archives, Atlanta, Records of the Atomic Energy Commission*)

Jean Finkelstein, the young woman who dated George Koval in New York City in 1948.

George Koval, as chemistry professor at the Mendeleev Institute in Moscow, late 1950s. (*Courtesy of Aleksandr Zhukov, part of the Koval family archive*)

George Koval with his grandniece, M.G. (Maya Gennadievna) Koval, in 2003.
(*Courtesy of Koval family archive*)

BOMBSHELL

Arnold Kramish's inscription in the 1997 book *Bombshell*, sent to George Koval in 2003. Kramish sought to renew their friendship even after discovering Koval's espionage activities. (*Courtesy of Maya Koval*)

On November 2, 2007, Russian President Vladimir Putin presents Defense Minister Anatoly Serdyukov Russia's highest civilian honor, the Hero of the Russian Federation award, posthumously, to George Koval for his role in the making of the first Soviet atomic bomb. (*Russian Presidential Press and Information Office, Press Photo*)

itself as its critics loudly called it a committee of headline-hunting political opportunists. Though Mississippi's Representative Rankin had continued his racist, anti-Catholic, and anti-Semitic tirades, his replacement as committee chairman, J. Parnell Thomas, was now drawing even more attention. A probe of Thomas himself was in progress, based on allegations of his taking kickbacks from his staff. The looming indictment of Thomas, in addition to the committee's tainted reputation, made the famed HUAC vulnerable to being eliminated if the Democrats took control of Congress. Thus, the committee avoided any attention-getting hearings—until late in the summer of 1948.

It was then that HUAC's renowned bluster would return, suddenly bolstered by new players and reinstated conspiracy theories. The fear of Communism's world domination replete with disturbing images of a Red plot to overthrow the US government had never really gone away. It had just been out of the spotlight. After all, most members of HUAC still believed that every Communist or left-leaning American was a spy reporting to Moscow, despite the fact that most Soviet spies in America steered clear of the Communist Party.

There was also the repeat performance of anti-Semitism, always lingering backstage since the Russian Revolution and the first Red Scare in 1919 when Jews in America were overtly labeled as Bolsheviks. Once again, in the aftermath of the Second World War, despite the horrors of the Holocaust, HUAC members and others were pointing fingers at Jews as a sinister force organizing to crush American democracy. Six of the indicted Hollywood Ten, as well as 90 percent of recently blacklisted teachers, were Jewish. It was an attack on two professions in which Jewish Americans thrived: entertainment and education. In 1948 the American Jewish Committee, an advocacy group established in 1906, conducted a nationwide survey revealing that 21 percent of Americans believed "most Jews are Communists," and more than 50 percent tied Jews to atomic spying.

When given an opportunity to prove any part of their theories, members of HUAC would grasp the moment in part to enforce their raison d'être which was to prove that the New Deal politicians brimmed with Communism. Such chances were increasingly important by late summer of 1948, when the Committee was trying to save its future as an established Congressional entity by proving to be crucial to American freedoms and thus unaffected by any potential outcome of the 1948 presidential election.

So it was that HUAC renewed its hunt for Communists in government on August 3, the green light being the testimony of Whittaker Chambers, a Soviet agent who defected two days after the Soviet-Nazi pact in 1939 and was now an editor at *Time* magazine. That day, Chambers testified in a closed executive HUAC inquiry. But when he revealed surprising details, the committee moved him to a much larger hearing room and opened the testimony to the public—including a large body of journalists, called in at the last minute. Soon Chambers read a lengthy statement that included such names as the current president of the Carnegie Endowment for International Peace. That person was Alger Hiss, a former assistant to the US assistant secretary of state.

Though Elizabeth Bentley had identified Hiss as a spy years before and Igor Gouzenko had pointed to Hiss's post in Roosevelt's State Department without naming him, Chambers's testimony that day was the first confirmation of the previous claims. Thus began the renowned Hiss-Chambers melee: HUAC's quest to force Hiss into admitting that he knew Chambers and to expose the 1930s role of New Dealer Hiss as a Soviet agent. Almost daily in August 1948, there were front-page stories about Soviet spies. And there were names "named," such as J. Peters, the man who ran an underground Soviet network in the US—known as the "secret apparatus"—until the late 1930s and who had met with Lassen occasionally in the Flatiron Building. After a month of hearings and publicity, HUAC's reputation was aglow, with a Gallup poll showing that four out of five Americans "approved HUAC's latest espionage inquiry and felt it should be continued."

But the drama of the HUAC hearings in DC wasn't the only espionage story making headlines. On August 12, the spotlight was turned on in New York City, where, at 7 East Sixty-First Street, home of the Soviet consulate, Oksana Kasenkina, a Soviet citizen who had been teaching chemistry to the children of Soviet diplomats in New York, jumped out of a window on the third floor. Telephone wires interrupted her fall, likely saving her life, as she collapsed onto a grassy courtyard, breaking both legs and her pelvis.

In the weeks leading up to this dramatic event, Kasenkina had fled Manhattan to seek refuge from a mandatory return to Moscow by hiding on a farm near Nyack, New York, owned by Countess Aleksandra Lvovna Tolstaya, the daughter of the Russian author Leo Tolstoy. The Soviet consul general found her and brought her back, and announced to the press that she had been kidnapped and held against her will by the Tolstoy Foundation. The question of her future became an international firestorm.

The Soviets claimed they were protecting Kasenkina from the American government while American officials insisted on helping her in what they firmly believed was her quest for asylum. To resolve the issue, she was scheduled to testify before HUAC on August 12, but Soviet officials would not allow her to leave the consulate. Hence at 4:19 p.m. that day, she escaped in the only way she could.

The Soviet government insisted that her fate was a consular matter and not the business of New York authorities who refused to release her from round-the-clock police protection at Roosevelt Hospital. When she regained consciousness, she proclaimed her wish to become an American citizen and slammed the Soviet Union when she told the press: "They call it paradise. I call it jail."

The widely publicized war of words continued for weeks. The Soviet ambassador issued a formal demand for the fifty-two-year-old teacher's release from America's so-called protection while claiming her leap was a suicide attempt instigated by the harassments of US officials. But the State Department refused. Soon, on August 23, hundreds of pounds of papers and personal belongings stuffed into canvas and leather duffle bags, well-secured cardboard boxes, and black briefcases were loaded into chauffeured cars lining up outside the consulate on East Sixty-First Street. Driven to Idlewild Airport in Queens, the consular officials were leaving New York to return home. Then, after President Truman revoked the credentials of the Soviet consul general, Stalin shut down the Soviet consulates in New York and San Francisco on August 25. He also demanded that the US consulate in Russia's Pacific port of Vladivostok close, and canceled plans to allow a US consulate in Leningrad.

On August 26, the Soviet vice consul in New York told the *New York Times* that Amtorg, the Russian commercial agency, "is definitely going to stay open. Amtorg offices remain—definitely." Still, the closing of the consulate would directly affect the espionage operations it had facilitated since it had opened in April 1934—and it would complicate life for Koval, Lassen, and all Soviet spies still working in Manhattan.

While the doors of the Soviet consulates in America were shutting, HUAC was continuing its investigation, having benefited immensely from the Kasenkina incident, which confirmed a sinister image of the Soviet Union. The committee was now moving quickly into the arena of stolen atomic bomb secrets, as *New York Times* headlines during the first two weeks of September revealed. September 1: "House Body to Sift Spying for Russia by Atom Scientists." September 8: "Atom Scientist Is Summoned in Spy Inquiry." September 10: "Atom Bomb Leaks Hinted by Groves." September 11: "Russians Got Data on Bomb." At the end of the second week, HUAC chairman J. Parnell Thomas issued a press statement: "What we started out to find out, we have accomplished."

Such news put the atomic bomb back into public awareness, stirring the curiosity that likely drew crowds to the monthlong "Man and the Atom" exhibit at New York's Grand Central Palace. But what caused Koval to visit the exhibit, with Jean, on the night of September 19, was the basic rule of espionage—the one about contacts in public places. He didn't go to see the display of fifty mousetraps triggered with corks snapping in sequence to demonstrate the chain reaction of fission, or the original scale models of the labs at Oak Ridge. He was concerned about one thing only: whether or not his contacts, whom he told Jean were his "war buddies from Oak Ridge," would show up.

It is possible that he was waiting to meet someone who had information for him to carry on his imminent return to the USSR; perhaps it was something he'd been waiting to receive. That could explain why, months after securing his passport in mid-March, he had not yet left America. Now things were heating up and he needed to leave, but for some reason he still was waiting.

The fact that his so-called war buddies didn't show up clearly sent a message of deep concern to Koval. On September 26 the *New York Times* noted that HUAC was preparing to unveil the details of its extensive investigation into the atomic espionage. Two days later when its massive twenty-thousand-word document was released, the *Times* printed excerpts that included the names of several suspected spies. The marrow of the document was disclosed at the beginning, in a quote from General Leslie Groves: "I have no hesitancy in saying that there was continued and persistent and well organized espionage against the United States, and particularly against the atom bomb project, by a foreign power with which we were not at war, and its misguided and traitorous domestic sympathizers. . . ." The last line of the excerpted transcript read, "The Committee [HUAC] believes that those who participated in the espionage conspiracy should be quickly placed where they can no longer jeopardize the security of the United States."

President Truman called the committee's demand for indictments "a proposal of election-year publicity-seekers." And the Republican-led committee accused Truman of issuing immunity to "the Communist conspirators in the United States and the many Soviet espionage agents who are still operating here." Even the gossip columns were focusing on the topic of Soviet spies: one claimed that presidential candidate Henry A. Wallace and alleged spy Alger Hiss were being dropped from the "social list" of Washington, DC.

In the October 4 issue of *Time*, a one-page article with the headline "The Atomic Spy Hunt" zeroed in on the question everyone was asking: Did the Soviet Union acquire US atomic secrets during the war? Then it reported the news of HUAC's account, which answered that hot question: "It probably did." Unveiling rich details from the committee's report, *Time* culled the part about "Arthur Alexandrovich Adams" and his Russian espionage strategies, especially how he connected to scientists, like Clarence Hiskey, active in atomic bomb research. The committee, the article said, recommended that Hiskey and Adams, among others, be prosecuted for conspiracy to commit espionage. By then Hiskey was teaching chemistry at Brooklyn Polytechnic Institute. Adams, having just retired from the GRU, was living in Moscow with his Boston-born wife, Dorothy Keen, and working for TASS, the Russian news agency.

The mention of names like Adams and Hiskey undoubtedly brought the topic of Soviet atomic bomb spies right to Koval's apartment door. Soon Adams and four others linked to his spy network were indicted for atomic espionage, and Adams, the *Times* noted, was "accused of obtaining highly secret information regarding the atomic bomb plant at Oak Ridge, Tennessee." If Koval read that article, which he likely did, he must have quickly packed his bags.

Surely Jean Finkelstein, who had been keeping her distance from Koval since their unhappy September 19 date at the Grand Central Palace, never connected these news stories to Koval. After Koval's wartime colleagues failed to arrive and his mood became icy, Jean had resisted contacting him, either by mail or phone, until October 7. It must have seemed like a good time to call, the day after a gripping first game in the 1948 Indians vs. Braves World Series. But that's when Jean learned from Mrs. Gardner that Koval had left. Later that day, the landlady said, an unidentified man had driven to the apartment house in what looked like "an army jeep." He went straight to Koval's apartment, unlocked the door, and left with a large trunk.

By the time Jean made the call, Koval was somewhere in the middle of the Atlantic in his cabin-class quarters on the SS *America*, a polished all-American liner with pine decks made from Oregon trees, silverware from Rhode Island, and murals and mosaics from the studios of New York artists. After nearly two weeks of travel, Koval would arrive at the port of Le Havre in France, where he would board a train to Paris. Then, just a few days later he would leave Paris on the Orient Express, and in a series of rail connections he would arrive in Moscow sometime during the first two weeks of November.

Before leaving France, Koval sent three postcards back to America. One went to a professor of electrical engineering at CCNY, Sadie Silvermaster, though the details are unknown. Another went to Herbie Sandberg with a simple note: "I'm in Paris. All is well. G." But no records document a return address or postal date. Then there was the card sent to Irving Weisman, a former classmate of Koval's at CCNY and a colleague in the ASTP. This one was postmarked October 21, 1948, with a return address of the Hotel Littre, a small Paris hotel in the Left Bank district.

Neither Weisman, Sandberg, nor Silvermaster would ever again hear from their old friend—or so they would later tell the FBI. It would be six years after they received the postcards that agents first contacted them. For it would take the FBI a long while to discover Koval.

The timing of Koval's escape in the autumn of 1948 was brilliant. He left New York before Lassen was uncovered. He traveled between the US and the Soviet Union before the escalating Cold War would immensely complicate such a journey. And he arrived in Moscow at a time when Russian scientists were feverishly at work on their nation's first atomic bomb, which would be detonated in August 1949.

Still, despite his adept escape, Koval would now face new uncertainties and challenges in Moscow. As Longfellow, one of Koval's favorite poets, wrote, "Thus at the flaming forge of life, our fortunes must be wrought."

PART III

THE HUNT

Even in chains we ourselves must complete that circle which the gods have mapped out for us.

—Aleksandr Solzhenitsyn,
   Nobel Prize acceptance speech, quoting
   Russian philosopher Vladimir Solovev

CHAPTER FOURTEEN

SOVERSHENNO SEKRETNO (TOP SECRET)

For eight years, George Abramovich Koval had lived in a mire of lies, about his past, his family, his work. And after escaping from the stresses of such artifice, he may have hoped for a new start. But when he returned to Moscow in November 1948, he found only a twisted, fearful culture steeped in propaganda and prejudice, mainly against Jews and Americans. As *New York Times* foreign correspondent C. L. Sulzberger wrote at the time, anyone "coming to Russia must always bear in mind the paradox that this country of revolution has become the most reactionary power on earth."

Almost daily, the newspaper of the Central Committee of the Communist Party, *Pravda* ("Truth") offered its readers examples of what it viewed as the decadence of a venomous America. Everything American was wicked enough to be attacked. US encyclopedias, readers were told, were filled with false information compiled for no other reason than to condemn socialist truths. Coney Island, detective movies, and cocktails were among the many "opiates used by capitalists to dull worker discontent" and to define the American lifestyle. Even comic books came under fire. "Superman" and

"Batman," very popular in the West, were the most flagrant examples for exposing America's so-called degenerate conditions. Such characters and their adventures did nothing more than teach children war-minded ways to treat one another, skills so necessary for survival in a capitalist system.

To be sure, Russia's fiery anti-American propaganda in 1948 was as predictable as the anti-Communist furor in the West. But far worse was the Russian anti-Semitism, which, by 1948, was ablaze once again. For Koval, there seemed to be no escape from the dredges of prejudice. He was six years old in the disquieting bigotry-filled aftermath of World War I; and now three years after the end of World War II, soon to be thirty-five years old, he would be dodging potential damage from a wave of Soviet anti-Semitism. In the very week he returned to Moscow, the Jewish Anti-Fascist Committee, which was established in the Soviet Union during the war to mobilize support from Jews worldwide, effectively shut down when the government arrested nearly all of its members. The head of the committee, who was also the director of the Moscow State Yiddish Theater, had been murdered in January. So too, there was an ongoing systematic removal of Jews from Soviet government posts, especially in foreign policy ministries, security services, and the Red Army.

Most damaging of all, perhaps, were the growing numbers of anti-Jewish details and comments dropped into news stories and other mass media—for example, depicting Jews as possessing dual national loyalties and "capable in times of crisis of betraying the socialist motherland and going over to her enemies." With the help of media tools, a vile stereotype was resurfacing: Jews as professional swindlers, smooth operators, and natural exploiters, unwilling to work, guilty of nepotism, and prone to evade military duty.

Russia's long-standing anti-Semitic tradition was returning with gusto, having been nourished by the Nazi propaganda machine, by the Soviets' xenophobic and anti-intellectual totalitarian regime, and by the public's need for a scapegoat to explain the dark economic conditions of the postwar Soviet Union. As one scholar wrote, "All the authorities had to do was to channel the people's wrath toward the Jews."

By the time Koval had returned, what could be best described as the "liquidation of Jewish culture" had begun. Leaders of the Jewish intelligentsia, from Jewish writers and literary critics to actors, composers, and artists, were arrested. Jews holding important posts at publishing houses, literary journals, and various cultural institutions were lambasted in articles and accused of being antipatriotic, "hostile to Soviet culture" and, worst of all at that time, "cosmopolitans." The campaign against cosmopolitans, meaning those who admired Western culture, especially Jews, was in full swing, throughout the radio, press, cinema, theater, and scientific lectures. Jews were viewed as the cosmopolitans threatening the stability of Stalin's regime.

Among those feeling the lash of Stalin's whip in 1948 were the residents of Birobidzhan, home to Koval's parents, his older brother Isaiah and wife, and their four children: a son and three daughters. Birobidzhan's once thriving Yiddish theater, its Jewish publishing house, its library of Yiddish and Hebrew books, its Jewish schools, and the periodical *Birobidzhan* all were shut down. In the aftermath of the war, there had been Jewish emigrations to the region bringing in at least ten thousand newcomers, with a high percentage being engineers, doctors, agronomists, technicians, and teachers, soon to become victims of the anti-Semitic purge nationwide, especially focused on intellectuals. And although the region's new flow of emigrants would be mostly penal exiles, propaganda advertised the region's vibrant image, always describing it as a land of prosperity and recounting the stories showing "the contented life of the Jews living there."

When exactly Koval was reunited with his parents and brother is unclear. His youngest brother, Gabriel, had died in 1943, fighting in the Red Army against the Germans. Mila had sent him the news in a letter smuggled through the New York consulate in late 1943. No doubt Mila was the first member of the family Koval saw after his November arrival. A survivor of the highest order, considering her years during the war working at the bomb factory in Ufa, Mila had moved in late 1945 with her mother to their previous space in apartment #1 at #14 Bolshaia Ordynka, in Moscow, once her grandfather's house.

Given the harsh biases of 1948 Russia, Koval's Jewish roots and American origins would block his path to a high GRU post or even to minor recognition. To be sure, his work during the war would become an enduring secret. Nothing seemed to be in his favor—except, as he would soon learn, the politics of the Soviet atomic bomb project.

Shortly after Koval's arrival in Moscow, he was instructed by the GRU to write a report about the American atomic bomb, based on his work at Oak Ridge and Dayton, eventually to be sent to Lavrentiy Beria, chief of the Soviets' atomic bomb project and head of the secret police. This would include parts of the information dispatched to Moscow earlier, through his handler, in 1944, 1945, and 1946, such as details about the functions of Oak Ridge plants K-25, Y-12, and X-10. As one GRU historian later wrote, "Everything that was happening in the sectors at Oak Ridge was known to the Soviet side from Agent Delmar."

After Lieutenant General Sudoplatov had received Delmar's accounts at "Department S"—at least the ones arriving in late 1945 and early 1946—they were stripped of any names, forwarded to the Scientific and Technical Council of the First Chief Directorate of the USSR (also called the Special Committee on the Uranium Problem), and then sent to the appropriate atomic project professionals. Igor Kurchatov, the project's scientific director, had read them, but without knowing the identity of the source. As Russian historians have noted, Koval's reports helped Kurchatov to formulate directions

in the Soviet atomic project, especially the decision to study plutonium fission in an implosion-designed bomb. Though he would
later be lauded most for delivering details about polonium, Koval,
in his report about the production of plutonium at Oak Ridge, had
confirmed what nuclear physicist Klaus Fuchs at Los Alamos had
already sent to Moscow, especially about the amount of plutonium
the Americans planned to use in the implosion bomb. And such confirmation allowed Kurchatov to move forward with the best strategy
and to allay his suspicions of possible misinformation, designed to
impede the Soviets' progress.

Koval's 1949 report consisted of at least a hundred pages, thirty-
nine of which were selected by the GRU to be sent directly to a
special committee within the USSR Council of Ministers, which
then forwarded the pages to Beria on March 1, 1949. Beria received
a diagram of the X-10 plant at Oak Ridge along with eighteen pages
bearing the heading "Atomic Center at Oak Ridge"; four pages under
the heading "Process for Production of Polonium in Dayton"; eight
pages with the heading "Safety Technology at the Factories of Oak
Ridge and Polonium Production Factory at Dayton"; and nine pages
titled "Working Conditions and Safety at the Sites of Oak Ridge."

On Friday, March 4, Beria sent the report, labeled "*Sovershenno
Sekretno*" (Top Secret), to Kurchatov and other leaders in the atomic
bomb project with a cover sheet of instructions to "familiarize yourself with the materials. . . . Consider how they can be used. Report
your conclusions and practical suggestions." And though B. L. Vannikov, the head of the First Main Directorate under the USSR Council of Ministers, was quite ill, Beria noted to Vannikov's replacement,
M. G. Pervukhin, that the report must be sent to Vannikov, whose
"illness could not serve as an excuse for eliminating his familiarizing
himself with this case."

Beria also showed parts of the report to his deputy aide, Lieutenant General Nikolai Sazykin, who had served as Sudoplatov's

deputy when Sudoplatov was head of "Department S" from 1944 to 1946—a time when reports from agent Delmar were arriving. Sazykin recognized the content of parts of Koval's 1949 report and may even have remembered the source, having seen the name on the earlier dispatches before it was stripped from the reports and the information was sent on to Kurchatov.

By March 1949, the Soviet Union's atomic bomb project had been in operation for six years, since early 1943, when Kurchatov was ordered to assemble a team of young, determined scientists to build the bomb in his newly established lab. Soon he would employ fifty scientists, though compared to the Manhattan Project's five hundred scientists at Los Alamos alone in 1943, it was a rather feeble effort. By the end of 1944 Kurchatov's team of scientists had doubled in size. But it wasn't until America dropped the bombs on Hiroshima and Nagasaki that an angry Stalin accelerated a full-scale project under Beria's overall control, with Kurchatov remaining as chief scientist, resulting in dramatically more progress. The Soviets built their first nuclear reactor in October 1946 and performed their first chain reaction in June 1948.

On February 8, 1948, the USSR Council of Ministers had ordered the production of enough plutonium by March 1, 1949, to conduct the first atomic bomb test. But the order was not met. Thus, the political atmosphere surrounding the atomic project at the time Koval wrote his report to the GRU was tense—described by one Russian writer as "smelling like a thunderstorm." Beria and Kurchatov, being the main players, had to explain to Stalin their failure to meet the deadline—each trying to shift the blame away from his own doorstep. Was ineffective intelligence work the reason for the delay? Or was it the fault of the scientists?

For Beria, it was a tricky situation. He was well aware of how crucial Kurchatov was to maintaining steady work on the bomb, which was close to completion. So he devised a plan that would draw attention to the value of his own work as intelligence chief without denigrating Kurchatov. He used Koval's 1949 report as a way to display the importance of the atomic intelligence that had been sent from the West to the Soviet nuclear scientists. To be sure, the March report did show how Soviet intelligence had delivered crucial, time-saving information, such as the advantages of using the bismuth method for producing polonium rather than the lead dioxide process, which could produce only minuscule quantities of the much-needed element. Such details would prove to Stalin that deficient intelligence work could not possibly be the culprit in the missed March 1 deadline.

Koval's report was also Beria's device for alerting Kurchatov to "how important the Koval materials of 1945–1946 were for the project." It could serve the purpose of what one scholar has noted as Beria's possible intention to order Koval to spy on Kurchatov's work at the Soviet plant where a reactor, said to be comparable to that at Oak Ridge, was producing plutonium. Koval would have had to agree to such a scheme. And Kurchatov would have to want to hire him. But would Kurchatov see the need to add another person to his team? And an American-born scientist, despite his Soviet espionage record, would likely never gain Stalin's trust or approval.

Nonetheless, Beria did set up a meeting with Koval and six of the main players of the atomic bomb project, all of whom had received the March 1 report. The gathering was designed to transfer useful information without revealing Koval's identity. The six leaders—best described as the atomic project brass—sat in one room while Koval was alone in another. Separated and unseen, he answered questions handwritten on sheets of paper delivered to him from the experts.

Koval, by then, was skilled at applying a professional mix of risk and logic in order to survive. He clearly knew the dangers of working for Beria on a clandestine assignment, and being a scientist he would not have wanted to betray Kurchatov. However, in the end,

Kurchatov did not ask to hire Koval, and thus, Beria released the American-born spy.

From then on, the secrets about what Zhorzh Abramovich Koval had accomplished on his "business trip" in America would last nearly to the end of his life. Any leaks of the truth could make him a target for revenge in the American intelligence community. And his American origins could put him—and his family—at risk of being accused by the Soviets of being traitors. Because of the Soviet anti-Semitism in late 1948, he would not be hired by the GRU and he could not reveal what he had achieved for the GRU on a résumé or in an interview for a job.

In July 1949, Koval was discharged from the Red Army as an untrained rifleman without any distinguished medals of achievement. To have been in the Red Army for nearly a decade, never rising above the rank of private, was not helpful in establishing a strong foothold in postwar Moscow. Koval was almost penniless. But from a positive perspective, his parents were still alive and Mila had waited for him. So too, he had never lost his lifelong passion for science and for schooling. He would now keep a low profile and enroll at Mendeleev, taking courses in chemistry in preparation for his doctoral degree.

Later that summer, on August 29, 1949, in northeast Kazakh SSR (Kazakhstan), on the steppe west of the town of Semipalatinsk, the Soviet Union successfully tested its first atomic bomb, referred to as "First Lightning." Nicknamed "Joe-One" (after Stalin) in America, the bomb was a duplicate of America's plutonium-based bomb with the polonium-beryllium initiator, tested as Trinity four years before.

In America, the news was greeted with disbelief. Only four years after Hiroshima? This was not possible, especially after intelligence and military experts had assured the public numerous times that for the Soviets to catch up with America would take five to ten years. Between August 1945 and August 1949, dozens of articles reported such a range. In November 1947, the *New York Times*'s military editor, the highly respected Hanson Baldwin, had written a piece headlined "Has Russia the Atomic Bomb?—Probably Not." The subheading was "Best American Opinion Is That She Will Need Years to Develop It." Baldwin's conclusion was based on "responsible government authorities."

Less than two years later, US secretary of defense Louis Johnson, refusing to accept the truth about the Soviets' sudden entry into the arms race, claimed that the sounds reported by intelligence sources to be a nuclear bomb were actually a Soviet reactor exploding. Such skepticism caused the Atomic Energy Commission to assemble a committee of experts to investigate what had just happened. It was headed by Vannevar Bush, the presidential science advisor under FDR later credited with founding the National Science Foundation. Among its members were the Manhattan Project's Robert Oppenheimer as well as the director of the British atomic bomb program. The task force soon concluded that the Soviets had indeed detonated an atomic bomb. Nonetheless, President Truman and Defense Secretary Johnson remained doubtful, which is why Truman did not inform the American public until September 23, 1949.

Still, skepticism persisted. General Walter Bedell Smith, the former ambassador to the Soviet Union, was quoted in a *New York Times* article saying that it would take Russia at least ten years to reach the US level in the atomic bomb race. American techniques and industrial skills, he said, were "far better than the best the Soviet[s] can offer." But, in response, a group of prominent American scientists wrote to the *Times* to say: "We, the undersigned, are aware of the problems involved in the large-scale production of atomic bombs. To our regret, we have to say that the above statement, attributed by *The New York Times* to General Bedell Smith, has no basis in fact."

American scientists were well aware of the number of Soviet physicists who in the 1930s had made significant contributions to the growing international studies of nuclear fission, several later winning Nobel Prizes. They also knew that Igor Kurchatov had built the Soviet Union's—and Europe's—first cyclotron. It was completed in 1937, after the one at Berkeley, patented in 1932 by Ernest O. Lawrence.

But while Soviet scientists were strong in the theoretical knowledge crucial to developing nuclear energy, they were less strong in the practical application of such knowledge to the actual building of an atomic bomb. That gap between theoretical and technical capabilities was filled by the Soviet espionage networks in Britain, Canada, and America. With the atomic bomb secrets slickly smuggled into the Soviet Union during the war, the Soviets saved an immense amount of time by eliminating unproductive experiments. Kurchatov would even say later that Soviet espionage accounted for "50% of the project's success." To be sure, the faster-than-expected 1949 detonation was undoubtedly a mix of Soviet scientific prowess and information relayed by Soviet spy networks in the West.

In the months following Truman's announcement, the unsettling reality of America losing its nuclear monopoly caused the predictable reaction of high-energy finger-pointing. Among the targets was the 1945 Smyth Report. Though General Groves had assured colleagues and readers that it contained a balance of "enough secrecy for safety, enough information for sound discussion," critics claimed that it provided the Soviets with ample information to speed up their bomb building.

At the same time, FBI director J. Edgar Hoover put the blame on the wartime Soviet atomic espionage in America, which he called "the crime of the century." Four years later, George Koval would be added to Hoover's list of culprits.

CHAPTER FIFTEEN

POSTCARDS FROM PARIS

In the August 1952 issue of *Reader's Digest*, J. Edgar Hoover wrote an article entitled "Red Spy Masters in America," informing the American public that "the FBI today is engaged in no work more important than protecting the United States against the threat of Soviet espionage. It is a task that requires much time and manpower. Meetings must be covered, identities of new agents discovered and underground informants installed. The Soviets are cunning, patient and meticulous operators; the FBI must be even more so."

Four months before, the cunning, patient, and meticulous craft of numerous FBI agents had matched the spy "Faraday" with the Manhattan electronics retailer and electrical engineer Benjamin William Lassen, aka Lassoff. The FBI had been aware of "Red Army Intelligence operating an illegal network, with headquarters in New York City, for some years, under a leader whose code name was Faraday," read the New York City bureau report issued on March 20, 1952. And now handwriting analyses, biographical details, travel timelines, passport applications, ship manifests, bank account records, interviews, and more had swayed the agency to declare Lassen to be Faraday. "Nothing has negated it," said the report, which included numerous "Top Secret" memos showing such details as recent findings from a probe into Lassen's banking habits, proving that he had been paid a commission on a regular basis out of the Broadway Savings Bank; that he had numerous accounts for Raven Electric at other banks; and that the ledger sheets at those banks showed deposits and withdrawals way out of line with the relatively small amount of business conducted at Raven.

One such memo had been issued in late January 1952 out of Washington to the New York bureau. Stamped "SECRET," it noted that the FBI first concluded in April 1951, as stated by Hoover in an April 9 letter, that "Lassen's background agrees favorably with all major background data furnished on Faraday." The evidence continued to build as agents collected countless details and pieced together revealing chronologies. They interviewed witnesses who recalled Lassen's meetings with such known spies as Jacob Golos, his muffled conversations about being a Soviet agent in Poland and Hungary before the war, his frequent trips to and from banks, and his use of aliases such as Rossoff, Roseff, and Losev.

One former store clerk at Raven Electric told the Feds that Lassen claimed he made his money in the stock market. The man remembered helping Lassen bring back cash from a bank one day, and told the Feds about the experience: "We entered the bank building and then went by an elevator to the sixteenth floor where Lassen presented a book and got the necessary funds. He would not let me go with him to the window where he presented the book. He told me that that bank always had all the money he needed. But it was a far-away account. And I convinced him that he should have a local bank account for payroll and business purposes, so that same day, he opened another account, one at the bank at Twenty-Eighth and Broadway. He must have had a dozen accounts at least."

Hoover's January 1952 memo briefly discussed the "papers which appeared to be ciphers found in Lassen's wallet in 1943 by two prostitutes," and the $10,000 in cash that "Lassen firmly denied belonged to him." Then the memo ordered the New York office to review all background information in their files relevant to both Gertrude and Benjamin Lassen and to "immediately institute a fugitive type investigation to locate them." The memo ended with orders that all FBI offices were instructed to send in reports on the case within fourteen days after the receipt of the January memo and every fourteen days thereafter "until advised to the contrary by the Bureau." Two months later, Hoover sent another memo to the New York bureau, ordering: "It is imperative that [Lassen's] present whereabouts be ascertained." But Lassen could not be found.

On April 4, 1952, the CIA officially entered the case and the hunt began to span the globe with the help of the bureau's liaison representatives in Germany, England, and France. This was a smart move considering that Lassen had sailed to Le Havre, France, in December 1950, likely taking a train to Paris where he appeared to have stayed at the Des Londres Hotel, in the Left Bank district, for at least a month.

From Paris in early 1951, in the tradition of his fellow spies, Lassen sent two postcards to America. One went to "Pyne, Kendall, and Hollister" addressed to 525 Fifth Avenue, minus an individual's name. This was the same location as the office of Jacob Aronoff, the attorney who devised the successful scheme to bring Arthur Adams back into the US from the Soviet Union via Canada in the late 1930s and who did legal work for the CPUSA. And it was directly across the street from Eric Bernay's office for Keynote Recordings, Inc. where Arthur Adams had worked as a cover.

The other card was sent to a friend in New Jersey whom, records note, Lassen had known since 1928, in Paris. The FBI would later note that the addressee on the card was simply "Clyder." And if the "r" was simply the result of a swoosh of the pen at the end of the name, the postcard recipient would have been "Clyde." The man's name at the New Jersey address where it was sent was "Carl Hyder."

By the time Lassen arrived in Paris, his son Seymour had been living there since the summer. A June 1950 MIT graduate in electrical engineering, Seymour had been an ardent member of the Youth for Wallace organization and the Young Progressives of America, during his school days. An FBI report later noted that in Paris, during the autumn months of 1950, Seymour had taken science courses at the University of Paris. And about three months after he had reunited with his father, his mother joined the family in Paris, after sailing to Cherbourg out of New York Harbor on April 6, 1951. Upon Gertrude's arrival, she sent a postcard photo of the Eiffel Tower to Benjamin Loseff, the jeweler running the cover shop on Nassau Street in Manhattan. It was signed by Seymour, Gertrude, and Benjamin.

The last known record of anyone in America hearing from the Lassens occurred in December 1951, when Benjamin sent a Christmas card from Paris to a former classmate at MIT. This was Philip Alger, who later told the FBI that he had introduced Lassen to "International GE officials when Lassen was trying to represent GE in Poland years before."

For several months after her husband's departure, Gertrude had stayed in New York to wrap up the financial affairs of Raven Electric. While it appeared that she was dealing mostly with the paperwork generated by Raven's bankruptcy, she was also draining funds from the numerous bank accounts tied to Lassen's operations, and eradicating as much account history as possible. And she was selling the US army surplus items Lassen had purchased: mostly maps and knapsacks plus at least one vehicle.

But it was not until Gertrude had left New York, a year or so later, that the FBI, through an attorney representing the Raven creditors, began to probe a large bundle of Raven financial and employee records, including a list of everyone who had worked there or had conducted business with Raven from 1942 to the end of 1950. There were hundreds of ledger sheets and several "telephone diaries."

It was then, perhaps late spring 1952, in response to Hoover's robust order to hunt down Lassen, that the FBI compiled another list of people considered to be Lassen/Faraday "associates." It included Arthur Adams and others, but there was no mention of George Koval. Not until the Raven employee roster was matched with lists of workers at government agencies and sites of the Manhattan Project would his name surface. It's unclear exactly when that match was discovered. However, on July 19, 1954, the FBI issued a report out of the New York office ordering a full-throttle investigation "to ascertain present whereabouts and employment of George Koval." The hunt had begun, nearly six years after Koval had left the US.

By the summer of 1954, the pursuits, captures, trials, and convictions of Soviet spies who had operated in networks touching on Koval's New York cell were over. Harry Gold, a Jacob Golos recruit who became a Soviet courier for several spies at Los Alamos, including Klaus Fuchs, was serving his fourth year of a thirty-year prison sentence. Fuchs, imprisoned in England with a fourteen-year sentence, was also in his fourth year. By 1954, David Greenglass, arrested on evidence provided by Gold, had been incarcerated for three years of his fifteen-year sentence. His sister and brother-in-law Ethel and Julius Rosenberg, whom he had exposed, were convicted in 1951; their appeals were denied in 1952; and tragically, they were executed on June 19, 1953. By 1954, Alger Hiss had been in prison for perjury for about three and a half years, soon to be released in November of that year.

Now came the intrigue of a new case: George Abramovich Koval, #65-16756 in the New York City field office and #65-62911 at FBI headquarters in DC. Their nationwide search would engage at least three dozen agents from field offices in New York, DC, Newark, Boston, Baltimore, Philadelphia, Buffalo, Cincinnati, Chicago, Saint

Louis, Kansas City, Omaha, New Orleans, Houston, Miami, Phoenix, San Francisco, and Los Angeles. It would eventually extend to France and Russia, among other nations, via CIA involvement, aimed at gathering a trail of clues that had been missed for years.

At the start, agents followed Koval's extensive paper trail, from records at the Veterans Administration to Manhattan Project security files at the Atomic Energy Commission to US State Department passport documents, and much more. Soon they located and tried to interview all those individuals whose names he had listed as references on his official records and applications. The list included Herbie Sandberg; Tillie Silver; two CCNY professors, Harry Hanstein and Harold Wolf; and Sarah Rose, one of the sisters of jeweler Benjamin Loseff. When questioned, Rose denied ever knowing Koval and she had no idea why a stranger would use her name as a reference.

As the first full year of the investigation unfolded, the agents moved ever deeper into Koval's past, unraveling his employment history, digging up every detail about the Atlas Trading Corporation; his CCNY fraternity and other club memberships; his Sioux City arrest record; his colleagues at Oak Ridge; and his family members. For his cousins and aunts and uncles, in Sioux City and Los Angeles, it was the beginning of many hours spent with federal agents who often asked the same questions again and again, always leading up to "Where is George now?" Then came the empty answers: "I don't know." "Haven't seen him or heard from him in years." "He left in 1932. Never saw him again." "Saw him on a street corner in New York in 1946, staring into space. Last time I saw him."

Interviews with CCNY classmates and Oak Ridge colleagues often zoomed into searches for answers to the question that appeared to obsess Hoover: How was it possible that a Red Army–trained spy got full US security clearance and ended up at the nation's highly secretive atomic bomb site at Oak Ridge? It was a question that the FBI could not answer, no matter how much information it acquired.

Hoover, however, in his 1952 *Reader's Digest* article, published a few years before the Koval case opened, may have answered his own question as well as anyone could. "The individual agent in America may be a 'principal' responsible for an entire espionage network. . . . Anonymity is standard practice."

In his detailed analysis of the machinations of Soviet spy networks, Hoover gave his readers a briefing on fundamental spycraft: "If an appointment had been arranged for Tuesday at 7:30 p.m. at Fifth Avenue and Fifteenth Street but could not be held, the appointment is automatically deferred to one week later at Sixth Avenue and Sixteenth Street, while a third automatic date would be the week after the second at Seventh Avenue and Seventeenth Street. The hour similarly would be advanced." And if an unexpected emergency occurred, demanding the spy to connect with his or her Russian boss whom the spy does not know how to locate, then "such contingencies are provided for long in advance. One spy, for example, was told to place this ad in a local newspaper: 'Biochemist, age 33, desires position in industry or research. Quality of work principal interest.' Reading that paper every day as routine procedure, the Russians would know that the agent desired an emergency meeting. The time and place would have already been determined."

But he and his "cunning, patient, and meticulous" crew could not unearth enough details to catch Koval. Even when FBI agents thought they might have him, they were wrong. In August 1954 agents visited the only George Koval listed in the Bronx telephone directory. It was about two weeks into the FBI's official investigation. This George Koval lived in the Bronx and had attended CCNY, though mostly taking courses in economics—never electrical engineering or chemistry—and only in 1935. This Mr. Koval had never worked for Raven Electric, nor was he a veteran of the US Army. At the time of his first FBI interview, in 1954, he was a fireman working in Manhattan at Engine Company 35, on East 119th Street between

Second and Third Avenues. He told the agents that on numerous occasions in recent years, perhaps since early 1949, he had been certain that he was mistaken for someone else. But he could never figure out why. This was especially true in 1949 when he had received "numerous telephone calls from females indicating they had met him in various cities around the United States." The fireman's wife had spoken to a few of the women callers, two having described someone who "had been wearing a Navy uniform of some type." Mrs. Koval and the callers concluded that "the other George Koval" must have been employed during the 1940s as a merchant seaman.

On one occasion, the wife of the wrong George Koval told agents about a woman who had met "George" in Albuquerque. This, interjected the fireman, was at first a problem because he had been out of town at the same time that the woman said she had met with the other Koval. He also said that in 1949 he had begun to receive an electrical engineering society magazine for which he had no reason to have a subscription, as well as copies of the *National Guardian*.

Months later, when agents contacted the fireman and his wife again, the couple added one detail they had forgotten during the first interview: that in the spring of 1950 or 1951 or 1952, the *New York Journal-American* listed "George Koval" as a winner of $500 in the Irish Sweepstakes. They knew they hadn't entered it, so they didn't attempt to claim the prize. The agents apparently never told the couple that this could have been a coded message written by a former comrade, perhaps in search of the missing spy.

At the start of the investigation's second year, Hoover sent a memo to the New York field office hammering the agents about grammatical and factual errors he had noticed in a recent report on the Koval case. He lambasted the carelessness and then pushed for more progress. "This investigation is of considerable importance and there are substantial leads which should be a challenge to interest and initiative," he wrote. Two months later agents had found Koval's

1931 arrest cards at the Woodbury County, Iowa, sheriff's office, and discovered the articles in the September 1931 *Sioux City Journal* about the poverty protest that caused his arrest.

In June that year, Hoover extended the hunt to France, when he sent a memo to the US embassy in Paris, attaching a report on the Koval investigation and asking for French records regarding the subject's arrival at Le Havre in 1948 and any evidence of his possible departure from France. He also sought known contacts Koval might have had in France and any hints of his present whereabouts.

That year too, the bureau tore into the Raven Electric bank accounts, and Hoover sent a memo to the New York field office, again likely to inspire progress, beginning it with new knowledge that could be helpful: "On May 25, 1945, Lassen wrote to Raven employee W. A. Rose, 71 Ridge Rd, Rutherford, NJ regarding 'the sale of Mexican twins.'" A week later a correction was sent: "twins" should have read "twine." "Codes," the memo noted.

But the busiest year of the investigation would be 1956, when agents submitted dozens of extensive field reports and interviewed nearly a hundred individuals, often multiple times. That was the year when the CIA was brought into the case, with a May memo from Hoover to CIA director Allen Dulles: "As you are aware, we are greatly interested in ascertaining the present whereabouts of George Koval. . . ." It was also the year that Hoover placed "a flash notice" about Koval in the Feds' massive fingerprint file, so that the bureau would be called "immediately" if there was a match anywhere in the nation.

One of the first interviews in early January was with Koval's former SED colleague, Arnold Kramish, who by then was living in DC working as a senior staff member in the Physics Division of the Rand Corporation. Kramish had been one of Koval's CCNY classmates in the ASTP who was assigned to Oak Ridge, though for a shorter time than Koval. He told the agent that he was "very close" to Koval both at CCNY and Oak Ridge. He commented on his friend being the oldest of the ASTP members and "a person who was hard drinking, liked women, and who knew New York City better than any of the group." He couldn't recall any occasion when Koval had engaged in a political discussion, and he had never questioned Koval's loyalty to America. The last time he saw Koval was in 1946, he said, at an apartment on Valentine Avenue in the Bronx.

Another former colleague from Oak Ridge interviewed that year was Seymour Block, who was the first to comment on the possible importance to the Russians of Koval's reports about safety issues. In 1956, Block worked at the Livermore site of the University of California Radiation Laboratory. At Oak Ridge he had been assigned to the health physics division. He told the agents that he and Koval, in their health physics routines, had been exposed to specific, classified information—for example, the details of why and how the plutonium was produced, where it was shipped, what was known about the large reactors in Hanford, Washington. Health physics data were classified, he said, and anyone working in the division had to have known that Oak Ridge was part of the project to create an atomic bomb.

Block also talked at length regarding the significance of what Koval knew about radiation monitoring techniques, tolerances, and instrumentation. Though health physics did not contribute in a direct way to the development of the bomb, it was "highly important" to the success of the project, he said. The threats and dangers of losing technicians and scientists exposed to radiation was a deadly risk to the project at all stages, especially as the bomb test drew near when it could be difficult to quickly replace well-informed experts.

The American bomb "could have been made faster if all the answers of health physics had been known in the beginning," said Block, who was confident that "if the Soviets obtained information concerning our health physics program, their development of the bomb would have been accelerated." Koval, he knew, had even published a well-researched article "on radiation contamination of the air," which could have been "very helpful," he said.

But what filled that year with countless leads came from the agent interviews with Jean Mordetzky, maiden name Finkelstein. It was Herbie Sandberg in his first meeting with agents, in April 1956, who steered them to Jean. By then she lived in La Verne, California, a suburb of Los Angeles, with her husband of four years, Alexander Mordetzky. During five or more lengthy interviews, in February, May, and October, the agents stirred her memories with questions that sculpted the profile of a man she likely had tried to forget. As her innocence must have dawned on her, curiosity seemed to drive her, and she unearthed as many details as she could to help with the investigation.

Jean described the bowling alley where her brother, now Leonard Field—changed from Finkelstein—had introduced her to Koval and how she was impressed that he was such an ardent fan of Walt Whitman. She talked about Koval's love of baseball, his tennis partners in Boston, his trips to Kansas City and to DC, a friend in the Zoology Department at Columbia, and many more details. As she rendered one story, another would suddenly surface, and then another. She told one agent about Koval's dedication to his fraternity, Eta Kappa Nu, and how members had sought his whereabouts by publishing a request for information about him in the fraternity's official magazine. She thought that might have been in 1949. There was also a photo she had kept of Koval with another woman whom Jean didn't know, but she thought he had told her it was taken during the summer of 1947. She gave the photo to the agents. It showed Koval and a lovely young woman leaning against each other, smiling on a sunny day as they sat in a park. Herbie Sandberg later identified the woman and said George had met her at a party at Herbie's apartment in 1947. The FBI would later interview her as they tried to find all the women who had dated Koval.

There is no evidence of Jean asking agents about Koval's current location or why the FBI had launched such an anxious hunt for him. But she must have had countless questions for each one she answered or couldn't answer. She did not know the names of his Boston tennis partners, or even if he played tennis on his trips to Boston. Baseball, yes, but no, she had never witnessed Koval on a tennis court. Whom did he meet in DC that March, or plan to meet at the Grand Central Palace on the night of their last date? She didn't know. Like in a dream, or nightmare, her memory had blurred edges with some details impossible to retrieve.

But soon the bureau turned from Jean to a new clue: the translation of a letter written by George's father, Abram Koval. Dated May 20, 1956, it was addressed to Abram's sister Goldie Gurshtel who, with her husband, Harry, lived in Sherman Oaks, California. And it contained facts that dramatically changed the direction of the FBI's hunt for Koval, effectively altering orders from "*Find* him" to "Get him *back* to the USA."

CHAPTER SIXTEEN

THE MARCH 1953 LETTERS

A bram Koval's May 20, 1956, letter informed his sister and brother-in-law, the Gurshtels, all about the side of the family living in the Soviet Union. "I am now about 75 and feel good, alive and well," Abram wrote. "Twenty years have passed since we have seen each other and during this time several changes have taken place in our family."

Abram wrote that his youngest son "Geybi" [Gabriel] had been killed on August 30, 1943, while "in a battle against the German fascists." Abram's wife, Ethel—George's mother—had died of cancer on August 28, 1952. On the bright side, his oldest son was married with four children, three girls and a boy—Gita, Sofiya, Galina, and Gennadi. "They are all good children," he wrote. But it was what came next that caused a stir at FBI headquarters: "George lives in Moscow, he still works for the Mendeleev Chemical Institute. . . . He is living with his wife Lyudmila (you saw them once in Moscow) but they have no children."

The letter set into motion endless follow-up interviews in the Koval case. There would be the Gurshtels again; Jean again; Arnold

Kramish; Herbie Sandberg; and Irving Weisman, one of Koval's 1948 postcard recipients—all interrogated for at least the third, fourth, or fifth time. More details could facilitate a deeper understanding of exactly what Koval had done in America for eight years. And because the Feds believed that Koval was a US citizen, it might be possible to extradite him and charge him with treason.

To be sure, the Bureau's strategy soon narrowed to one focus: the tricky process of extradition. Hoover wanted to force Koval's return to his country of origin to face an official interrogation. Taking this step, Hoover enlisted the help of other government agencies and divisions. Any action, he wrote in a memo, was "believed warranted in consideration of [Koval's] known activities in the U.S., 1940–1948, which strongly suggests his involvement in Soviet espionage during that period. . . . It is believed that any practical approach that could possibly effect [Koval's] denaturalization should be fully exploited. . . . This would appear particularly desirable if the necessary liaison poses a situation of 'maximum to be gained as opposed to nothing to be lost.'"

There was no documented, legal proof that Koval had renounced his US citizenship. However, in 1932 when he left America with his parents and two siblings to live in the Jewish Autonomous Region, Soviet law at that time stated that if both parents became citizens of the Soviet Union, their children also acquired Soviet citizenship if they had not reached the age of fourteen, like Koval's younger brother, Gabe. If older than fourteen, all that was required was the consent of the children through their parents. It was therefore quite probable that Koval's acquisition of Soviet citizenship had occurred in 1932. The only way to confirm this, from Hoover's viewpoint, was to interview Koval, in person, at the US embassy in Moscow. So, in early 1959, Hoover sent a memo to the director of the Office of Security at the US Department of State requesting that he [the director] "arrange to have [Koval] interviewed in Moscow in order to determine his present citizenship status and to determine whether he plans to remain in Moscow or whether he plans on returning to the United States. This Bureau would be interested in determining whether Koval has committed an act which would expatriate him."

On May 21, after finding Koval's place of employment at the Mendeleev Institute, Lewis W. Bowden, consul at the American Embassy in Moscow, wrote to Koval asking him to come to the embassy to be interviewed. "The Embassy's files indicated that you are an American citizen residing in the USSR. It would be appreciated if you would call at the Embassy at your convenience in order that your citizenship status may be clarified. The Embassy is located at 19/21 Chaikovsky Street and is open from 0900 to 1800 Monday, Tuesday, Thursday and Friday and from 0900 to 1300 Wednesday and Saturday."

Two months later, the embassy received a written response from Koval in which he declined "to discuss his American citizenship status with the American consulate in the USSR." And he wrote, "I have been a citizen of the USSR since 1932." In November the chief of the Foreign Adjudications Division of the US State Department sent a letter to Hoover acknowledging that "all logical action has been taken to effect [Koval's] expatriation." Koval's July 1959 letter was "sufficient enough to deny him recognition as a citizen of the U.S. until such time as he may present himself at the Embassy at Moscow and submit to appropriate interrogation." That said, he suggested that the extradition case be closed. However, Hoover would insist that the "lookout notice" placed with customs officers throughout the US be firmly maintained in the event of any attempt by Koval to enter America.

What happened next was quite predictable: not a dramatic halt to the hunt, but a slow drift into obscurity. Hoover knew the crucial role of good timing in the fine art of self-promotion as well as Koval did in the craft of spying. By the end of 1959, it must have been obvious that Koval, like Lassen, was out of reach. The targets had fled the country years before, apparently never returning. And to have missed a Soviet military trained spy with US top-security clearance driving an Army jeep on the grounds of a highly secretive weapons project during the war could only embarrass the FBI. Best to let the case, the names, and the clues simply fall through the cracks of history. If someday a telling or surprising detail suddenly surfaced, check it out—but quietly.

In the aftermath of the final memo on the extradition effort, "the citizen case against Koval" was closed, though the Koval investigation did not shut down. From 1961 through 1966, a few reports trickled in, some introducing new leads and directions. For example, in 1961, the FBI began an analysis of the known activities of several "illegals," including Koval, to help devise "methods of logical approaches to the problem of detection of Soviet illegals in the U.S." This included a probe into possible Soviet use of the Bronx 126 Selective Service station where Koval was processed for entry into the U.S. Army, where he received a Selective Service registration card, and where Lassen filed applications for Koval's deferment. The Bureau found one more Raven worker who had received his selective service card at the Bronx 126. And that spurred a deeper probe into the dealings of Raven Electric with a renewed investigation of its former employees—still looking for the tracks of Koval's espionage.

That was also the year when an informant told an agent that, according to one of his sources, Koval had done nothing for the Soviets while in America, except to waste GRU time and money. The informant was described as "sometimes reliable and sometimes not." But if the informant's tip had been true, then Koval, having returned to Moscow in the midst of a harsh anti-Semitic period and facing an intelligence chief known for his vile ways, especially regarding inept agents, would have been liquidated or sent to the gulag. Instead, the GRU had helped him.

The FBI file containing the claim of Koval's incompetence did not include the March 1953 GRU letter that proved the error of such skepticism. After Koval was discharged from the Red Army in June 1949, he began his work toward an advanced degree in chemistry at Mendeleev. And by the end of September 1952, he had defended his doctoral dissertation and was ready for the job placement committee to find him a teaching post. But by the spring of 1953, after months of waiting, he had been repeatedly told that there were few, if any, openings for scientists in his field. His record in the Red Army, as available to the employment committee, was thin, bland, and unimpressive. Because he had been ordered never to reveal what he had done during the war for the GRU, he could not explain his army record. At the same time, Russian anti-Semitism had only worsened. As one Russian scholar described Koval's situation: "Russia in the spring of 1953 was so saturated with anti-Semitism that the only hope of salvation was an attempt to find protection by making contact at the very top."

Then on March 5, Stalin died, and rumors were rampant about a possible plan to purge Jews and send them to Siberia. So it was that on the day after Stalin's death, as Soviets were crowding into the Kremlin to view the body, Koval wrote the first draft of a letter to the head of the GRU, asking officials to contact Beria, who would know all about his contributions to the atomic bomb project and about their "conversation in 1949." He desperately wanted help in securing an academic post, but only the GRU could release him from the silence that blocked his future. On March 10, the day after Stalin's funeral, he sent the letter:

Dear Comrade,

I am writing to you because of the difficult situation I find myself in. At the end of September of 1952, I got my graduate degree. I should have been sent to a job but the committee that should have

sent me, didn't do anything and left the question open. I didn't want
to bother you but the 10 years [1939–1949] I worked for you is a
blank spot now on my biography because I can't tell anyone what
I did in the army. Only you know about the challenge and responsibility of my job for you and how I completed it with honesty.

By one account, the letter was "a decorative cover for the real
plea to save his life." It ended with a request to meet in person. He
noted that he could be reached through his wife's telephone number
VI3440.

Despite the unsurprising chaos in the early days after Stalin's
death, the GRU's response was immediate. On March 16, the Soviet
minister of higher education received a letter from the director of the
GRU telling him to "gainfully employ" George Koval. "According to
the non-disclosure agreement of military security, he cannot explain
the details of what he did under special conditions. If this fact had any
effect on the Ministry not giving him a good job, then we'll send our
representative who will give you whatever details you need." Quickly
after that, Koval was hired at Mendeleev as a lab assistant, soon to
be a chemistry teacher for nearly thirty-five years. This was not the
way the GRU would have treated a spy whose mission had failed.

Other FBI leads in the Koval case during the 1960s included the
New York bureau getting a tip in 1966 that the GRU was reactivating
old agents and may have been doing so since 1956. This hastened a
reminder for the nation's immigration services and ports of entry
to be on the lookout for Koval. But nothing came of it. No one
appeared. And for the next twelve years, there was not a single report
added to the files of case #65-16756.

Then, in 1978, a strange detail about Koval suddenly surfaced
with the first publication of the uncensored version of Aleksandr
Solzhenitsyn's novel *The First Circle* in Russian, under the title *In
the First Circle*. In the novel, Solzhenitsyn used true incidents and

real-life people he had come across in his eight years as a Soviet prisoner. In the first chapter, he used a name he had heard, "Georgy Koval," possibly believing it was a code name for a spy.

By 1978, Solzhenitsyn was an internationally recognized author who was scheduled to give the commencement speech at Harvard University that spring. In 1970 he had won the Nobel Prize in Literature, "for the ethical force with which he has pursued the indispensable traditions of Russian literature." Then, shortly after the 1973 publication in Paris of his nonfiction masterpiece *The Gulag Archipelago*, in which he chronicled life in the Soviet forced-labor camp system, he was deported from Russia to West Germany, soon moving to America to live for nearly two decades.

The Gulag Archipelago was based on the testimony of at least 250 former prisoners and on Solzhenitsyn's own eight-year sentence in the gulag, beginning in 1945. Several of those years were spent in one of the gulag system's *sharashka*s. These were special research labs staffed by prisoners with engineering, mathematical, or scientific training who were ordered to help advance Soviet military and intelligence technologies. His *sharashka* was in the town of Marfino, on the outskirts of Moscow, in a converted church once with a name that translated as "Ease My Sorrows."

During his time there, Solzhenitsyn had been on a team assigned to work with a voice-recognition device for the purpose of identifying a Soviet traitor on a tape sent to the *sharashka*. The tape, from an intercepted call possibly made in December 1949, to the US embassy in Moscow, revealed a Soviet diplomat anxiously trying to warn an American attaché about a Soviet spy who was planning an espionage rendezvous with a Soviet courier at a radio shop in Manhattan to spill secrets about the US atomic bomb. The spy's name was "Georgy Koval."

Solzhenitsyn would use the details of what was heard on the tape as the central motif for *In the First Circle*. At the start of the book, at a phone booth in the Moscow metro station, the Soviet diplomat calls the US embassy and after a struggle to reach an attaché, he says: "Do not put the receiver down! This is a life-and-death matter for your country! And not only your country! Listen! Within the next few days a Soviet agent called Georgy Koval will pick something up at a shop selling radio parts."

After some hesitation on the other end, he cries out in despair, "Listen! Listen! In a few days' time the Soviet agent Koval will be giving important technological information about the production of the atomic bomb, at a radio shop—" The click on the phone and a sudden disconnection signaled to the Soviet diplomat that the secret police were listening to the call.

For that first version of the book to pass through Soviet censors, Solzhenitsyn cut nine chapters and altered several essential scenes, including the one about the atomic spy. Even to find a publisher for the toned-down version, he had to smuggle the manuscript out of the country to the US, where it first appeared in 1968 under the title *The First Circle*, published by Harper & Row. Ten years later the uncut, original edition, entitled *In The First Circle*—with its plot focused on the hunt for the errant Soviet diplomat who had betrayed his nation by exposing the Soviet agent Koval—was published for the first time. The timing of the narrative, though possibly off by a year or two, its action, and its setting were close enough to Koval's work in the US to cause a stir at both the CIA and FBI.

On March 2, 1978, the newly appointed FBI director, William Webster, sent a memo to the New York City and Albany, New York, bureaus alerting them to a CIA memo about the book just received at FBI headquarters. He reminded them about Koval, "the Soviet GRU illegal who operated in the U.S. from approximately 1938 [*sic*] to 1948." And he said that an interview with Solzhenitsyn at his home in Vermont "would be justified for historical and operational reasons." Next, Webster ordered the New York bureau to select its "most knowledgeable and experienced Special Agent" to conduct the interview, on April 19.

That day, before the session formally began, Solzhenitsyn asked about the purpose of the interview and requested that no notes be taken at any time. He was told that the interview concerned the telephone conversation described at the start of the uncensored version of *In the First Circle*: the exchange between an unknown individual and the US embassy in Moscow, about a spy named Koval. The author "appeared very reluctant to converse on this topic and inquired why should he explain these details in April 1978?" He was then asked if he had a personal fear of retaliation by the KGB. But he did not respond.

The interview lasted one hour, and when asked if he would agree to another meeting soon, Solzhenitsyn said that would not be necessary. He assured his interrogator that he could not recall more details than those in the book. He did confirm the date as December 1949 or 1950—a detail of concern to the FBI, considering there was no record of Koval returning to America after his documented exit in 1948. The FBI did know that during that period the Raven Electric shop was open for business and Faraday was still in New York—in fact, until December 16, 1950. If it could ever be proven that Koval had continued his work as a spy after returning to Moscow, the Soviets could have used the information on the tape to quickly warn Koval to cancel plans for travel to America.

There were other possible explanations: that the caller to the US embassy was trying to defect from the Soviet Union by making up an urgent story about a spy whose name he had heard at the Soviet embassy; that Soviet security officials had created a false tape, using the telephone call as a way to test the progress of the voice-recognition research at the *sharashka*; or that the taped call could have occurred in 1947 or 1948, but had not been sent to the *sharashka* until 1949.

A few years after the 1978 interview, Lev Kopelev, Solzhenitsyn's teammate working on the voice-recognition devices at the *sharashka*, published his memoir *Ease My Sorrows*—1981 in Russian and 1983 in English. In the chapter "Phonoscopy, Hunting for Spies," Kopelev showed that his memory of the incident exposing the spy Koval matched with Solzhenitsyn's account in *In the First Circle*.

But the mismatch between the 1949 date and the Koval records might never be resolved. What was of lasting significance, however, was the fact that Solzhenitsyn and Kopelev both confirmed hearing a tape identifying George Koval as an atomic spy in America. The mystery of the December 1949 timing would never discount the accuracy of naming Koval.

Koval would never be formally interviewed about *In the First Circle* or any of the details in Solzhenitsyn's story. However, one of his star Mendeleev students, the Russian author Yuri Lebedev, later recalled having asked Koval about his presence in the book. It was at a gathering of close friends, and Lebedev, who had waited a long while for the right moment to bring up the topic of Solzhenitsyn's novel, broke the silence. When he did, Koval simply smiled and said, "Where did he get it?"

By the time Kopelev's memoir was published in English, the FBI's case #65-16756 had shut down in New York, and nationwide: quietly, without notice. No more interviews by FBI agents seeking leads to flesh out the seemingly undetectable details. No more reports exposing clues missed by classmates, girlfriends, or Manhattan Project colleagues. No more attempts to catch, or even locate, the deep-cover Agent Delmar.

But the hunt wasn't over.

CHAPTER SEVENTEEN

EXPOSED

The grand opening of the newly constructed US embassy in Moscow in May 2000 was one of those events that seem to exalt and shame simultaneously. Pride must have glazed the walls as the speeches rolled out and the glasses clinked, for there was no doubt that the postmodern building of stone and glass was quite an architectural and political accomplishment. At the same time, the occasion was a disturbing reminder that the entire project had taken more than thirty years to complete, a time during which high-profile gaffes had earned America's Moscow embassy such headline images as "bungled and bugged."

After a 1969 agreement to proceed with a new embassy, the construction finally began in the fall of 1979 with directives calling for the Soviet Union to use its own labor and materials to build the basic structure. The host country was also given the right to review architectural drawings for the building's frame "to ensure that it met local (Soviet) building codes and standards." But six years later, the Soviet workers were ejected from the site and work was suspended, after Soviet listening devices implanted in concrete pillars were found in the structural shell of the building. Then, it would take many more years for the US and the USSR to agree to a solution for dealing with such permanent eavesdropping systems, while Americans debated the prickly issue of slipshod scrutiny. As former defense secretary and CIA chief James Schlesinger said at the time of the discovery, "The culprit is American complacency, the tendency to assume that the Russians are technically inferior to us and that we can handle them." In his testimony after investigating the blunder, he called it "the best-bugged building ever built."

Through the years there had been attempts to plant devices at the old embassy, which had opened in 1953—such as the Soviets' gift of a large replica of the Great Seal of the United States, replete with a tiny listening mechanism found only after it had been hanging on the wall of the US ambassador's study for nearly two decades.

Then, in the 1960s, forty microphones had been found in the embassy walls, and in the 1980s, bugs were discovered in at least a dozen electric typewriters, one of them used by the secretary of the second-ranking embassy diplomat. These were sensors capable of picking up the contents of typed documents. There were also the "honey trap" cases, including a scandal around the same time as the shocking find at the new embassy construction site; this one involved a Marine security guard arrested and soon convicted of espionage after his affair with a Soviet woman working at the US embassy. The woman had a KGB handler.

Perhaps there would always be walls with ears at the embassy, though what was learned by such astute listening was not always picked up by the press. In 1999, for example, a somewhat significant spy story moved across the embassy landscape, missed by the media searchlight. In early June, a thin, stooped, bespectacled, eighty-five-year-old George Koval entered the American embassy without notice, forty years after US officials had invited him there. By then, Koval had retired from his post as an esteemed professor in the Department of Chemical Technology at Mendeleev, where he had studied or taught since the autumn of 1949. In 1952, his mother had passed away and, in 1964, he lost his father, both having lived on the collective farm at the Jewish Autonomous Region since their 1932 arrival. In 1987, his older brother, Isaiah, died, also at the JAR. And on May 26, 1999, a short time before his trip to the US Embassy, Mila, his wife of sixty-three years, passed on.

During the time he managed Mila's care, Koval was told about a special benefit available to US Army veterans who had served in World War II. His Russian army pension was based on a record that identified him only as a Red Army private—not as a veteran of Red Army intelligence who had conducted a valuable mission to the United States. It was surely meager, and the value of the ruble had recently collapsed, so money must have been the incentive for Koval's venture to the embassy. Specifically, he wanted to know how to apply to the US Social Security Administration for the benefit.

Exactly when the GRU learned that Koval had visited the American embassy is difficult to document, though one historian's account suggests it must have been early in the summer of 1999. Around that same time the agency encouraged a GRU historian to research the work of Agent Delmar—likely not a coincidence. Then in August, a Russian magazine article noted Soviet espionage "illegals" who had "saved the planet from nuclear terror." Delmar was on the list.

The article was written by Vladimir Lota, the pseudonym for the GRU historian who was also a former GRU colonel and whose real name was Vladimir Ivanovich Boyko. Right before the deadline for the August publication, Lota added paragraphs about Delmar to the section devoted to Arthur Adams, code name Achilles. He wrote, "The actions of Achilles and Delmar were coordinated by the chief *rezident* P. Melkishev of military intelligence, known as Moliere, who worked in New York as vice consulate under the name Mikhailov."

And he told readers that "Delmar is alive. He is 85 years old. He is a doctor of sciences. And it's not time yet to reveal his name."

According to the Russian writer Lebedev, who has tried to piece together this episode in the spy's elderly years, Koval's trips to the embassy that summer had "caused anxiety" at the GRU, and from Koval's first visit in June onward, Russian military intelligence knew his every move: when he arrived and when he left the embassy, as well as when he sent and received envelopes from the US and sometimes, but not always, their content. All the while Koval was likely aware that he was being watched. But it was not until after the arrival of the September 4 envelope from the US Social Security Administration—containing the necessary application forms—that the simmering concern of Russian intelligence likely began to boil.

Lebedev claimed that the GRU was not sure about Koval's intentions, but knew that his actions could be something "of a black stain for the GRU. No one considered the possibility that he was a traitor, but the fact that this former spy could be asking the U.S. for monetary compensation could be spun by the media as a heavy hit for the GRU. The GRU feared that he would discredit the intelligence structure to which he had given ten years of his young life." And whoever was tasked with the problem of what to do about Koval decided that calling him to the GRU headquarters was not a good idea. "They didn't dare. Could have turned out badly," wrote Lebedev. Instead, they made the smart decision to make him their ally—effectively to court him. They raised his pension. They started a monthly food delivery to his home. And they added him to their advisory committee for intelligence veterans.

Then, in February 2000, the GRU apparently learned that Koval had received another letter from America, this one from the Office of Central Operations of the Social Security Administration in Baltimore, Maryland. Dated February 7, it was the response to his application for the special benefit. It consisted of one sentence only: "We are writing to tell you that you do not qualify for retirement benefits." But the GRU, according to one account, knew only that he had received another letter from the US government—not the content. Next they decided to honor him with an award pin typically presented only to acting GRU officers. As Lebedev later commented, it was also good public relations, as it showed that the GRU cared about its veterans. A closed award ceremony was planned for late April 2000.

Next, the GRU authorized a book to be written about Koval's years as a spy in America: the story of "a brilliant GRU operation to insert its own agent into the super secret atomic operation." The title would be "GRU and the Atomic Bomb" and the author would be Vladimir Lota, who had met Koval for the first time at the April 2000 awards event. A few days later, using a password suggested by a GRU veteran who had known Koval for many years, the fifty-nine-year-old writer visited him at his home. The meeting, however, lasted barely an hour. Koval was hesitant to be under Lota's spotlight. With time, that changed as Lota would write about the life and accomplishments of Zhorzh Abramovich Koval in six magazine pieces and two books—half using only the Delmar code name and a false identity, "Dmitry," while Koval was alive.

Several weeks after Koval received his GRU award pin, a former colleague in America reappeared in his life: Arnold Kramish, the physicist, historian, and author who had been an ASTP classmate of Koval's at CCNY and a fellow member of the SED at Oak Ridge. Kramish would later tell the press that at Oak Ridge Koval "had access to everything. He had his own Jeep. Very few of us had our own Jeeps. He was clever. He was a trained GRU spy." He would refer to Koval as "the biggest" of the atomic spies, a comment that had to be respected as it was coming from a man who was an expert on the topic, fluent in Russian, knew Koval quite well. And he would say that Koval's greatest contribution to the Soviet bomb project was "shedding light on the polonium production and purification."

Kramish's résumé of scientific and government work was as thick as a book, brimming with intriguing accomplishments. As one writer later put it, Kramish "rubbed shoulders with spies and scientists." In the early 1950s, he worked with the renowned physicist Edward Teller on the hydrogen bomb, and he was the only scientist who participated in the questioning of Julius Rosenberg's brother-in-law, David Greenglass. He was also the Atomic Energy Commission's liaison with the CIA. And when the FBI had interviewed him in 1956 about Koval, he worked as a senior staff member at the Rand Corporation in DC, which started in 1946 as a think tank focusing on keeping America's technology ahead of all other nations, especially in nuclear energy and weapons systems. As Richard Rhodes wrote in his book *The Making of the Atomic Bomb*, Kramish was "a scientist involved with the more clandestine parts of the government."

As an expert in nuclear intelligence, Kramish wrote numerous articles and books on the topic, such as his 1959 book *Atomic Energy in the Soviet Union* and *The Griffin*, on the life of a spy working for the British in World War II who sought details about the German atomic bomb effort. In his seventy-seventh year, Kramish was writing his own memoir, "of which my friendship with Koval is very much an integral part," as he noted in a letter to the Mendeleev Institute in late April 2000 addressed to the institute's director, Professor Pavel D. Sarkisov. In the letter, Kramish described Koval as "my old friend." And could the school help him to locate Koval? To assure the director of his respectability, Kramish added that a "Dr. Sergei Kapitza" knew him and would "supply a personal and professional reference," if necessary. Kapitza was a renowned Soviet scientist who at the time of the letter was the host of a popular television show in Moscow about the miracles of science called *Evident but Incredible!*

In response, Professor Sarkisov quickly located Koval and mailed the contact information to Kramish, who then called Koval. He introduced himself and Koval said, "Ah, Arnold!" "Is that you,

George?" Kramish said. There was a pause and then they both burst out laughing, according to Kramish, who would later say, "It was an emotional moment for both of us."

What partly had inspired Kramish's quest to reconnect with Koval was something he had read that awakened him to misconceptions about who did what during the years of Soviet spying in America's top-secret bomb project. Knowledgeable about the history of Soviet espionage and the American atomic bomb, Kramish had discovered a recent biography of the atomic spy Theodore Hall, a brilliant young physicist at Los Alamos who leaked details about the plutonium bomb to the Soviet Union. And while impressed with the scholarship of its authors, Joseph Albright and Marcia Kunstel, Kramish, who had worked at both Oak Ridge and Los Alamos during the war, believed he could solve a mystery for them.

In the book, titled *Bombshell*, the authors described an intelligence report that "made a difference in the arms race." Marked "Top Secret," it "had been forwarded to Beria on March 1, 1949." The report, which the authors had obtained from the Russian Ministry of Atomic Energy archives, "divulged an industrial process for manufacturing polonium 210, the isotope that serves as the key ingredient in the triggering mechanism of a nuclear bomb. . . . As the report to Beria disclosed, the Americans were artificially creating polonium 210. . . ." The report, the authors wrote, went on to describe the process of irradiating slugs of bismuth at the nuclear reactor in Hanford, Washington, and sending the irradiated bismuth to a plant in Dayton, Ohio, where the "polonium 210 was recovered by acid treatments inside five-foot-tall glass-lined vats." Then, "Just four days after receiving the report on the American polonium process, Beria passed it to Igor Kurchatov and Boris Vannikov, the chief scientist and top administrator of the Soviet atomic bomb project."

The authors wrote: "There is no evidence linking Ted Hall and his friends to any of this—either in declassified Russian archives or anywhere else." But if Hall had nothing to do with the report, then "Who did?" they asked.

Kramish was sure he could answer that question. The person who wrote the report had to be his former colleague, Koval. As Kramish knew, Hall wasn't stationed at Oak Ridge or at the Monsanto operations in Dayton, nor was he an expert on "safety technology" or methods of detecting radiation contamination (two of the sections of the report). Hall was not a health physicist. Koval was.

After their reunion by telephone in 2000, Kramish and Koval began a correspondence, first by letters and then, at the suggestion of Koval's grandniece, Maya Gennadievna Koval, by emails. He said that he wanted to write Koval's biography and hoped that Koval would cooperate. Though likely gratified by the reconnection, Koval kept a distance. In response to Kramish's comments about his work and life, Koval wrote, "It's interesting." He never denied his involvement in the espionage work, but he also did not share any details. And he never answered Kramish's questions directly. He had clearly made a decision about what to reveal and when to keep quiet.

Then, in April 2003, Kramish sent Koval a copy of the book about Hall and at the same time, separately, a letter dated April 6, 2003. In the letter, Kramish explained his discovery of the book and his view of its significance to Koval. "I sent you the biography of Theodore Alvin Hall whom I worked with at Los Alamos. He died three years ago in Cambridge, but before that I went to visit him, and his wife. We had a very interesting conversation, including about his motives. The authors of this book were scrupulous in their research and wording of the text. But I think they made a mistake in noting the author of one of their reports. On pgs. 194–195, the authors say there's reason to assume that Hall gave the Soviets some secret information that affected the arms race. That same winter when Hall met with a Soviet agent in snowy New York, the spy report describing

American developments reached Moscow, which allowed Soviets to organize a mass production of atomic bombs. I put two pages of this report in the book; I think you will be very interested." On the two pages were the four categories of the report and the cover page of the March 4 memo Beria had sent to ministry officials ordering them to read the report.

Shortly after sending the book and the letter, in 2003, Kramish emailed Koval about writing his biography. "To write your complete biography, I will have to ask you questions that you will not want or will be unable to answer. . . . In particular, I'd like to question you about the Dayton materials." Kramish knew the questions to ask, but he understood that Koval could say little about his work as a spy. They continued their written exchanges, but they would never again meet in person. In late January 2006 Koval died at his home in Moscow, with family members by his side.

On February 2 at noon, a bus left Mendeleev transporting "those wanting to say goodbye to George Koval" to a wake at the morgue in the First City Gradskaya Hospital. The announcement about the planned event described him as "a veteran of the Great Patriotic War, a person of legendary fate, a teacher in the Department of General Chemistry technology." He was cremated and the name "Zhorzh Abramovich Koval" was added to the gravestone shared by Mila and her mother. There were no obituaries.

To be sure, at the time of his death, few people knew about Koval's intriguing double life. Because he was skilled enough never to be caught in America and because he was hit hard by the politics of prejudice upon his return to the Soviet Union, his story went unnoticed in the history of both nations.

In Russia, after moving back to Moscow in 1948, Koval didn't receive awards of distinction nor was he offered a respectable post in the GRU. But such fate was not because he lacked accomplishments. If, in fact, his 1940s "business trip" had been a failure, he would have been severely punished. And the director of the GRU would not have responded so quickly to Koval's March 10, 1953, letter in which he sought an official acknowledgment of his espionage work as a way to boost his job security. As Koval had written, "Only you know about the challenge and responsibility of my job for you and how I completed it with honesty." The GRU director's letter to the Soviet minister of higher education, more than hinted at Koval's impressive, yet hidden, record: "According to the nondisclosure agreement of military security, [Koval] cannot explain the details of what he did under special conditions. If this fact had any effect on the Ministry not giving him a good job, then we'll send our representative who will give you whatever details you need."

Those "details" would have included facts from GRU files that could prove Koval's contribution to the Soviet bomb project. His reports sent to "Department S" contained information about Manhattan Project sites, including plant structures, layouts, and worker numbers at Oak Ridge, and the volume of fuel production at both Oak Ridge and Dayton. There was also his diagram of X-10, the plant at Oak Ridge producing plutonium and irradiating the bismuth to produce polonium. Working often at X-10 from August 1944 to June 1945, Koval had been able to inform Moscow about plutonium production details. Consequently Kurchatov could trust earlier intelligence about plutonium sent from America and would choose the plutonium-implosion bomb for the Soviet Union's first nuclear weapon.

Koval's move to Dayton in June 1945 greatly "expanded his opportunity to gather new intelligence," as GRU historian Lota later pointed out—especially regarding the processes for synthesizing and purifying the polonium from the irradiated bismuth sent to Dayton from Oak Ridge and Hanford. For the Soviets, this priceless information eliminated certain time-consuming and costly experiments that the Americans had conducted in their pursuit of the fuel used to initiate the chain reaction of the bombs. Koval's explanation of the industrial process for making polonium in his March 1949 report to Beria was later described by two historians as having "made a difference in the arms race."

There were also Koval's contributions as a health physicist in the new realm of radiation research. As the physicist Seymour Block had commented, "if the Soviets obtained information concerning our health physics program, their development of the bomb would have been accelerated." They did—from Delmar.

Koval's espionage went unrecognized in the US because he got away. He followed the rules and didn't mingle socially with anyone in his network. He fit easily into the American scene, never attracting counterintelligence. As one scholar later wrote, Koval was most skilled at "predicting dangerous situations and reacting in a timely manner." The FBI did not discover him until nearly six years after he left America in 1948. And they never could bring him back. Also, only a small percentage of the cables sent between Moscow and its intelligence sources in the US in the 1940s that were decrypted in America's top-secret Venona project exposed GRU spies.

Whatever the reasons, Koval's double life would remain buried for many decades. And though Aleksandr Solzhenitsyn in his novel *In the First Circle* and Lev Kopelev in his memoir *Ease My Sorrows* were the very first to name the spy "Georgy Koval," the identity of Koval as agent Delmar was first exposed by the spy himself. It happened at a party in Moscow in 2003 celebrating his ninetieth birthday. Two of his former students at Mendeleev asked him to sign copies of Vladimir Lota's recent book, *The GRU and the Atomic Bomb*, which revealed the spy with the code name Delmar, though never mentioning Koval. His signature on both copies of the book was "Zhorzh Abramovich (Delmar)."

Four years later Lota would be credited with disclosing Delmar's identity in a July 2007 magazine piece entitled "They Called Him Delmar." Its audience was largely Russian readers. Within a few months, however, Koval would become known internationally as a star performer in the history of Soviet espionage—his spying, a successful dance of skillful pirouettes.

EPILOGUE

Early one afternoon in late autumn 2006, Russian president Vlad-imir Putin visited the new Moscow headquarters of Russia's Military Intelligence Directorate, the GRU, for the grand opening of an exhibition featuring portraits of the nation's military heroes, including Cold War spies. With a host of bodyguards, top cabinet officials, and journalists hovering closely, he walked from hall to hall. His schedule was tight and his stride was swift as he moved with the cadence of a confident leader who had made many such appearances. So when he suddenly stopped and abruptly turned around, there was a slight fuss. His entourage, like the swirl of a royal cloak, turned with him as he backtracked to the previous exhibit where he stood in front of the portrait of a Soviet spy and said, effectively, "*Kto eto*?" ("Who's that?")

One year later, on November 2, 2007, at Novo-Ogaryovo, the Russian president's estate on the outskirts of Moscow, Putin bestowed Zhorzh Abramovich Koval, the man in the portrait, with Russia's highest civilian honor, the Hero of the Russian Federation gold medal, for his role in the making of the first Soviet atomic bomb. At the ceremony, after presenting Koval's posthumous award to Russia's defense minister Anatoly Serdyukov, Putin proclaimed that Koval, was "the only Soviet intelligence officer to penetrate the U.S. secret atomic facilities producing the plutonium, enriched uranium and polonium used to create the atomic bomb" and that the American secrets Koval sent to Moscow "helped speed up considerably the time it took for the Soviet Union to develop an atomic bomb of its own, thus ensuring the preservation of strategic military parity with the United States."

The news about the award sent a shock wave through intelligence communities worldwide, especially in Russia and America. It was a startling reminder that the story of Soviet espionage during World War II was far from being a closed chapter, as the experts well knew. This was especially true for spies of the GRU whose activities in America during the 1930s and 1940s were still locked away in Russian archives. Even decryptions from the Venona project, which had released its findings for public access in 1995, barely touched upon the GRU. "We knew next to nothing about the extent of the GRU's espionage operation against the Manhattan Project until the Koval thing came up," according to John Earl Haynes, a respected American scholar of Cold War history.

As the shock wore off, the questions mounted. Who was this deep-cover agent, this "plant" of the Soviet military intelligence? What was the magnitude of his spying? How was it possible that he was undetected for so many years in America? As Haynes commented in 2007, "Koval was a trained agent, not an American civilian. He was that rarity, which you see a lot in fiction but rarely in real life—a sleeper agent. A penetration agent. A professional officer." Stewart Bloom, a nuclear physicist at the Brookhaven National Laboratory on Long Island and a former ASTP and SED colleague of Koval's during the war, said, "He played baseball and played it well. He didn't have a Russian accent. He spoke fluent English, American English. His credentials were perfect." And when the US government finally discovered him, after he had returned to the Soviet Union, there was no fanfare because "it would have been highly embarrassing for the US government to have had this divulged," explained historian Robert S. Norris in a 2007 interview.

At the same time, the naysayers emerged. There were the skeptics who suspected Putin had embellished Koval's prowess and accomplishments to boost the image of the GRU. There were the defensive ones who, having missed the clues, perhaps wanted to dull the shine on Koval's spy career. And there were others who had known Koval but were less forgiving than his former colleague Kramish. "Oh wow, I don't think you'd want to hear what I'd say to him," said James Schoke, a fellow SED member, when asked how he would respond if he were to see Koval again. "I wouldn't be very friendly. Would not be very friendly, yeah, I have no tolerance for that, none at all," he said.

In multiple interviews with the press, Kramish showed only respect for Koval, and restraint, never revealing details from their correspondence in recent years. The only comment Kramish made that showed even a hint of the depth of their bond was, "Koval never had any regrets. He believed in the system." What he meant was twofold: a system of scientists whose quests and beliefs transcended politics and a system of collective idealism that Koval's parents had taught him from the start.

In the summer of 2014, Koval's grandniece, Maya Koval, was arranging books on the shelves of her Moscow home, including some having once belonged to Koval. Among the English-language works were a 1911 set of Shakespeare's sonnets and plays, a translated collection of Balzac's poetry, some chemistry books, and a worn 1930 edition of Walt Whitman's *Leaves of Grass*, inscribed "George Koval, 1931."

There was also a book stuffed with papers written in Russian, one of them marked "*Sovershenno Sekretno*" (Top Secret), and a letter, in English, dated April 2003. This was the book Kramish had sent to Koval. Tucked under its cover were copies of the top page of the

March 1, 1949 report written by Koval for the GRU and then sent to Beria, plus Beria's March 4, 1949, memo to high officials in the Soviet ministries ordering them to read the full intelligence report from the Red Army spy who had gained top-security clearance at the Manhattan Project. Those were the Soviet documents Kramish would have shown to the world to prove Koval's significance in the making of the Soviet bomb, if he had lived to write the biography of Zhorzh Abramovich Koval. But Kramish had died in 2010.

On the title page of the book was an inscription, written by Kramish, in English: "George, Ours is a friendship forged in wartime, fallow during a 'Cold War'—but now renewed! In a way, it has been a 'closing of the circle'—memorable and treasured."

Kramish didn't tell reporters about the book he sent to Koval in 2003 or the content of the documents folded under its front cover. He steered attention to Koval's personality, the Oak Ridge job, the jeep, and the overlooked signs. At CCNY, during the war, he said, fellow classmates noticed that Koval was ten years older than everyone else and wondered why, but no one suspected he was a sleeper agent with a hidden agenda. As Kramish well knew, the clues that should have been warnings were there all along.

ACKNOWLEDGMENTS

Writing a book is an all-embracing, step-by-step process—a marathon, not a sprint. And the author's reward for reaching the finish line is to compose the acknowledgments, a special honor that requires remembering each stage of the book's progress to appreciate who contributed what and when. For *Sleeper Agent*, I could write a book about the process and the people involved, but for now, I will simply sing some praises.

First, as always, is my agent, Alice Martell, whose wisdom, diplomacy, and diligence are cherished gifts to her writers. There is also Alice's voice of reality, which is a major motivator. I am indebted to her. Thanks also to her assistant Stephanie Finman.

An exceptional editor respects a writer's individual style and route, and yet catches potential wrong turns at just the right moment. That's Bob Bender, my editor, a fine mix of sensitivity and sharp vision. From the start, he understood my determination to unravel the complexities and to answer the long-standing questions about the life of George Koval. He tolerated my spurts of excitement after big discoveries, discouraged occasional attempts to dig too deeply, and knew the best times to inspire endurance. I'm hugely grateful to Bob and to his assistant, Johanna Li.

For the long, demanding years of the project, I was fortunate for the excellent contributions of the following individuals:

Masha Stepanova's superb work in finding and translating relevant Russian-language letters, books, and articles provided crucial details in the narrative, such as the story of Koval's journey back to America in 1940, and the 1953 letters revealing the respect of Soviet military intelligence for his espionage work. In short, Masha, who is Miami University's Slavic librarian, is truly remarkable.

Also outstanding is Joanne Drilling, a skilled researcher with a never-give-up approach who uncovered useful, often surprising, details, especially about the spy Arthur Adams and about buried ties in several Soviet spy networks. Loyal and invaluable, she also indexed thousands of pages of FBI reports and compiled numerous timelines, allowing me to discover intersecting events and locations among the players and organizations in the narrative.

Research librarian Alison Gibson, whom I often have called a national treasure, discovered rare publications that helped to unravel a few conundrums, especially regarding Benjamin W. Lassen. And her astute awareness of resources potentially useful to the story was priceless.

Also treasured is June Zipperian, who reads at least a book a week, proving that the habit of reading nurtures adept skills for critiquing a piece of writing. I'm honored that June has been a first reader for many a chapter I've written in four of my books, including *Sleeper Agent*.

And colossal thanks to Marlay B. Price, who read countless pages of FBI reports to flag specific details and who joined me on several of the research trips. When a spouse understands the daily work of a writing partner, the seemingly endless hours of solitude in a writer's life transform from loneliness to fulfillment. Thank you, Marlay.

Next, I am grateful to Duane M. Weise, who was a military colleague of George Koval's at both Oak Ridge and CCNY, and who generously shared stories and memories with me. I thank Bridget M. Vis who, at the beginning of the research, gave the book its working title, "Undetected." Also, in the book's early stage, Sari Ewing shared her expertise on ship manifests and ancestry research plus her sheer elation regarding the topic. I thank Sari especially for her quick realization that George Koval's "A mighty man is he" in his high school yearbook is a line from Henry Wadsworth Longfellow's poem "The Village Blacksmith." Gratitude also to Victoria Baird for her excellent translations of Russian articles at the very start of the project. Much appreciation also to Robin Gilbert, Melody Kokensparger, Sonja Cropper, and Ron Ralston who generously helped with tasks in the midst of crucial deadlines. And immense gratitude to James Ralston for sharing his knowledge of nuclear physics, to Josh Karpf for his skillful copyediting, and to Lisa Healy for her expertise as the book's production editor.

Throughout the research, librarians and archivists were so often helpful. What the future can know about the past is clearly in their hands: the documentary evidence of history in letters, diaries, reports, government documents, personal records, photos, newspapers, magazines, broadsides, and more. I am grateful to the following:

Amy Reytar, archivist at the National Archives, in College Park, Maryland. Dr. Gary Zola, executive director, and Dr. Dana Herman, director of research, at the Jacob Rader Marcus Center of the American Jewish Archives at Hebrew Union College-Jewish Institute of Religion in Cincinnati; and librarian Alice Finkelstein at the Klau Library, at Hebrew Union College. Archivist Ilya Slavutskiy at the Center for Jewish History and YIVO Institute for Jewish Research, in New York City. Head archivist of the City College of New York, Sydney C. Van Nort. Archivist David Clark at the Truman Library. Aaron Novelle at the Institute of Electrical and Electronics Engineers. At Oak Ridge: Teresa Fortney in the Oak Ridge Room at the Oak Ridge Public Library; D. Ray Smith, historian at the Y-12 National Security Complex; Mark Dickey at the Oak Ridge National Laboratory; and Robbie Meyer, at the Manhattan Project National Historical Park. Curator Tom Munson at the Sioux City Public Museum and Kelsey Patterson at the Sioux City Public Library.

Regarding the myriad files sent from the Federal Bureau of Investigation archives by way of the Freedom of Information Act (FOIA), I must thank Leanna Ramsey, the FBI public information officer, who was always as gracious and efficient as the system would allow. Also, thanks to attorney Adam Marshall at the Reporters Committee for Freedom of the Press for advice on how best to use the FOIA for administrative appeals regarding redacted FBI files. And a special thanks to attorney and author Mark Cymrot.

Other libraries and archives: The New York Public Library Reading Room and Reference Desk, Main Branch. The Municipal Library at 31 Chambers Street in New York City. The New York City Department of Records and Information Services. The New-York Historical Society. The archives at Columbia University, the University of Wisconsin, the University of Notre Dame, the University of Chicago, and the Massachusetts Institute of Technology. New York University's Tamiment Library. Washington University's Special Collections. The Galveston Historical Foundation's archive. The Atomic Heritage Foundation. The Wright Memorial Public Library. The National Museum of Nuclear Science & History. The National Academy of Sciences Archives. The US Department of State, Passport Office. The *New York Times* archive. The Central Archives for the History of the Jewish People, in Jerusalem. Ancestry.com. The Mound Science and Energy Museum in Miamisburg, Ohio. The General Electric digital archive. The Massachusetts Land Records site. The Ohio Northern University Archives, Heterick Memorial Library. Pinsk City Archive. Freedom of Information Act Reading Room: cia.gov/library/readingroom.

Regarding Russian resources, I am grateful to Maya Koval, George's grandniece, especially for sending me photos of George's copy of *Leaves of Grass* with his signature in 1931 on the frontispiece. And I respect the Russian scholars Aleksandr Petrovich Zhukov and Yuri Aleksandrovich Lebedev for their research and writings about George Koval—plus a posthumous thanks to Vladimir Lota, the GRU historian who also wrote extensively about Koval.

Thanks also to Dr. Stephen Norris, the director of Miami University's Havighurst Center for Russian and Post-Soviet Studies, and Russian language professor Dr. Benjamin Sutcliffe, also an interpreter at the Center—both so very helpful.

For generous assistance in specific parts of the research, I am grateful to the following: Don and Brian Connelly, Ron Ellis, Peter Fischer, Corey Flintoff, Matthew Francis, Richard Hacken, Peter Houk, David Katzman, Paul Lamberger, Mark Neikirk, Lori Stacel, Michael Stallo, Jim Tobin, Bill Tuttle, Jim and Ann Veith, Jon Warner, and Jocelyn Wilk. Special thanks also to: Chase Beach, Scott and Sarah Byers, Richard Campbell, Scarlett Chen, Jenny and Perry Clark, Nick and Nina Clooney, Jeremiah Costa, Jeffrey and Carol Donohoo, Ceílí Doyle, Lynn Fraze, Tim and Christine Gilman, Lisa Haitz, Pam Houk, Mark Jones, Tom and Alice Laurenson, Lois Logan, Keith McWalter, Joe Prescher, Chris Singer, Emily Williams, Joe Worrall—and a posthumous thanks to George W. Houk.

I must close with a note of gratitude to my editors from many years ago at the *Wall Street Journal*—Don Moffitt, Norm Pearlstine, Paul Steiger, and Steve Adler—from whom I learned the enduring discipline of a daily writing routine and the value of humility.

NOTES

To unearth the truth about anyone's life requires extensive research into the motives, desires, fears, beliefs, and hopes that drive decisions and accomplishments. Buried in letters, journals, postcards, news clips, yearbooks, photos, maps, tax records, ship manifests, passports, even inscriptions in books, such details are not always easy to find. And telling the story of a spy is doubly difficult because the main players in the narrative have used their expertise to block all potential paths to the truth, during their lifetimes and ad infinitum. In researching the biography of George Koval, there was the added complication that he was a spy for the GRU (Soviet military intelligence), whose records for work in America during the 1940s are still largely inaccessible. As noted in the *Sleeper Agent* epilogue, Cold War expert John Earl Haynes—a prolific writer on the US counterintelligence project, code name "Venona," to decipher the Soviet spy exchanges—has said that "next to nothing" was known about the GRU in the Manhattan Project before Koval surfaced. And as Soviet intelligence historian Jonathan Haslam wrote in his 2019 book *Near and Distant Neighbors*, the history of the GRU "has yet to reach the public eye."

So how to research the life of an undetected GRU atomic spy in America in the 1940s? Proceed with the wisdom that the story

of Soviet espionage in the West during World War II is in the early
stages of discovery. And accept that there will be unanswered questions. Then, move forward with extensive, resolute goals to explore
primary sources and records, seek FBI case reports, compile detailed
chronologies of the narrative's major players, chart the addresses of
cover shops and residences, disprove coincidences, and study the
excellent books and articles by espionage experts thus far.

For *Sleeper Agent*, the far-reaching FBI case files of George
Koval, Benjamin Lassen, and Arthur Adams—also several hundred
pages of the Nathan Gregory Silvermaster reports and a multitude
of J. Edgar Hoover memos—were immensely helpful, especially
regarding interviews with people across a vast landscape of former
colleagues, bosses, employees, landlords, classmates, girlfriends,
relatives, and teachers. There were also the FBI agents' thorough
surveys of official documents, such as passport applications, army
registrations, security files, and legal records of all sorts. Sifting
through the nearly seven thousand pages of reports did indeed
lead to significant primary sources as well as links for the chronologies and descriptions of major players in the narrative. However, it
must be said that the files do contain contradictions and occasional
errors as well as repetitions and redactions. Facts often must be
double-checked.

I also consulted exceptional secondary sources, as listed in the
selected bibliography, ones with research notes almost as stimulating
as the texts and worthy perhaps of a future book revealing the best
methods and resources for extensive research into wartime Soviet
espionage in America. And, as noted in the acknowledgments, I
sorted through many documents in archival collections nationwide.

My quest was to get as close to the truth as possible, of course,
and to answer at least a few of the long-lingering questions about
Koval's GRU "business trip" in America. For example, the narrative
shows that it was not sheer luck that Koval ended up at the Oak

Ridge site of the Manhattan Project in August 1944. Also, Koval's difficulties after returning to Moscow in 1948 had nothing to do with a failed mission, and his known reports to Soviet intelligence in Moscow regarding the Oak Ridge site, the polonium production, and the radiation safety efforts helped to shorten the Soviets' project to build their first atomic bomb.

But there is the frustration of unanswered questions. How many reports did Koval send to Soviet military intelligence and exactly when? Were Koval's postcard recipients in 1948 connected to his espionage work, or at least aware of his double life? Was the courier "Clyde" another code name for Benjamin Lassen? And who didn't meet Koval at the Grand Central Palace in September 1948? This is the type of book that prompts obsession. But there must always be a stopping point.

My hope is twofold: that *Sleeper Agent* will deepen the reader's understanding of the intriguing psychology of a spy and of the timeless costs of oppression; and that it will be helpful to future researchers by contributing to the step-by-step process of prying open the closed chapters in the story of Soviet espionage in America.

PROLOGUE

1 About New York City's 1948 Golden Anniversary Exposition: Robert W. Potter, "Three Big Shows for City's Jubilee," *New York Times*, June 6, 1948, 13; William L. Laurence, "Public to Witness Atom Explosions: First Demonstration of Actual Uranium Blasts Scheduled Here for Golden Jubilee," *New York Times*, August 9, 1948, 21; "Far Star to Open City Jubilee Show," *New York Times*, August 16, 1948, 21; Associated Press, "Starlight of 50 Years Ago to Open New York Exhibit," *Kingston Daily Freeman* (Kingston, NY), August 20, 1948, 1; Paul Blauvelt, "Visitors at Exposition to See Atom-Splitting," *Brooklyn Daily Eagle*, August 22, 1948, 3; Walter Sullivan, "City's Exposition for Jubilee Opens in Blaze of Lights," *New York Times*, August 22, 1948, 1.

2 "It is highly appropriate": Sullivan, 21.

2 " 'Man and Atom': Best Show in New York": Bob Considine, International News Service, September 16, 1948, 14.

3 "a shocking chapter in Communist espionage in the atomic field": C. P. Trussell, "House Body Plans to Expose Details of Atomic Spying," *New York Times*, September 18, 1948, 1.

3 Details about George Koval and Jean Finkelstein and about the exposition date: FBI case #65-16756, agents' interviews with Jean throughout March 1956 and once in October 1956; additional details in FBI case #65-14743, reports in January, February, and March 1954. The "near CCNY" bowling alley was on the Upper West Side in the basement of Riverside Church, which was built with two underground floors that contained four bowling alleys, a theater, and an auditorium. From Peter J. Paris, ed., *The History of the Riverside Church in the City of New York* (New York: New York University Press, 2004).

3 "interesting and rare friend": FBI case #65-16756, March 1956 interview with Leonard Finkelstein.

4 "It was serious from the start": Ibid., interview with Jean Finkelstein Mordetzky.

5 Viewers' hair stands on end: Blauvelt, 3.

5 "a lovers' quarrel": FBI case #65-16756, March 1956.

5 "seemed to be picking a fight": Ibid.

6 "Spies in U.S. are 'On Run' ": Irving Spiegel, "Clark Holds Spies in U.S. Are 'On Run,' " *New York Times*, September 19, 1948, 28.

6 "yesterday morning": FBI case #65-16756, interviews with the landlady April 1955, and Jean Mordetzky, in March 1956.

6 Herbie Sandberg and the power plant in Poland: Ibid., March 1956.

PART I: THE LURE

CHAPTER ONE: THE DREAM ON VIRGINIA STREET

11 Sioux City newsboys: *Sioux City Journal*, June 18, 1924, 7. Susan Marks Conner, ed., *I Remember When . . . Personal Recollections and Vignettes of the Sioux City Jewish Community, 1869–1984* (Sioux City, Iowa: Jewish Federation of Sioux City, 1985), 30–35.

11 Description of cramped quarters and black flies on walls: Bernard Marinbach, *Galveston: Ellis Island of the West* (Albany: SUNY Press, 1984), 26.

11 1,600 steerage passengers on the SS *Hannover*: "S/S Hannover (2), Norddeutscher Lloyd," Norway Heritage, norwayheritage.com/p_ship.asp?sh=hann2.

11 Abram Koval: Dates of his trip from Telekhany to Bremen to Galveston to Sioux City on the SS *Hannover* are in FBI reports, regarding case #65-609, April 17, 1955.

12 Abram Koval's name and destination as it was written on his immigration form at Galveston: Filed in the Woodbury County District Court after his arrival in Sioux City on May 5, 1910. His birth date was confirmed on his naturalization papers, petition #853, filed in the same district court, on May 8, 1919. His certificate of naturalization, #1247809, was issued on September 4, 1919, and he officially became a US citizen on September 8, 1919.

12 Details of the Galveston Movement: Marinbach, *Galveston*. Marinbach, in describing the new Jewish communities in the West, mentions on page 188 Abram Koval arriving in Sioux City in 1910 "as an immigrant at the port of Galveston."

12 More about the Galveston Movement: Edward Allan Brawley, "When the Jews Came to Galveston," *Commentary*, April 2009, 31–36. *Galveston Daily News*, March 22, 1931, 1; Henry Cohen, "The Galveston Immigration Movement: A 1909 Report," *B'nai B'rith Messenger*, Los Angeles, March 26 and April 16, 1909; Henry Cohen Papers at the Jacob Rader Marcus Center of the American Jewish Archives, box 1, folder 4, Galveston Movement, 1907–1916.

12 Concerns about immigration restrictions: Cyrus L. Sulzberger, "Immigration Restriction: Its Fallacies," *The Menorah: A Monthly Magazine for the Jewish Home*, New York, April 1906, 193–202.

13 What the society paid for the immigrants' voyage: Brawley, "When the Jews Came to Galveston," 33.

13 Statistics about the placement of Russian immigrants: Ibid., 35.

13 Pale of Settlement restrictions: Inna Shtakser, *The Making of Jewish Revolutionaries in the Pale of Settlement: Community and Identity during the Russian Revolution and Its Immediate Aftermath, 1905–07*, Palgrave Studies in the History of Social Movements (London: Palgrave Macmillan, 2014), 1–18; Azriel Shohat, *The Jews of Pinsk, 1881 to 1941* (Stanford, CA: Stanford University Press, 2013).

13 The czar's army requirements being a reason for flight: New York attorney Sidney Naishtat's descriptions in FBI case #65-14743, January 1954.

13 The October Manifesto, the pogroms, the Russian Revolution of 1905, and the Bund: John D. Klier and Shlomo Lambroza, eds., *Pogroms: Anti-Jewish Violence in Modern Russian History* (New York: Cambridge University Press, 1992). Note that on page 220 of that book, there is a 1905 photo of

the Bund self-defense organization in Pinsk, the town near Telekhany, and one of the gentlemen deeply resembles Abram Koval, though no individuals are identified. See also Hilary L. Rubinstein, Dan Cohn-Sherlock, Abraham J. Edelheit, and William D. Rubenstein, *The Jews in the Modern World: A History Since 1750* (London: Hodder Education, 2002), and Henry Jack Tobias, *The Jewish Bund in Russia* (Stanford, CA: Stanford University Press, 1972).

14 Statistics of pogroms and towns attacked: Victoria Khiterer, "The October 1905 Pogroms and the Russian Authorities," *Nationalities Papers* 43, no. 5 (2015), 788–803.

15 Teenagers in the Bund: Tobias, *The Jewish Bund in Russia*, 237.

15 Ethel Shenitsky: From George Koval's biographical essay sent to the GRU in the summer of 1939, in IU. A. Lebedev, *Dva vybora . . . ob istorii verbovok Zh. A. Kovalia* [*Two Choices . . . The History of George Koval's Recruitments*], Moscow: RKhTU, 2014.

16 1910 violence: Herman Bernstein, "Expulsion of Jews from Russia Begins Afresh," *New York Times*, April 17, 1910, 8; "The New Martyrdom of the Jews in Russia," *New York Times*, June 5, 1910, 14.

16 "even taking babies from their mothers": "Expulsion of Jews Goes On, German Jews Association Makes the Charge," *Vossische Zeitung* (Berlin), May 21, 1910.

16 "bloodless pogroms": "Jews Sent into Exile," United Press Wire, May 21, 1910.

16 Early-twentieth-century Sioux City Jewish community: Marinbach, *Galveston*, 187–89; Conner, ed., *I Remember When . . .*, 10–56; Bernard Shuman, *A History of the Sioux City Jewish Community, 1869 to 1969* (Sioux City, IA: Jewish Federation, 1969); William L. Hewitt, "So Few Undesirables," *Annals of Iowa* 50, no. 2 (Fall 1989), 158–79.

17 Koval family home in Sioux City: Abram Koval purchased the 619 Virginia Street house on December 30, 1922. The deed was filed on March 7, 1923 at the Woodbury County (Iowa) Courthouse.

17 Birth dates of all Koval children: Woodbury County (Iowa) courthouse records.

CHAPTER TWO: "NOTHING BUT THE TRUTH"

19 George's upbringing: Details come from various accounts of childhood friends and relatives interviewed by FBI agents in case #65-16756, December 1954 and March 1955.

19 Baseball in Sioux City: Hewitt, "So Few Undesirables," 158.

19 Baseball greats at Sioux City Stock Yards Ball Park: Marcia Poole, *The Yards: A Way of Life* (The Lewis and Clark Interpretive Center Association, Sioux City, Iowa: 2006), 98–101.

20 Anti-Semitism in the aftermath of the 1917 October Revolution and the post–World War I Red Scare: Ann Hagedorn, *Savage Peace: Hope and Fear in America, 1919* (New York: Simon & Schuster, 2007), 185–87, 222–23.

21 1924 immigration law: Linda Gordon, *The Second Coming of the KKK: The Ku Klux Klan of the 1920s and the American Political Tradition* (New York: Liveright, 2017), 195.

21 Statistics on KKK membership in Iowa: Robert J. Neymeyer, "In the Full Light of Day: The Ku Klux Klan in 1920s Iowa," *The Palimpsest*, Summer 1995, 59.

21 Summer 1924 KKK in Sioux City: Hewitt, "So Few Undesirables," 177–79.

22 Anti-Semitic newspaper ads: Albert Lee, *Henry Ford and the Jews* (New York: Stein & Day, 1980), 150.

22 "the greatest barrage of anti-Semitism": Ibid., 14.

22 The ninety-one-part series about "the Jewish menace": Boris Brasol, *The International Jew* (Dearborn, MI: The Dearborn Publishing Company, 1920–1922).

23 "We are Jewish and . . . ": The Barish brothers' full-page ad: *Sioux City News*, September 30, 1921.

23 Ford's six-hundred-word retraction: Lee, *Henry Ford and the Jews*, 80–81.

23 Koval's personality was popular but private: Interviews of high school friends, in FBI reports regarding case #65-16756, March 1955.

23 Role in "Nothing But the Truth": *Maroon & White* (Sioux City, Iowa: Central High School Yearbook, 1929), vol. 25, 51.

24 "Interscholastic debater": "Youngest Member of Central High Graduating Class an Honor Student," *Sioux City Journal*, June 1, 1929, 7; *Maroon & White*, 30.

24 "A mighty man is he": *Maroon & White*, 119.

24 Henry Wadsworth Longfellow, *The Village Blacksmith* (New York: E.P. Dutton, 1890), 10.

24 Koval at University of Iowa: He entered the College of Engineering on September 19, 1929, and attended until May 1932, according to Octavia Pratt at the Registrar's Office, University of Iowa. Pratt's interview is from an FBI report regarding case #65-16756, December 1954.

25 American Vigilant Intelligence Federation: *Objects and Purposes of the American Vigilant Intelligence Federation* (Chicago: AVI, 1900).

25 Minutes of the Communist Party, Iowa State Nominatic [sic] Convention, August 17, 1930: American Vigilant Intelligence Federation, Chicago,

August 28, 1930; also published in "Investigation of Communist Propaganda," US Congress, House of Representatives, Special Committee on Communist Activities in the United States (1930), 94–95.

25 Hoover memo, and details about Hoover receiving reports from the American Vigilant Intelligence Federation: Regin Schmidt, *Red Scare: FBI and the Origins of Anti-communism in the United States, 1919–1943* (Copenhagen: Museum Tusculanum Press, University of Copenhagen, 2000), 326–27.

CHAPTER THREE: THE ARREST

27 Grasshopper Plague: Allen Parker Mize Jr., "High Mercury Blamed for Hopper Army," *Des Moines Tribune*, July 27, 1931, 1, 3; Associated Press, "Planes May Be Used to Kill Pests," *Iowa City Press-Citizen*, July 29, 1931, 1.

27 Unemployment statistics: Stanley Lebergott, "Labor Force, Employment, and Unemployment, 1929–39: Estimating Methods," US Bureau of Labor Statistics, www.bls.gov/opub/mlr/1948/article/pdf/labor-force -employment-and-unemployment-1929-39-estimating-methods.pdf; see table 1 on page 2.

27 Farmers facing foreclosures: Ferner Nuhn, "The Farmer Learns Direct Action," *The Nation*, March 8, 1933, 254–56.

27 Iowa during the Great Depression: Linda Mason Hunter, "The Farmer Feeds Us All: Making Do During the Great Depression," *The Iowan*, March/April 2004, 13–20.

28 Unemployed Councils: Harvey Klehr, *The Heyday of American Communism: The Depression Decade* (New York: Basic Books, 1984), 50; *Labor Unity* (the official organ of the Trade Union Unity League, an industrial union umbrella organization of the Communist Party of the USA from 1929 to 1935), February 8, 1930, 8.

28 September 4, 1931, arrest: Long before Newspapers.com, the FBI discovered a file with the news articles about Koval's arrest at a private investigation agency, The Lewis System, run by Paul Lewis, in Sioux City. The articles were quoted verbatim in an FBI report regarding case #65-16756, March 1955.

29 IKOR and Birobidzhan: Masha Gessen, *Where the Jews Aren't: The Sad and Absurd Story of Birobidzhan, Russia's Jewish Autonomous Region* (New York: Schocken, 2016); Henry Felix Srebrnik, *Dreams of Nationhood: American Jewish Communists and the Soviet Birobidzhan Project, 1924–1951* (Brighton, MA: Academic Studies Press, 2010); Robert Weinberg, *Stalin's Forgotten Zion: Birobidzhan and the Making of a Soviet Jewish Homeland* (Berkeley: University of California Press, 1998).

30 "determined struggle against bloody Fascism": A. Rovner, *The "Icor" and the Jewish Colonization in the U.S.S.R.* (New York: ICOR, 1934), 13.

30 "the Jewish masses liberty, equality, and equal share": M. J. Wachman, *Why the Jewish Masses Must Rally to the Defense of the Soviet Union* (New York: ICOR, 1932), 16.

30 The Brigham Young University commission: From the pamphlet *Birobidjan*, published by ICOR (at YIVO Institute for Jewish Research at the Center for Jewish History), 1; Rovner, *The "Icor,"* 4.

30 "great agricultural and industrial wealth": "Excerpts from the Report of the American Icor Commission of Biro-Bidjan," ICOR Yearbook, 1932, xviii.

31 "Wasn't easy to be for [IKOR], not at all": Interview with Morris Lefko, FBI report regarding case #65-16756, March 1955.

31 Real estate sold by the Koval family in 1932: September 1931 transaction, lots record #367, page 419. The parcel is noted as lot 5, block 48, Middle Sioux City Addition. Then in May 1932, lots record #167, page 467, docket #4139.

32 Shipping companies traveling to Birobidzhan, shown in ads, in ICOR Yearbook, 1932.

32 The ship *Majestic* and journey to the Soviet Union: IU. A. Lebedev, *Vetvleniia sudby Zhorzha Kovalia* [Branches of Fate of George Koval] (Moscow: Tovarishchestvo Nauchnykh Izdanii KMK, 2019), vol. 1, 247.

PART II: THE DECEPTION

CHAPTER FOUR: "THE BUSINESS TRIP"

35 "A letter from a young man": *Nailebn* (*New Life*), vol. 9, no. 2, 1935, 45. Note that Mendeleev is now D. Mendeleev University of Chemical Technology of Russia.

36 Birobidzhan settler statistics and conditions: Henry Srebrnik, "The Other Jewish State," *Jewish Advocate*, September 7, 1972, A21–22.

37 "work first and": Ibid., A22.

37 Rumor of protecting the USSR from a Japanese invasion: Ibid., A21.

37 "Not every settler who," "Housing and roads," "the Kovals from Sioux City, Iowa," and "Koval is one of": Henry Srebrnik, *Dreams of Nationhood*, 249–53; also, Paul Novick, *Jews in Birobidzhan* (New York: 1937), available in the Papers of Paul (Pesakh) Novick, YIVO Institute for Jewish Research, Center for Jewish History, RG1247, Folder 17.

38 Interview with Novick: Julia Older, "Jewish Pioneers Creating Rich, Fertile Homeland, Secure Future with Soviet Aid," *Moscow News and Moscow Daily News*, November 7, 1936, 4, 30–31.

38 Details of George Koval's life in the Soviet Union in the summer of 1936: FBI interviews with Harry and Goldie Gurshtel about their trip to Russia that summer; FBI report regarding case #65-16756, January–September 1958.

39 Details about Mila: From her autobiographical essay, written in November 1938 and from the same by George for the GRU in August 1939. A. P. Zhukov, *Atmosfera deistvii: Zhorzh Abramovich Koval (1913–2006)* [*The Atmosphere of Action: George Abramovich Koval (1913–2006)*] (Moskva: RKhTU, 2013).

39 Physical description of Mila: FBI reports regarding case #65-16756, April 1958.

39 Mila and George's address in Moscow: IU. A. Lebedev, "Paradoksy sud'by" ["Paradoxes of Fate"], *Vesti* (Tel Aviv), January 10, 2008, 18, 22.

40 Statistics on the purges: Michael Ellman, "Soviet Repression Statistics: Some Comments," *Europe-Asia Studies* 54, no. 7 (November 2002), 1151–72.

41 The letter "my dear friend, Zhora . . . ": Zhukov, *Atmosfera deistvii*, 92.

42 The cousin whose parents were into "gold speculation work": Ibid.

42 The purge and the Soviet Union's military intelligence corps: Jonathan Haslam, *Near and Distant Neighbors: A New History of Soviet Intelligence* (New York: Farrar, Straus & Giroux, 2015), 85.

42 "I was told to go to a room": V. I. Lota, "Zvezda 'Del'mara'" ["The Star of 'Delmar'"], *Rossiiskoe Voennoe Obozrenie*, no. 10, 40–44, and no. 11 (2008), 34–49; and Levedev, *Dva vybora* [*Two Choices*], 38.

43 "to send characteristics regarding student George Koval": Ibid.

43 "He is soon finishing Mendeleev": Ibid.

43 The GRU likely received the report by June 1: Ibid., 39.

43 "Why and who was inviting me": Ibid.

44 "I believe that the" and "I knew that Mila did not": Ibid.

46 Spy training: Viktor Suvorov, *Inside Soviet Military Intelligence* (New York: Macmillan, 1984), 77–78.

46 "to recruit sources of information": V. I. Lota, "Spetskomandirovka . . . v Ok-Ridzh" ["Special Assignment . . . to Oak Ridge"], *Krasnaia Zvezda* 238 (December 25, 2013), 6; Lebedev, *Dva vybora* [*Two Choices*], 40.

47 "They just saw each other": Zhukov, *Atmosfera deistvii*, 86.

CHAPTER FIVE: UNDERCOVER IN THE BRONX

49 Koval's reentry to America in 1940: From a letter written on "three yellow leaves" and found by the Russian scholar Yuri Lebedev in the Koval family archives. He included it in his published writings about the life of

George Koval. The letter from George begins "Mila, You're [*sic*] probably worried." George gave the letter to the ship's captain to mail to Mila upon the ship's return to Vladivostok. IU. A. Lebedev, *Vetvleniia sudby Zhorzha Kovalia* [*Branches of Fate of George Koval*], 2 vols. (Moscow: Tovarish-chestvo Nauchnykh Izdanii KMK, 2019), vol. 1, 246.

50 Aliases: Throughout the FBI interviews in case #65-14743, "Faraday" and case #65-16756, "George Abramovich Koval," there are occasional inform-ers claiming names Koval used. One, in the July 1958 Koval file, said he sometimes went by "Sam." And in FBI case #65-14743, March 1954, a few former Raven Electric employees remembered his name when he first came to New York City as "George Rose." There is no proof of either claim.

50 Selective Service details: Order #12928, serial #2987. From FBI report regarding case #65-16756, October 1954.

50 George Koval addresses after his 1940 return to America: Ibid.

51 Workmen's Circle: David Margolick, "Workmen's Circle: 85 Years of Aid to Jews," *New York Times*, November 10, 1985; *Reform Advocate*, vol. 44, no. 2, August 24, 1912, 15; Oliver B. Pollak, "Keeping Yiddish Alive: The Workmen's Circle in Des Moines, Iowa, 1930–1952," *Shofar* 16, no. 3 (Spring 1998), 118–31.

51 Benjamin Loseff: Details from FBI reports regarding case #65-14743, April 1952.

51 Tillie Silver, as Loseff's sister: Ibid., January 27, 1954.

51 The cell structure of Lassen's spy network, "agent group leader," and "each member knew little": Svetlana Lokhova, *The Spy Who Changed History* (London: William Collins, 2018), 215–16. Lokhova writes that the best description of the cell structure can be found in Fyodor Dostoevsky's novel *The Devils*.

52 Banks: FBI reports regarding case #65-14743, October 1951 and March 1952; Lassen's compensation from the Broadway Savings Bank from the February 1950 report. The banks included Manufacturers Trust Company on Broadway, a block from West 24th Street; the Public National Bank and Trust Company at the corner of Broadway and West 24th Street; Modern Industrial Bank at 249 West 34th Street; the Corn Exchange Bank and Trust at 1 East 42nd Street; and the New York Trust Company on Broadway near Vesey Street, just five minutes walking distance from Loseff's jewelry store.

52 Description of Lassen: Compiled from his Ohio Northern University 1912 yearbook photo, from numerous passport shots in equally numerous FBI reports, and from FBI interviews with former Raven Electric tenants and employees in FBI case #65-14743. February, March, and May 1952; Sep-tember 1954; October 1955.

52 "very private" and "due to some unknown fear of him": From interviews in FBI reports regarding case #65-14743, September 1954.

53 Biographical details of "Lassen, as Lassoff": From FBI reports regarding case #65-14743, February and March 1952. Lassen became a citizen under the name Lassoff on February 15, 1912, in the Common Pleas Court, Hardin County, Kenton, Ohio, certificate #23435.

53 "all Russia's troubles": Klier, *Pogroms: Anti-Jewish Violence in Modern Russian History*, 88.

53 Lassoff at Ohio Northern University, including membership in several clubs, "flourishing chapter," and "make an intelligent": "Socialist Study Club Organized," *Ada Record* (Ada, Ohio), March 6, 1912, 2.

53 ONU branch of the AIEE: Ohio Northern University yearbook, 1912, 166.

54 List of Lassen's memberships with photo: Ohio Northern University yearbook, 1912, 43.

54 "Junior electrical engineer" for New York's Public Service Commission: From a January 31, 1920, archival record located at cityrecord.engineering.nyu.

54 State Committee of Electrification of Russia and Charles P. Steinmetz: Edison Tech Center digital archives, edisontc.org; FBI reports from case #65-14743, February 1950 and March 1952; Stephen Millies, "GE's 'Moral Fabric' and Its Forgotten Socialist Wizard," *Workers World*, April 15, 2016.

54 *Electrical World* magazine article about the project: Charles P. Steinmetz, "The Soviet Plan to Electrify Russia," *Electrical World*, September 30, 1922, 715–19.

55 Lassoff at ARCOS: From FBI reports regarding case #65-14743, March 1952.

55 Amtorg: Joseph Albright and Marcia Kunstel, *Bombshell: The Secret Story of America's Unknown Atomic Spy Conspiracy* (New York: Times Books, 1997); John Earl Haynes and Harvey Klehr, *Early Cold War Spies: The Espionage Trials That Shaped American Politics* (Cambridge, UK: Cambridge University Press, 2006); Lokhova, *The Spy Who Changed History*; Henry L. Zelchenko, "Stealing America's Know-How: The Story of AMTORG," *American Mercury*, February 1952, 75–84.

56 Name change, from Lassoff to Lassen: Supreme Court records, Bronx County, New York, September 7, 1931.

56 Lassen as "Faraday": From FBI files regarding case #65-14743, March and April 1952.

56 Lassen's GRU assignment "in the Fourth Section" and "Chief Illegal Resident Agent of the 4th Section": From a Hoover memo dated November 9, 1954. The same memo states that "Soviet Intelligence personnel dispatched

to the United States were sent to 'Faraday,' who established them in his business or elsewhere."

57 "conspiratorial headquarters": Ibid., September 1954.

57 Michael Burd, money "from Russian sources," addresses and American Merchandising Co.: Ibid., November 1954.

58 Raven Electric certificate of incorporation: Records of the New York State Department of State, Albany, vol. 5645, no. 92, signed certificate.

58 World Tourists: John Earl Haynes and Harvey Klehr, *Venona: Decoding Soviet Espionage in America* (New Haven, CT: Yale University Press, 1999), 93–97; Andrei Soldatov and Irina Borogan, *The Compatriots: The Brutal & Chaotic History of Russia's Exiles, Émigrés, and Agents Abroad* (New York: Public Affairs, 2019), 58–59; Haslam, *Near and Distant Neighbors*, 132–34.

58 American passports: Haynes and Klehr, *Venona*, 79, 95.

59 The FBI had barely three hundred agents: Ibid., 87.

59 "the Justice Department had little interest in prosecuting Soviet espionage, and the popular press paid scant attention": Ibid., 82.

60 "was not, in fact, a single apparatus, but several networks": Ibid., 93.

60 Lassen meeting Golos at World Tourists: FBI reports regarding case #65-14743, April 1952.

60 "had a habit": Soldatov and Borogan, *The Compatriots*, 59.

61 The case against World Tourists and Golos's indictment: Haynes and Klehr, *Venona*, 93–96.

61 Golos and the CPUSA open the U.S. Service and Shipping Corp.: FBI case file #65-56402. The address is located in the Nathan Gregory Silvermaster summary (part 4 of 7) for the Julius Rosenberg case, page 2.

61 "weapons design work and their belief": From FBI reports regarding case #65-14743, March 1952.

62 Koval's enrollment at Columbia: from Ms. Madeline Scully, Records Division, Registrar's Office, Columbia University, noted in a November 1954 FBI report, case #65-16756. (He received a "Grade B.")

CHAPTER SIX: GENERAL CHEMISTRY

63 Details about the Columbia University Extension program in 1941 and 1942: *Columbia University Catalogue*, 1941–42, 1942–43.

63 Details about the times and location of Columbia University classes, Pupin Hall and Havemeyer Hall: Columbia University Archives with the assistance of Jocelyn Wilk.

64 "Enormous kicks": Laurence Lippsett, "The Manhattan Project: Columbia's Wartime Secret," *Columbia College Today*, Spring/Summer 1995, 18.

64 "each fission produced," and "If fission released": Ibid., 20.

65 "Believe we have observed": Ibid., 18.

65 "liberate a million times": Ibid., 20.

66 "Some recent work by E. Fermi": For the letter, Linda Carrick Thomas, *Polonium in the Playhouse* (Columbus: Ohio State University Press, 2017), 30–31. For the steps leading to the letter: Richard Rhodes, *The Making of the Atomic Bomb* (New York: Simon & Schuster, 1986), 303–9.

66 "This requires action": Ibid., 314.

66 The $6,000 grant to Columbia would be $100,000 in 2020: the inflation calculator on saving.org/inflation/.

67 "A natural substance found": William L. Laurence, "Vast Power Source in Atomic Energy Opened by Science," *New York Times*, May 5, 1940, 1, 51.

67 Even the popular magazine *Collier's*: Dr. R. M. Langer, "Fast New World," *Collier's*, vol. 106, no. 1 (July 6, 1940), 18–19, 54–55.

67 "the long dreamed of age": Laurence, "Vast Power," 1, 51.

68 "the science community acted as a club": Lokhova, *The Spy Who Changed History*, 214.

69 "to network as broadly as possible": Ibid., 305.

69 Clarence Hiskey: *Hearings Regarding Clarence Hiskey Including Testimony of Paul Crouch* (United States: US Government Printing Office, Congress, House Committee on Un-American Activities, 1949). The Atomic Heritage Foundation (atomicheritage.org) also has several articles referencing Hiskey's education, personal background, and HUAC testimony. Also, regarding Hiskey at the reserve commission in the Chemical Warfare Service: FBI case file #101-2118, a document dated August 21, 1940, supplied by the Military Intelligence Division to the FBI, in a September 1944 report.

70 "worked under and received his directions and payment through 'Faraday'": A former GRU member informant from an FBI report referencing case #65-14743, October 1955.

70 Arthur Alexandrovich Adams: There are 2,840 pages of FBI reports referring to Adams, mostly in the New York bureau case #100-16821. Case numbers 100-6277, 100-17841, 100-63983, and 100-331280 are the Adams case numbers for other bureaus nationwide. Details about Adams can also be found in relation to Lassen, in FBI case #65-14743, March 1952, July 1953, August and September 1954, and October 1955. Helpful secondary sources that also reference Adams include Haynes and Klehr, *Venona*; Lokhova, *The Spy Who Changed History*; Haslam, *Near and Distant Neighbors*; and Herbert Romerstein and Eric Breindel, *The Venona Secrets: Exposing Soviet Espionage and America's Traitors* (Washington, DC: Regnery History, 2001).

71 Dorothy Keen Adams: Robert Gottlieb, *Avid Reader: A Life* (New York: Farrar, Straus & Giroux, 2016), 313–14, 316. Details, including several passport numbers can also be found in FBI case #100-16821, March 1945.

71 "for a time after her arrival in Soviet Russia": A detail documented from the American Legation in Riga, Latvia, dated April 12, 1923, and found in FBI report case #100-16821, March 1945.

72 "false statements on Adams' behalf": Sam Novick's failed attempt, and the letter showing Jacob Aronoff's success in returning Adams to the US in 1938, can be found in FBI reports regarding case #65-14743, March 1952.

73 The meeting at The Music Room: Hiskey was interviewed by FBI agents on June 11, 1946, in the New York field office, at which time he said he first met Adams "in a casual manner" at the music shop in September 1941. FBI reports from case #100-16821, June 1946.

75 Koval's enlistment and deferments: Details can be found in FBI reports from case #65-16756, April, May 1954; March 1956; and March 1957.

75 Raven Electric's war contracts: listed in FBI case #65-14743, September 1954.

75 George's letter to Mila with "April 27, 1942" penciled in: A. P. Zhukov, "Mendeleyevets v Oak-Ridge (st. Tennessee USA)" ["A Mendeleevite at Oak Ridge (Tennessee USA)"], *Istoricheskii Vestnik RKhTU* 3, no. 5 (2001), 32.

77 William Rose and his travels: In the FBI reports referencing case #65-14743, there are financial reports from Raven Electric, Lassen's cover shop, October 1955. Further information can be found in FBI files for case #65-16756, April 1954, and the visitor records at Oak Ridge, March 1957.

78 Details about Oak Ridge: Rhodes, *Making of the Atomic Bomb*, 427, 486.

78 "In late fall 1942": The land details come from the notice to landowners in Roane and Anderson Counties in Tennessee, dated November 2, 1942. Civil action no. 429, subject "Eminent Domain Manhattan Project."

78 Initial tons of uranium purchased: Thomas, *Polonium in the Playhouse*, 40.

CHAPTER SEVEN: LIES AND TIES

79 Rose Stephenson, Marian Greenberg, and the Lassen "roll" episode: In FBI reports regarding case #65-14743, October 1953. There are interviews with Lieutenant Louis Sklarey, of the Essex County, New Jersey, Prosecutor's Office, who established the date of the incident as March 8, 1943, with Chief of Essex County Detectives Clarence Merrill. Reports from New York and Newark Police Department files are also attached.

81 The hundred folded $100 bills: With inflation, $10,000 would be worth approximately $166,000 in 2020. And the $4,000 spent by Marian and her boyfriend would be worth about $66,000 in 2020.

82　The layout of the Raven Electric building, located at 20 West Twenty-Third Street: FBI reports regarding case #65-14743, September 1954.

82　"somewhat harshly": Ibid.

83　Raven Electric inventory: FBI reports regarding case #65-14743, February and March 1952, and October 1955.

83　"[Lassen] often just sold," and "he [Lassen] did not do business in the American way": Ibid., March 1952.

83　The man who played cards with Lassen, "an ordinary shop owner . . . at a profit": Ibid.

83　Raven Electric employee and the *Daily Worker* episodes, "I hadn't any reason to open his secrets": Interviews with former Raven employee Alexander Doniger from FBI reports regarding case #65-14743, November 1954 and June 1955.

84　"had observed rare spontaneous fissioning in uranium" and silence "convinced the Russians that": Rhodes, *Making of the Atomic Bomb*, 327.

84　"evidence on possible work": Albright and Kunstel, *Bombshell*, 74. Note further that *Bombshell*'s helpful information on early Soviet intelligence work on atomic weapons in America is based in part on primary sources on pages 316–18 of that book.

84　"In a number of capitalist countries . . .": Ibid.

84　"the resumption of pre-war investigations of radioactive elements": Ibid., 75.

85　"to pursue all leads": Ibid.

85　"Stalin's government openly asked": Ibid., 104.

85　"an inestimable value to our country": From Ovakimian's report "About Use on a New Source of Energy—Uranium," Ibid., 76.

86　"indisputable that the Soviets": Ibid.

86　The duties of the War Production Board: J. A. Krug, "Production, Wartime Achievements and the Reconversion Outlook," *A Report to the War Production Board* (Washington, DC: October 9, 1945), 38–39.

86　The sixty-one deciphered cables and "huge quantities of War Production Board": FBI case #65-56402, in the Nathan Gregory Silvermaster summary (part 4 of 7).

86　Ties between Coe and Silvermaster on the War Production Board: Haynes and Klehr, *Venona*, 136, 143.

87　Adams meeting with Hiskey five or six times: FBI reports regarding cases #63983 and #16821, July 1944.

87　"sophisticated camera equipment": Haynes and Klehr, *Venona*, 175.

87　"Adams is known to be," "it would be most undesirable," and "did not wish to have Adams prosecuted": In a February 27, 1945, memo to J. Edgar Hoover,

FBI agent D. M. Ladd explains that Lieutenant Colonel John Lansdale Jr., head of the Manhattan Project's security, was the first to tell the bureau about Adams. This memo is filed in FBI case #331280. February 1948.

CHAPTER EIGHT: THE MAN IN THE JEEP

89 Koval's "Manhattan Engineering Security File": From FBI reports regarding case #65-553 (the Koval case out of Knoxville), February 1954.

90 "key man": FBI reports regarding case #65-16756, March 1956 and March 1957.

90 Details of Koval's early months in the US Army and his test scores: Ibid., May 1955.

90 About the Army Specialized Training Program: Dwight Ink, "The Army Goes to College," in *Ohio State Engineer*, vol. 27, no. 1 (November 1943), 15–16.

91 The Army Specialized Training Program at City College of New York was officially the "3225th 'STAR' Unit," Army Specialized Training Unit: FBI reports regarding case #65-16756, October 1955.

91 More ASTP details: The CCNY weekly newspaper *The Campus*, February 8, 1943, and October 6, 1943; and the CCNY *Bulletin*, 1942–1943.

91 Statistics about the ASTP at CCNY and a list of officers from Koval's ASTP unit: FBI case #65-16756, July 1957.

91 "There was no better man than George": Arnold Kramish, in Michael Walsh, "George Koval: Atomic Spy Unmasked." *Smithsonian*, May 2009, 44.

91 CCNY ASTP required course on advanced camouflage techniques: *The Campus*, February 25, 1944, 1.

91 Special Engineer Detachment: *District Circular Letter to All Area Engineers and Division Heads* (Knoxville, TN: War Department, US Engineer Office Manhattan District, September 1, 1943), 1–7. This file was stamped "CONFIDENTIAL" and can be found in the Oak Ridge Room, Oak Ridge Public Library.

91 Details on the SED at Manhattan Project sites: atomicheritage.org/history/special-engineer-attachment.

92 Selection of SED members at CCNY: FBI reports regarding case #65-16756, February–August 1957.

92 "extremely secretive," "in view of the highly technical training we had," "the discharge of assignments," "no knowledge of an ASTP," and "would have been so top secret": Ibid.

93 "could have been the result of a preconceived plan," "highly placed member," "someone with such a tie," "a goodly number," and "could have resulted": from the interview with Col. Raymond Cook, ibid., February 1957.

93 The jingle: Ibid., March 1958.

94 "a formidable array of factories": Bertrand Goldschmidt, a French chemist, quoted by Rhodes, *Making of the Atomic Bomb*, 605.

94 About the University of California, Berkeley, cyclotron: Thomas, *Polonium in the Playhouse*, 54.

94 Details about Oak Ridge: Rhodes, 486–95; also, General Leslie M. Groves, *Now It Can Be Told: The Story of the Manhattan Project* (Boston: Da Capo Press, 2009), 94–124; Charles W. Johnson and Charles O. Jackson, *City Behind a Fence: Oak Ridge, Tennessee 1942–1946* (Knoxville: University of Tennessee Press, 1981); and Robert S. Norris, *Racing for the Bomb: The True Story of General Leslie R. Groves, The Man Behind the Birth of the Atomic Age* (New York: Skyhorse Publishing, 2014).

94 Three main plants at Oak Ridge when Koval arrived: Note that facility S-50 had been closed by then.

96 "instituted remote handling of": "Karl Z. Morgan: Man on a Mission," *ORNL Review* 9, no. 4 (Fall 1976), 44.

96 Health physics: Karl Z. Morgan, "The Responsibilities of Health-Physics," *Scientific Monthly* 63, no. 2 (August 1946), 93–100.

96 "mathematical problems in connection with radiation" and "would have been given access": K. Z. Morgan interview from FBI reports regarding case #65-16756, July 1955.

97 "determine where hazard exists," and "Know all operations in your area": W. H. Ray, "Health Physics Building Surveying at Clinton Laboratories," Manhattan District, 1946. This typewritten document can be found in the Oak Ridge Room, Oak Ridge Public Library. The "Job Break-Down Sheet" is listed on pages 7–11.

97 "A person in his position": FBI reports regarding case #65-16756, November 1956.

97 "Safety Forces": Johnson, *City Behind a Fence*, 137–40.

98 Security forces at Oak Ridge: Ibid., 137–66.

98 General Groves and the FBI: Norris, *Racing for the Bomb*, 270.

98 Intelligence and Security Division, "the primary unit for assuring secrecy," the "queer ray," the stories about the Superman comic strip and the Maryville, Tennessee, minister: Ibid., 145–46.

99 Security manual and "individuals whose background": *Security Manual: Manhattan District*, US Engineer Office, November 26, 1945, Restricted, National Archives, College Park, MD, file #160259, 11. Declassified for the author on April 7, 2017.

99 "individuals having membership": Ibid., 30.

99 "restricted documents" and "by an authorized employee": Ibid., 32.

99 "Classified waste": Ibid., 34.

100 "was the presence in the collected sample": G. Koval, "Determination of Particulate Air-Borne Long-Lived Activity," June 22, 1945. This document was later published by the Technical Information Division, Oak Ridge Operations, 1947.

100 About Koval's leaves and "three main sectors": V. I. Lota, "Ego zvali 'Del'mar'" ["They Called Him 'Delmar'"], *Krasnaia Zvezda* 128 (July 25, 2007). Note that Lota claimed Koval met with "Faraday" once before leaving New York City for Oak Ridge, and at least once while at Oak Ridge.

101 Koval's trip to New York City with his Oak Ridge colleague in late May or early June 1945: from the author's interview with Duane M. Weise in September 2020.

101 Thirty-four SEDs in Dayton: Thomas, *Polonium in the Playhouse*, 72.

101 code name "Firm K": V. I. Lota, GRU *i atomnaia bomba* [*The* GRU *and the Atomic Bomb*] (Moscow: Olma-Press, 2002), 255.

CHAPTER NINE: THE PLAYHOUSE SECRET

104 Code name "Postum": B. Cameron Reed, "Rousing the Dragon: Polonium Production for Neutron Generators in the Manhattan Project," *American Journal of Physics* 87 (5) (May 2019), 377–83.

104 "a visionary with pioneering ability": Thomas, *Polonium in the Playhouse*, 9.

105 "the amount of chemistry in the project had been underestimated": Ibid., 51.

105 June 1943 letter from Oppenheimer to Groves about the need for polonium for the neutron detonation: Thomas, *Polonium in the Playhouse*, 58.

105 About the polonium: Harvey V. Moyer, ed., *Polonium* (Oak Ridge: US Atomic Energy Commission Technical Information Service Extension, TID-5221, July 1956); Rhodes, *Making of the Atomic Bomb*; Thomas, *Polonium in the Playhouse*; Keith V. Gilbert, *History of the Dayton Project* (Miamisburg, OH: Monsanto Research Corporation, 1969); Reed, "Rousing the Dragon."

105 "No trigger, no bomb": George Mahfouz, an engineer who worked at Unit IV, the Runnymede Playhouse, in an interview for Voices of the Manhattan Project, Atomic Heritage Foundation archives, manhattanprojectvoices .org/oral-histories/george-mahfouzs-interview.

106 "the minuscule innermost component": Rhodes, *Making of the Atomic Bomb*, 578.

106 Reed, in "Rousing the Dragon," notes that the initiator in the uranium bomb did not need to be as strong as the one in the plutonium bomb, and the initiators in both bombs used the polonium/beryllium fuel.

106 "high alpha activity": Gavin Hadden, ed., *Manhattan District History: Book VIII, Los Alamos Project (Y)*, vol. 3, chapter 4: "Dayton Project," 1947, 4.

106 "a very difficult assignment": Ibid., 111.

107 50 curies of polonium: Thomas, *Polonium in the Playhouse*, 104.

107 70,000 pounds of lead oxide: Ibid., 88.

107 0.2 or 0.3 milligrams of polonium from six tons of the Port Hope lead dioxide: Ibid., 64.

107 The lead dioxide vs. irradiated bismuth methods: Moyer, *Polonium*, 3.

107 Details about the Dayton Project and its units: Thomas, *Polonium in the Playhouse*; Charles Allen Thomas Papers, Washington University Special Collections; Gilbert, *History of the Dayton Project*; Hadden, ed., *Manhattan District History*; Howard Shook and Joseph M. Williams, "Building the Bomb in Oakwood," *Dayton Daily News Magazine*, September 18, 1983; Jim DeBrosse, "Russian Spy Lived in Dayton, Stole Secrets," *Dayton Daily News*, April 28, 2012.

108 "the only suitable structure": Shook and Williams, "Building the Bomb in Oakwood."

108 "a film laboratory for the US Army Signal Corps": Thomas, *Polonium in the Playhouse*, 90.

109 Polonium being highly radioactive: Interviews with sources; Traci Pedersen, "Polonium: A Rare and Highly Volatile Radioactive Element," Live Science, December 6, 2018, livescience.com/39452-polonium.html; Moyer, ed., *Polonium*, 342.

109 "Routine surveys consisting of thirty or more spot checks": *Monsanto Chemical Company—Unit III*, "Progress Report," September 1–15, 1945; Thomas, *Polonium in the Playhouse*, 116.

111 The Fishers: FBI reports regarding case #16756, April 1956.

112 "most promising" design for the initiator: Thomas, *Polonium in the Playhouse*, 123.

112 "only a full-scale test culminating in a chain reaction": Rhodes, *Making of the Atomic Bomb*, 580.

112 Code name "cases" for curies: Reed, "Rousing the Dragon," 379.

112 "quantities and delivery dates" and "the immense importance of the polonium": Thomas, *Polonium in the Playhouse*, 125.

112 "Some deadlines were so close": Gilbert, *History of the Dayton Project*, 6.

113 "We knew the world would not be the same": Rhodes, *Making of the Atomic Bomb*, 676.

114 "The atomic bomb is news to": Thomas, *Polonium in the Playhouse*, 141.

114 "A detailed description of your efforts": Arthur Holly Compton, *Atomic Quest: A Personal Narrative* (New York: Oxford University Press, 1956), 103.

115 The War Department's Bureau of Public Relations's announcement to radio commentators issued on August 11, 1945: General Leslie M. Groves, *Now It Can Be Told: The Story of the Manhattan Project* (New York: Harper & Row, 1962), 351.

115 "Laymen with even elementary scientific knowledge": General Leslie R. Groves, foreword to Henry DeWolf Smyth, *Atomic Energy for Military Purposes: The Official Report on the Development of the Atomic Bomb under the Auspices of the United States Government, 1940–1945.*

115 "dumfounded": General Leslie R. Groves, "The Atom-General Answers His Critics," *Saturday Evening Post*, June 19, 1946, 101.

115 "principal breach of security": Ibid., 15.

115 "It might have been possible," "We started to build": Ibid., 101.

116 "Secrecy requirements": Smyth, *Atomic Energy for Military Purposes*, preface.

116 "enough secrecy for safety": Groves, "The Atom-General Answers His Critics," 102.

116 Aleksandr Solzhenitsyn and the Scientific and Technical Society of Cell 75: Alex Wellerstein, "Solzhenitsyn and the Smyth Report," *Restricted Data: The Nuclear Secrecy Blog*, February 12, 2016, blog.nuclearsecrecy.com/2016/02/12/solzhenitsyn-smyth-report/.

117 Smyth Report translated into Russian: Albright and Kunstel, *Bombshell*, 154; and also see chapter 10 of *Sleeper Agent* regarding "Department S."

117 The polonium future at Monsanto: Compton, *Atomic Quest*, 103.

117 The underground structure on the 178-acre site: Hadden, ed., *Manhattan District History*, 9. Note that the production of polonium continued at the Mouno Laboratory twelve miles southwest of Dayton until 1972.

118 The four-hundred-page document: Harvey V. Moyer, ed., *Polonium* (Oak Ridge: US Atomic Energy Commission on Technical Information Service Extension), TID-5221, July 1956. Note that most of the Manhattan Project records on polonium were classified until 1983.

118 Koval invited to be on team to collect radiation data in Japan: Lota, GRU *i atomnaia bomba*, 257.

CHAPTER TEN: SPYCRAFT

119 "Safeguarding Information," "after relief from assignment," and "the characteristics of the bomb": *Security Manual* (Manhattan District: US Engineer Office, November 26, 1945), 35 and Exhibit IV.

120 "Department S": Pavel Sudoplatov and Anatoli Sudoplatov with Jerrold L. and Leona P. Schecter, *Special Tasks: The Memoirs of an Unwanted Witness—A Soviet Spymaster* (New York: Little, Brown, 1994), 184–87; Albright and Kunstel, *Bombshell*, 154–55; IU. A. Lebedev, "Novye dokumenty po istorii sovetskogo atomnogo proekta" ["New Documents on the History of the Soviet Atomic Project"], *Voprosy istorii estestvoznaniia i tekhniki* 37, no. 4 (2016), 719.

121 "The intelligence department of the Red Army": Lota, GRU *i atomnaia bomba*, 26.

121 "walk-ins": William Broad, "A Spy's Path: Iowa to A-Bomb to Kremlin Honor," *New York Times*, November 12, 2007, A18.

121 Three hundred forty-nine Americans later identified in decrypted cables: Haynes and Klehr, *Venona*, 9.

121 "direction remains unsatisfactory" and "The Moscow leadership": IU. A. Lebedev, "O doblesti, o podvige, o slave . . . Paradoksy syd'by Geroia Rossii Zhorzha Kovalia" ["Valor, Feat, Glory . . . The Paradoxes of the Fate of George Koval, the Hero of Russia"], *Istoricheskii Vestnik RKhTU* 28, no. 3 (2009), 23.

122 Details about plants and specialists given to courier Clyde: Thomas, *Polonium in the Playhouse*, 115; Lota, "Spetskomandirovka," *Krasnaia Zvezda*, no. 238 (201,3), 6, and no. 4 (2014), 6; Lota, *Kliuchi ot ada* [*The Keys to Hell*] (Moscow: Kuchkovo pole, 2008), 255–56; and details given to Faraday: V. I. Lota, "Ego zvali 'Del'mar' " ["They Called Him 'Delmar'"], *Krasnaia Zvezda*, 128 (July 25, 2007).

122 "The polonium is sent to the state of New Mexico" and that we received from a reliable source": Lota, "Spetskomandirovka," Krasnaia Zvezda, no. 238 (2013), G, and no. 4 (2014), 6.

122 About methods of delivery: Lota, GRU *i atomnaia bomba*, 30; and Walsh, "George Koval," *Smithsonian*, 45.

123 "personnel would obtain": Compton, *Atomic Quest*, 103.

125 HUAC: Walter Goodman, *The Committee: The Extraordinary Career of the House Committee on Un-American Activities* (Farrar, Straus & Giroux, 1968); Haynes and Klehr, *Early Cold War Spies*; Haynes, *Red Scare or Red Menace*; Weinstein, Allen. *The Haunted Wood: Soviet Espionage in America—The Stalin Era* (New York: Modern Library, 2000).

CHAPTER ELEVEN: DEFECTIONS AND DETECTIONS

127 "a dazzling cache of stolen GRU documents": Amy Knight, *How the Cold War Began: The Gouzenko Affair and the Hunt for Soviet Spies* (New York: Basic Books, 2007), 5.

128 "the obtaining of complete": Ibid., 1.

128 "For the Russians, the defection": Ibid., 10.

128 "G.'s defection has caused great damage" and "The work must be organized":
     Romerstein and Breindel, *The Venona Secrets*, 16.

129 "no. 1 project" and "to run down *all* angles very promptly": Knight, *How
     the Cold War Began*, 6.

129 Elizabeth Bentley and the significance of her defection: Dickey, Christopher,
     "The 'Red Spy Queen' Who Shocked America—and the Soviets," *Daily
     Beast*, July 28, 2019.

130 Elizabeth Bentley: Sulick, Michael J., *Spying in America* (Washington, D.C:
     Georgetown University Press, 2012), 185, 191.

130 "Alfred Adamson" and Eric Bernay, The Music Room, Clarence Hiskey, and
     Pavel Mikhailov, "no action on his arrest," and "The real name": Howard
     Rushmore, "Russian Atom Spy Trailed by FBI Here," *New York Journal-
     American*, December 3, 1945, 1.

131 Description of Mikhailov and his blond pompadour: from J. Edgar Hoover
     memo, April 10, 1947, in FBI case #100-331280, June 1947.

132 "some trouble," "Don't you feel that this thing you were working on belongs
     to humanity?" and "only if the world were well ordered": March 1949
     interview with Edward T. Manning, a former employee at the Met Lab in
     Chicago, from FBI reports regarding case #100-63983, November 1949.

132 "for the purpose of eliciting his comments": Memo from J. Edgar Hoover
     to the New York FBI bureau. The memo is filed with FBI case #100-16821,
     December 23, 1946.

133 The last hours of the FBI's surveillance of Arthur Adams on January 23,
     1946: FBI report regarding case #100-63983, March 5, 1946.

133 "Victoria Dearest": Ibid., March 1946.

134 "The ring leader of the international Soviet spy network" and "is now also
     under surveillance": Howard Rushmore, "Red Atom Spy Eludes FBI as
     Canada Nabs 22," *New York Journal-American*, February 16, 1946, 1.

134 "network of undercover agents": *New York Times*, March 5, 1946, 1.

134 "How Many of These Are in the U.S.?": Photo legend, *New York Journal-
     American*, March 15, 1946.

CHAPTER TWELVE: THE JOINER

135 "urgent": Hoover memo, FBI report regarding case #100-16821, March 24,
     1946. (The memo includes a reprint of the March 24 *New York Journal-
     American* article about an Oak Ridge leak.)

136 "The Canadian disaster alone": Albright and Kunstel, *Bombshell*, 180.

136 Never socialize: Sudoplatov, *Special Tasks*, 213.

137 Eta Kappa Nu at CCNY: FBI files regarding case #65-16756, June and July 1956. Note that several individuals in FBI interviews recalled Koval's leadership in the fraternity, one noting he was president. But the fraternity's chapter records were inaccessible during the book research, preventing the confirmation of his post.

137 "He was extremely interested in fraternity affairs": Interview with Henry Hanstein, ibid., September 1956.

137 "it is correct to say that": Regarding Hanstein, ibid., March 1956.

137 "List of Faculty on Atom Bomb Project": *The Campus*, October 4, 1945.

138 Comments from the landlady, Mrs. G. Gardner: FBI report regarding case #65-16756, April 1955.

139 "As editor of *The New Republic* I shall do everything": Wallace, Henry, *New Republic*, October 21, 1946.

139 "I say that the century on which we": John C. Culver and John Hyde, *American Dreamer: A Life of Henry A. Wallace* (W.W. Norton, 2000), 266–68.

140 "purely out of curiosity," "only a short while," "I sought him out," "continuing engineering studies," and "friend from Oak Ridge": FBI reports regarding case #65-16756, April 1957. These quotes come from an interview on March 22, 1957, and a follow-up interview on April 4, 1957.

141 "a deliberate whitewash": Robert Mayhew, *Ayn Rand and* Song of Russia: *Communism and Anti-Communism in 1940s Hollywood* (Lanham, MD: Scarecrow Press, 2004), 182.

142 "If I have any doubt that": Sam Wood's testimony as quoted in *Time* magazine, "The Congress: From Wonderland," October 27, 1947, 4.

142 "for a period of approximately five years": statement of Herbert J. Sandberg on passport application form #170092, US Department of State, Passport Office, March 15, 1948.

143 "Refused permission": decrypted Venona 1944 cable: Wilson Center, wilsoncenter.org.

143 Rincones and Petrinovic: FBI case file #65-16756, January and April, 1955, and December 1956.

143 Confirmation of "Viktor" code name in CIA-DRP00M01914R00100000 40050-6, decrypted Venona cable sent from New York to Moscow, December 6, 1944, with notes date June 23, 1971, identifying Viktor.

CHAPTER THIRTEEN: THE ESCAPE

145 The landlady's views and "He supposedly had one aunt": From FBI case file #65-16756, two interviews in June 1954 and one in April 1955.

145 "He was very popular at school": Arnold Kramish, ibid., November 1955.

146 "quite the ladies' man": Leonard Field, ibid., March 1965.

146 "I thought, not exactly the typical American way": Ibid.

146 "a rather mysterious person," "nobody knew much about him," and "very conservative politically": Interview with Abraham Fuchs (not Klaus Fuchs), in FBI case #65-2384, August 1956. Note that Abraham Fuchs's sister dated Koval.

146 About AYD: in *New York Times*, February 19, 1949, 2.

147 "intellectuals who," "potential for foreign travel," "an art show," and "business purposes": In FBI case file #65-16756, the March 1956 interviews with Jean Finkelstein Mordetzky. Note that Jean's three brothers were Sheldon, Leonard, and George.

148 About HUAC in 1948: Goodman, *The Committee*, 227–71.

149 About six of the Hollywood Ten: American Social History Project, *Who Built America?*, vol. 2 (New York: Pantheon Books, 1992), 503; Michael Freedland, "Hunting Communists? They Were Really After Jews," *Jewish Chronicle*, August 6, 2009.

149 The American Jewish Committee's 1948 survey: Laurence Bush, "McCarthyism and the Jews," *Jewish Currents*, May 1, 2011.

151 "approved HUAC's latest espionage inquiry": Allen Weinstein, *Perjury: The Hiss-Chambers Case* (New York: Knopf, 1978), 51.

151 Soviet consulate image: Albright and Kunstel, *Bombshell*, 96.

151 Details of the Oksana Kasenkina story: Oksana Kasenkina, *Leap to Freedom* (Philadelphia: Lippincott, 1949); and coverage in the *New York Times* for weeks.

151 "They call it paradise": *New York Daily News*, as part of the "Big Town" series on "old New York," July 26, 1998.

152 The scene with duffle bags and briefcases: Alexander Feinberg, "3 Russians Go Home as Lomakin Stays," *New York Times*, August 23, 1948, 1, 5.

152 "is definitely going to stay open": Ibid., August 26, 1948, 1, 3.

152 "What we started out": William A. Reuben, *The Atom Spy Hoax* (New York: Action Books, 1955), 141.

153 Display of fifty mousetraps: Blauvelt, 3.

153 "I have no hesitancy": General Leslie Groves in the text of the September 27, 1948, "Text of Report by House Committee on Un-American Activities Relating to Atomic Espionage," in *New York Times*, September 28, 1948, 22–23.

153 "The Committee [HUAC] believes that those": Ibid., 23.

154 "a proposal of" and "the Communist conspirators": William S. White, "Clark Agency Hits Spy Investigations, Bars Trials Now," *New York Times*, September 30, 1948, 1, 15.

154 "social list": "Wallace, Hiss Off Capital Social List," *New York Times*, October 3, 1948, 38.

154 "It probably did": "The Atomic Spy Hunt," *Time*, October 4, 1948, vol. 52, no. 14, 24.

154 "accused of obtaining": *New York Times*, September 30, 1948, 1.

155 SS *America* decks, silverware, and murals: "S.S. America, S.S. United States: Sailing on the 'All American' Team to Europe," united-states-lines.org/america-first-class.

155 "I'm in Paris," and the postcards: in FBI case #16756, March and August 1956.

156 "Thus at the flaming forge of life": Longfellow, *The Village Blacksmith*, 20.

PART III: THE HUNT

CHAPTER FOURTEEN: *SOVERSHENNO SEKRETNO* (TOP SECRET)

159 "coming to Russia must always": C. L. Sulzberger, "Russia—A Land of Paradox," *New York Times*, January 2, 1949, 26.

159 "opiates used by capitalists," "Superman," and "Batman": Harry Schwartz, "What Russians Read in Their Newspapers," *New York Times*, January 9, 1949.

160 "capable in times of crisis of betraying": Benjamin Pinkus, *The Jews of the Soviet Union: The History of a National Minority* (Cambridge, UK: Cambridge University Press, 2008), 141.

161 "All the authorities had to do," "liquidation of Jewish culture," "hostile to Soviet culture," and "cosmopolitans": Ibid., 144, 149; see also Oleg Yegorov, "Fighting the 'Rootless Cosmopolitan': How Stalin Attacked Soviet Jews after WWII," Russia Beyond, www.rbth.com/history/327399-stalin-versus-soviet-jews, January 26, 2018; and Walter Bedell Smith, *My Three Years in Moscow* (New York: Simon & Schuster, 1949), about anti-Semitism in early 1949, pages 273–75.

161 "the contented life of the Jews living there": Pinkus, *Jews of the Soviet Union*, 193.

162 "Everything that was happening": V. I. Lota, "Spetskomandirovka," *Krasnaia Zvezda*, no. 238 (December 25, 2013), 6, and no. 4 (January 15, 2014), 6.

163 The contents of Koval's 1949 report: described by Albright and Kunstel, *Bombshell*, 194; note that Albright and Kunstel obtained the report from the Soviet Ministry of Atomic Energy Archives in Moscow on November 19, 1993; listed in detail in Lebedev, *Vetvleniia sudby Zhorzha Kovalia*, 710.

163 "familiarize yourself with the materials": Lavrenti Beria, memo to USSR Council of Ministers, March 4, 1949, ibid., 711.

163 "illness could not serve as an excuse": Note from Beria to M. G. Pervukhin, March 4, 1949, ibid.

164 Statistics for early stage of Soviet bomb project: Michael I. Schwartz, "The Russian-A(merican) Bomb: The Role of Espionage in the Soviet Atomic Bomb Project," in *Journal of Undergraduate Sciences* 3 (Summer 1995), 104.

164 "smelling like a thunderstorm": Lebedev, *Dva vybora* [*Two Choices*], 3.

165 "how important the Koval materials" and the meeting of six main players of the atomic bomb project: Lebedev, "Novye dokumenty po istorii sovetskogo atomnogo proekta," 722–24.

167 "responsible government authorities": Hanson W. Baldwin, "Has Russia the Atomic Bomb?—Probably Not," *New York Times*, November 9, 1947, E3.

167 About the task force: Vince Houghton, *The Nuclear Spies: America's Atomic Intelligence Operation against Hitler and Stalin* (Ithaca, NY: Cornell University Press, 2019), 166.

167 Walter Bedell Smith: "Did the Soviet Bomb Come Sooner Than Expected?" *Bulletin of the Atomic Scientists*, October 1949, 264.

167 "We, the undersigned, are aware": Ibid.

168 "50% of the project's success": Schwartz, 106.

168 the Smyth Report as a target: Houghton, *Nuclear Spies*, 153.

168 "enough secrecy for safety": Groves, "The Atom-General Answers His Critics," 102.

168 "the crime of the century": J. Edgar Hoover, "The Crime of the Century: The Case of the A-Bomb Spies," *Reader's Digest*, May 1951.

CHAPTER FIFTEEN: POSTCARDS FROM PARIS

169 "the FBI today is engaged in": J. Edgar Hoover, "Red Spy Masters in America," *Reader's Digest*, August 1952, 87.

170 "Nothing has negated it": in FBI case #65-14743, March 28, 1952. Note that the FBI reports in the Lassen case were not labeled with his name after the match with "Faraday" was announced. All were labeled "Unknown Subject; Faradej; Faraday; Espionage R."

170 "Lassen's background agrees favorably": letter from J. Edgar Hoover to the New York bureau, on April 9, 1951, in Ibid., January 12, 1952.

170 "We entered the bank building": Ibid., March 12, 1952.

171 "papers which appeared to be ciphers" and "Lassen firmly denied" and "immediately institute a fugitive type" and "until advised": Ibid., January 12, 1952, memo.

171 "It is imperative that": Ibid., March 20, 1952.

171 The postcards: Ibid., several reports in March 1952.

172 The Eiffel Tower postcard from Gertrude to Benjamin Loseff: Ibid., July 23, 1953.

172 Christmas card to Alger: Ibid., January 1953. Note that Benjamin Lassen died in Russia in 1967, exact location unknown. The fates of Gertrude and their son Seymour, after leaving Paris in late 1951 or early 1952, are yet to be discovered.

172 About US Army surplus items: From interviews with a former Raven Electric bookkeeper, Elizabeth Barry, ibid., March 1953.

173 "to ascertain present whereabouts": Hoover memo, ibid., July 19, 1954.

174 "I don't know. . . . Last time I saw him on a street corner": all from FBI case #65-16756, in many interviews in reports filed in 1954 and in the first half of 1955.

175 "The individual agent in America," "If the appointment had been arranged," and "such contingencies": Hoover, "Red Spy Masters," 83–84.

176 "numerous telephone calls" and "had been wearing": FBI case #65-16756, first interviews with the "wrong" George Kovals in September 1954 and then more in January 1956.

176 "This investigation is of considerable importance": Hoover, memo to New York bureau, ibid., January 13, 1955.

177 "'the sale of Mexican twins'": Ibid., Hoover, two memos in August 1955.

177 "As you are aware": Ibid., Hoover memo, May 10, 1956.

177 "a flash notice" and "immediately": Ibid. Hoover memo, January 6, 1956.

177 "very close" and "a person who was": Ibid., January 22, 1956.

178 "could have been made faster," "if the Soviets obtained," and "on radiation": Ibid., November 19, 1956.

179 Multiple interviews with Jean (Finkelstein) Mordetzky: Ibid., throughout the month of March, 1956.

CHAPTER SIXTEEN: THE MARCH 1953 LETTERS

181 "I am now about 75," "Twenty years have passed," and "George lives in Moscow": In the May 20, 1956, letter from Abram Koval to the Gurshtels. FBI case #65-6124, August 26, 1956.

182 "believed warranted in consideration": Hoover memo, FBI case #65-16756, February 24, 1959.

182 "arrange to have [Koval] interviewed in Moscow": Hoover memo, ibid., April 2, 1959.

183 "The Embassy's files indicated": May 21, 1959 letter to Koval from Lewis W. Bowden, consul at the American Embassy in Moscow, ibid., June 1959 report.

183 "to discuss his American citizenship status" and "I have been a citizen": Koval letter in ibid., July 1959.

183 "all logical action has been taken" and "sufficient enough": Ibid., November 1959.

184 "The citizen case against Koval": FBI case #65-16756, June 1962.

184 "methods of logical approaches": Ibid.

184 Informant on allegation of Koval incompetence: FBI case #65-16756, November 1962.

185 "Russia in the spring of 1953": Ibid.

185 "conversation in 1949": Lota, GRU *i atomnaia bomba*, 259.

185 "Dear Comrade, I am writing to you": Ibid., 260.

186 "a decorative cover for the real plea to save his life": Lebedev, "Paradoksy sud'by," 18.

186 "gainfully employ" and "According to the non-disclosure agreement": March 16 letter, in Lota, GRU *i atomnaia bomba*, 262.

186 Koval first hired as a lab assistant. From an email he sent to Arnold Kramish: Walsh, "George Koval," *Smithsonian*, 47.

186 About Aleksandr Solzhenitsyn: Michael Scammell, *Solzhenitsyn: A Biography* (New York: W.W. Norton, 1984), 262–65; and about the two versions of his *First Circle*: Alla Latynina, " 'Genuine Occurrence' and 'Overworked Soviet Plotline': The Two Versions of [*The First*] *Circle* as Viewed from the Present," *Russian Studies in Literature* 43, no. 4 (Fall 2007), 82–97.

187 "Georgy Koval" and "Do not put the receiver down!": Aleksandr I. Solzhenitsyn, *In the First Circle*, translated by Harry T. Willets (New York: HarperCollins, 2009), 5.

188 "the Soviet GRU illegal," "would be justified," and "most knowledgeable": FBI director William Webster memo to New York City and Albany, New York, bureaus, FBI case #65-16756, March 1978.

189 "appeared very reluctant," "appears to be an eccentric," "time reference," and "1949/1950": Ibid., May 4 and May 16, 1978.

190 "Phonoscopy, Hunting for Spies": Lev Kopelev, *Ease My Sorrows: A Memoir*, translated by Antonina W. Bouis (New York: Random House, 1983), 72–105.

190 "Where did he get it?": Lebedev, "O doblesti," 16.

CHAPTER SEVENTEEN: EXPOSED

191 "bungled and bugged": from John Barron, June 1987, 100. "Our New Moscow Embassy," *Reader's Digest*.

191 Details about the bugging history, in Michael A. Boorstein. *History of the Construction of the American Embassy in Moscow: The History, Politics and*

Planning Behind the Construction of the Most Costly American Embassy in the World. Lecture given on November 18, 1989, at Fellows Breakfast for the Harvard University Fellows Program at the Weatherhead Center for International Affairs in Cambridge, Massachusetts, 9.

191 "to ensure that it met": Ibid., 5.

192 "The culprit is American" and "the best-bugged building": in Saul Pett, "Bugged U.S. Embassy Stands—for Now—as a Reminder of the Cold War," *Los Angeles Times*, February 25, 1990, 1.

192 The bug in the Great Seal: Albert Glinsky. *Theremin: Ether Music & Espionage* (Urbana: University of Illinois Press, 2000), 260–64.

192 forty microphones in the embassy walls: Harrison Salisbury, " 'Bugged' Embassy in Moscow Was Viewed as Security 'Dream,' " *New York Times*, May 21, 1964, 1.

192 Bugs in the typewriters: Stephen Engelberg, "Embassy Security," *New York Times*, April 19, 1987, 1, 15.

192 "honey trap" cases: Boorstein, 9.

193 "saved the planet from nuclear terror" and "The action of Achilles and Delmar" and "Delmar is alive": V. I. Lota, "Kliuchi ot ada" ["The Keys to Hell"], *Sovershenno Sekretno* 8, no. 124 (1999), 18 and 19.

194 "of a black stain" and "they didn't dare": Lebedev, *Dva vybora [Two Choices]*, 44.

194 "We are writing to tell you": Claim #052-18-0975, Social Security Administration, Office of Central Operations, Baltimore, MD, February 7, 2000. More details about the Social Security application in Andrei Soldatov, "The Soviet Atomic Spy Who Asked for a U.S. Pension," in *Daily Beast*, May 28, 2016.

195 "a brilliant GRU operation": Lebedev, *Dva vybora [Two Choices]*, 45.

195 Lota met Koval for the first time at the 2000 awards ceremony: Lota, "Ego zvali 'Del'mar' " ["They Called Him 'Delmar' "].

195 Lota's first time at Koval's home (in detail): Ibid.

195 Using the password: Lota, GRU *i atomnaia bomba*, 17.

195 "had access to everything": Broad, "A Spy's Path."

195 "the biggest": Ibid.

195 "shedding light": Andrei Shitov, "Agent Del'mar vykhodit na sviaz' " ["Agent Delmar Makes Contact"], *Rossiiskaia gazeta*, no. 4575, January 30, 2008.

196 "rubbed shoulders with spies and scientists": Jascha Hoffman, "Arnold Kramish, Expert on Nuclear Intelligence, Dies at 87m," *New York Times*, July 15, 2010.

196 "was a scientist involved": Ibid.

196 "of which my friendship with Koval," "my old friend," and "supply a personal and professional": letter from Kramish to Mendeleev director in late April 2000. From *Historical Bulletin of the Mendeleev Institute*, issue 3, no. 5, vol. 3 (2001), 34.

196 "Ah Arnold!" and "Is that you, George?": Lebedev, "O doblesti," 20; Zhukov, "Mendeleyevets v Oak-Ridge (st. Tennessee USA)," 32.

197 "It was an emotional moment": Walsh, "George Koval," *Smithsonian*, 44.

197 Note that the Hall biography *Bombshell* revealed that Hall and his courier devised a code for communicating dates to meet by using verses from the poet Walt Whitman's *Leaves of Grass*, the same book Koval carried with him for decades, though any further connection has never been established.

197 "made a difference in the arms race": *Bombshell*, 194.

197 "divulged an industrial process for": Ibid.

197 "polonium 210," "Just four days after," and "There is no evidence linking": Ibid., 195.

197 "Who did?" Ibid.

198 "It's interesting": Ibid., 24.

198 "I sent you the biography": letter from Kramish to Koval in 2003, ibid.

199 "To write your complete biography": email from Kramish to Koval in 2003, ibid.

199 "a veteran of the Great Patriotic War": IU. A. Lebedev, "The Character of Solzhenitsyn," in *Historical Bulletin of the Mendeleev Institute* 50 (2017), 27–43.

201 "predicting dangerous situations": Lota, GRU *i atomnaia bomba*, 261.

202 his inscription in Lota's book in 2003: Lebedev, *Dva vybora [Two Choices]*, 48.

202 Koval's public exposure: Lota, Vladimir: "They Called Him Delmar" in *Red Star* magazine, July 2007.

EPILOGUE

203 Scene at the grand opening of the GRU exhibit: Lota, "Ego zvali 'Del'mar,'" ["They Called Him 'Delmar'"], 25.

203 "Who's that?": Walsh, "George Koval," *Smithsonian*, 40.

203 November 2, 2007, award (order #1404): "President Vladimir Putin Handed Over to the GRU (Military Intelligence) Museum the Gold Star Medal and Hero of Russia Certificate and Document Bestowed on Soviet Intelligence Officer George Koval," press release, President of Russia: Official Web Portal, web.archive.org/web/20140116194923/archive.kremlin.ru/eng /text/news/2007/11/150176.shtml, November 2, 2007.

203 "the only Soviet intelligence officer" and "helped speed up": Ibid.

204 "We knew next to nothing": Walsh, "George Koval," *Smithsonian*, 40.

204 "Koval was a trained agent": Ibid., 40, 42.

204 "He played baseball and": Broad, A18.

204 "it would have been highly embarrassing": Ibid.

205 "Oh wow, I don't think you'd": "James A. Schoke's Interview (2014)," Voices of the Manhattan Project, November 7, 2014, manhattanprojectvoices.org /oral-histories/james-schokes-interview-2014. 1/4/20.

205 "Koval never had any regrets": Walsh, "George Koval," *Smithsonian*, 47.

205 The books in Maya Koval's collection: a list from Maya Koval sent to the author in June 2020.

206 "George, Ours is a friendship": The inscription was written in English, and after discovering it, Maya Koval translated it to Russian for Lebedev, who placed it in his books *Dva vybora . . . ob istorii verbovok Zh. A. Kovalia* (*Two Choices . . . The History of George Koval's Recruitments*) and *Vetvleniia sudby Zhorzha Kovalia* (*Branches of Fate of George Koval*), and then Masha Stepanova translated it back to English to appear in this book.

SELECTED BIBLIOGRAPHY

Akhmedov, Ismail. *In and Out of Stalin's GRU: A Tatar's Escape from Red Army Intelligence.* Frederick, MD: University Publications of America, 1984.

Albright, Joseph, and Marcia Kunstel. *Bombshell: The Secret Story of America's Unknown Atomic Spy Conspiracy.* New York: Times Books, 1997.

Andrew, Christopher, and Oleg Gordievsky. KGB: *The Inside Story of Its Foreign Operations from Lenin to Gorbachev.* New York: HarperCollins, 1992.

Andriushin, I. A., A. K. Chernyshev, and IU. A. Iudin, "Khronologiia osnovnykh sobytii istorii atomnoi otrasli SSSR i Rossii" ["The Chronology of Key Events in the History of the Nuclear Industry in the USSR and Russia."] In *Ukro-shchenie iadra: stranitsy istorii iadernogo oruzhiia i iadernoi infrastruktury SSSR* [*Taming the Nucleus: The Pages of the History of Nuclear Weapons and Nuclear Infrastructure in the USSR*], edited by R. I. Il'kaev. Sarov and Saransk: Krasnyi Oktiabr', 2003.

Baggott, Jim. *The First War of Physics: The Secret History of the Atom Bomb, 1939–1949.* New York: Pegasus Books, 2010.

Baldwin, Neil. *Henry Ford and the Jews: The Mass Production of Hate.* New York: PublicAffairs, 2001.

Bird, R. Byron. *Charles Allen Thomas, 1900–1982: A Biographical Memoir.* Washington, D.C.: National Academy of Sciences, 1994.

Blum, Howard. *In the Enemy's House.* New York: HarperCollins, 2018.

Bush, Vannevar. *Modern Arms and Free Men.* New York: Simon & Schuster, 1949.

Campbell, Craig, and Sergey Radchenko. *The Atomic Bomb and the Origins of the Cold War.* New Haven, CT: Yale University Press, 2008.

Chambers, Whittaker. *Witness.* New York: Random House, 1952.

Cohen, Adam. *Nothing to Fear: FDR's Inner Circle and the Hundred Days That Created Modern America.* New York: Penguin Press, 2009.

Cohen, Rabbi Henry II. *Kindler of Souls: Rabbi Henry Cohen of Texas.* Austin: University of Texas Press, 2007.

Committee on Un-American Activities, U.S. House of Representatives. *The Shameful Years: Thirty Years of Soviet Espionage in the United States.* December 30, 1951.

Compton, Arthur Holly. *Atomic Quest: A Personal Narrative.* New York: Oxford University Press, 1956.

Conner, Susan Marks, ed. *I Remember When . . . Personal Recollections and Vignettes of the Sioux City Jewish Community, 1869–1984.* Based on Oscar Littlefield's History. Sioux City, Iowa: Jewish Federation of Sioux City, 1985.

Coryell, Julie E., editor. Interviews by Joan Bainbridge Safford. *A Chemist's Role in the Birth of Atomic Energy: Interviews with Charles DuBois Coryell.* Portland, OR: Promethium Press, 2012.

Culver, John C., and John Hyde. *American Dreamer: The Life and Times of Henry A. Wallace.* New York: W. W. Norton, 2000.

Gentry, Curt. *J. Edgar Hoover: The Man and the Secrets.* New York: W.W. Norton, 2001.

Gessen, Masha. *Where the Jews Aren't: The Sad and Absurd Story of Birobidzhan, Russia's Jewish Autonomous Region.* New York: Schocken, 2016.

Gilbert, Keith V. *History of the Dayton Project.* Miamisburg, OH: Monsanto Research Corporation, 1969.

Glinsky, Albert. *Theremin: Ether Music & Espionage.* Urbana: University of Illinois Press, 2000.

Goodman, Walter. *The Committee: The Extraordinary Career of the House Committee on Un-American Activities.* New York: Farrar, Straus & Giroux, 1968.

Gordon, Linda. *The Second Coming of the KKK: The Ku Klux Klan of the 1920s and the American Political Tradition.* New York: Liveright, 2017.

Gornick, Vivian. *The Romance of American Communism.* New York: Basic Books, 1979.

Gottlieb, Robert. *Avid Reader: A Life.* New York: Farrar, Straus & Giroux, 2016.

Groueff, Stephane. *Manhattan Project: The Untold Story of the Making of the Atomic Bomb.* New York: Little, Brown, 1967.

Groves, General Leslie M. *Now It Can Be Told: The Story of the Manhattan Project.* New York: Harper & Row, 1962.

Hadden, Gavin, ed. *Manhattan District History: Book VIII, Los Alamos Project (Y).* Volume 3, Auxiliary Activities, Chapter 4, Dayton Project. 1947.

Haslam, Jonathan. *Near and Distant Neighbors: A New History of Soviet Intelligence.* New York: Farrar, Straus & Giroux, 2015.

Haynes, John E. *Red Scare or Red Menace? American Communism and Anti-communism in the Cold War Era*. Chicago: Ivan Dee, 1995.

Haynes, John Earl and Harvey Klehr. *Early Cold War Spies: The Espionage Trials That Shaped American Politics*. Cambridge, UK: Cambridge University Press, 2006.

Haynes, John Earl and Harvey Klehr. *In Denial: Historians, Communism & Espionage*. San Francisco: Encounter Books, 2005.

Haynes, John Earl and Harvey Klehr. *Spies: The Rise and Fall of the* KGB *in America*. New Haven, CT: Yale University Press, 2009.

Haynes, John Earl and Harvey Klehr. *Venona: Decoding Soviet Espionage in America*. New Haven, CT: Yale University Press, 1999.

Herken, Gregg. *Brotherhood of the Bomb: The Tangled Lives and Loyalties of Robert Oppenheimer, Ernest Lawrence, and Edward Teller*. New York: Henry Holt, 2013.

Hoddeson, L., P.W. Henriksen, R.A. Meade, and C. Westfall, *Critical Assembly: A Technical History of Los Alamos During the Oppenheimer Years*. Cambridge: Cambridge University Press, 1993.

Holloway, David. *Stalin and the Bomb: The Soviet Union and Atomic Energy, 1939–1956*. New Haven, CT: Yale University Press, 1994.

Hoover, J. Edgar. *Masters of Deceit*. New York: Henry Holt, 1958.

Houghton, Vince. *The Nuclear Spies: America's Atomic Intelligence Operation against Hitler and Stalin*. Ithaca, NY: Cornell University Press, 2019.

Howe, Irving. *World of Our Fathers*. New York: Open Road Media, 2017.

Johnson, Charles W. and Charles O. Jackson. *City Behind a Fence: Oak Ridge, Tennessee 1942–1946*. Knoxville: University of Tennessee Press, 1981.

Kasenkina, Oksana. *Leap to Freedom*. Philadelphia: Lippincott, 1949.

Kelly, Cynthia, and Richard Rhodes. *The Manhattan Project: The Birth of the Atomic Bomb in the Words of Its Creators, Eyewitnesses, and Historians*. New York: Black Dog & Leventhal, 2007.

Klehr, Harvey. *The Heyday of American Communism: The Depression Decade*. New York: Basic Books, 1984.

Klehr, Harvey. *The Soviet World of American Communism*. New Haven, CT: Yale University Press, 1998.

Klehr, Harvey, and John Earl Haynes. *The American Communist Movement: Storming Heaven Itself*. Woodbridge, CT: Twayne Publishers, 1992.

Klehr, Harvey, John Earl Haynes, and Fridrikh Igorevich Firsov. *The Secret World of American Communism*. New Haven, CT: Yale University Press, 1995.

Knight, Amy. *Beria: Stalin's First Lieutenant*. Princeton, NJ: Princeton University Press, 1993.

Knight, Amy. *How the Cold War Began: The Igor Gouzenko Affair and the Hunt for Soviet Spies.* New York: Basic Books, 2007.

Kopelev, Lev. *Ease My Sorrows: A Memoir.* Translated by Antonina W. Bouis. New York: Random House, 1983.

Kotkin, Stephen. *Stalin: Waiting For Hitler, 1929–1941.* New York: Penguin Press, 2017.

Kramish, Arnold. *The Griffin.* New York: Houghton Mifflin, 1986.

Krivitsky, W. G. *I Was Stalin's Agent.* London: The Right Book Club, 1939.

Krivitsky, W. G. *In Stalin's Secret Service.* New York: Enigma Books, 2000.

Latynina, Alla. "Istinnoe proisshestvie" i "Raskhozhii sovetskii siuzhet" ["A Real Event" and "A Popular Soviet Story"], *Novyi mir,* no. 6, 2006.

Lebedev, IU. A. *Dva vybora . . . ob istorii verbovok Zh. A. Kovalia [Two Choices . . . (the History of George Koval's Recruitments].* Moscow: RKhTU, 2014.

Lebedev, IU. A. "Novye dokumenty po istorii sovetskogo atomnogo proekta" ["New Documents on the History of the Soviet Atomic Project"], *Voprosy istorii estestvoznaniia i tekhniki* 37, no. 4 (2016), 702–35.

Lebedev, IU. A. "O doblesti, o podvige, o slave . . . Paradoksy syd'by Geroia Rossii Zhorzha Kovalia" ["Valor, Feat, Glory . . . The Paradoxes of the Fate of George Koval, the Hero of Russia"]. *Istoricheskii Vestnik RKhTU* 28, no. 3 (2009), 13–29.

Lebedev, IU. A. "Paradoksy sud'by" ["Paradoxes of Fate"]. *Vesti* (Tel Aviv), January 10, 2008, 18, 22; January 17, 2008, 20, 33; February 14, 2008, 38–39; February 21, 2008, 26–27.

Lebedev, IU. A. *Vetvleniia sudby Zhorzha Kovalia [Branches of Fate of George Koval].* 2 vols. Moscow: Tovarishchestvo Nauchnykh Izdanii KMK, 2019.

Lebedev, IU. A. and G. I. Koval. "Pishchat' nel'zia . . ." ["Squeaking Is Not Allowed . . ."]. *Istoricheskii Vestnik RKhTU* 44, no. 2 (2014), 20–21.

Lee, Albert. *Henry Ford and the Jews.* New York: Stein & Day, 1980.

Lokhova, Svetlana. *The Spy Who Changed History.* London: William Collins, 2018.

Longfellow, Henry Wadsworth. *The Village Blacksmith.* New York: E.P. Dutton, 1890.

Lota, V. I. "Ego zvali 'Del'mar' " ["They Called Him 'Delmar' "]. *Krasnaia Zvezda* 128, July 25, 2007.

Lota, V. I. GRU *i atomnaia bomba [The* GRU *and the Atomic Bomb].* Moscow: Olma-Press, 2002.

Lota, V. I. "Kliuchi ot ada" ["The Keys to Hell"]. *Sovershenno Sekretno* 8, no. 124 (1999).

Lota, V. I. *Kliuchi ot ada [The Keys to Hell]* (Moscow: Kuchkovo pole, 2008).

Lota, V. I. "Operatsiia "Del'mar'" ["Operation 'Delmar'"], *Krasnaia zvezda*, no. 71 (23616), April 19, 2002.

Lota, V. I. "Spetskomandirovka . . . v Ok-Ridzh" ["Special Assignment . . . to Oak Ridge"]. *Krasnaia Zvezda*, no. 238 (December 25, 2013), 6, and no. 4 (January 15, 2014), 6.

Lota, V. I. "Vklad voennykh razvedchikov v sozdanie otechestvennogo atom-nogo oruzhiia, 1941–1945 gg" ["The Contribution of Military Intelligence Agents to the Creation of the Soviet Atomic Weapons. 1941–1945"], *Voenno-istoricheskii zhurnal*, no. 11 (2006).

Lota, V. I. "Zvezda 'Del'mara'" ["The Star of 'Del'mar'"]. *Rossiiskoe Voennoe Obozrenie*, no. 10, 40–44, and no. 11 (2008), 34–49.

Macintyre, Ben. *A Spy Among Friends: Kim Philby and the Great Betrayal.* New York: Crown, 2014.

Macintyre, Ben. *The Spy and the Traitor: The Greatest Espionage Story of the Cold War.* New York: Crown, 2018.

Marinbach, Bernard. *Galveston: Ellis Island of the West.* Albany: SUNY Press, 1984.

Maroon & White, 1929, vol. 25. Central High School yearbook, Sioux City, Iowa.

Mayhew, Robert. *Ayn Rand and* Song of Russia: *Communism and Anti-Communism in 1940s Hollywood.* Lanham, MD: Scarecrow Press, 2004.

McCullough, David. *Truman.* New York: Simon & Schuster, 1992.

"Iz mendeleevtsev XX veka" ["Of Mendeleevites of XX century"], *Mendeleevets*, no. 10 (2299), December 2013.

Moyer, Harvey V., ed. *Polonium.* Oak Ridge: US Atomic Energy Commission Technical Information Service Extension, TID-5221, July 1956.

Norris, Robert S. *Racing for the Bomb: The True Story of General Leslie R. Groves, The Man Behind the Birth of the Atomic Age.* New York: Skyhorse Publishing, 2014.

Olmsted, Kathryn S. *Red Spy Queen: A Biography of Elizabeth Bentley.* Chapel Hill: University of North Carolina Press, 2003.

Ossian, Lisa L. *The Depression Dilemmas of Rural Iowa, 1929–1933.* Columbia: University of Missouri Press, 2011.

Pinkus, Benjamin. *The Jews of the Soviet Union: The History of a National Minority.* Cambridge, UK: Cambridge University Press, 2008.

Pondrom, Lee G. *The Soviet Atomic Project: How the Soviet Union Obtained the Atomic Bomb.* Singapore; Hackensack, NJ: World Scientific Publishing Co., 2018.

Reed, Thomas C., and Danny B. Stillman. *The Nuclear Express: A Political History of the Bomb and Its Proliferation.* London: Zenith Press, 2009.

Reuben, William A. *The Atom Spy Hoax.* New York: Action Books, 1955.

Rhodes, Richard. *Dark Sun: The Making of the Hydrogen Bomb*. New York: Simon & Schuster, 1995.

Rhodes, Richard. *Energy: A Human History*. New York: Simon & Schuster, 2018.

Rhodes, Richard. *The Los Alamos Primer: The First Lectures on How to Build an Atomic Bomb*. New York: Chump Change, 2018.

Rhodes, Richard. *The Making of the Atomic Bomb*. New York: Simon & Schuster, 1986.

Richelson, Jeffrey T. *Spying On the Bomb: American Nuclear Intelligence from Nazi Germany to Iran and North Korea*. New York: W.W. Norton, 2007.

Rockaway, Robert A. *Words of the Uprooted: Jewish Immigrants in Early 20th Century America*. Ithaca, NY: Cornell University Press, 1998.

Romerstein, Herbert, and Eric Breindel. *The Venona Secrets: Exposing Soviet Espionage and America's Traitors*. Washington, DC: Regnery History, 2001.

Rovner, A. *The "Icor" and the Jewish Colonization in the U.S.S.R.* New York: ICOR, 1934.

Rubinstein, Hilary L., Dan Cohn-Sherlock, Abraham J. Edelheit, and William D. Rubenstein. *The Jews in the Modern World: A History Since 1750*. London: Hodder Education, 2002.

Sakmyster, Thomas. *Red Conspirator: J. Peters and the American Communist Underground*. Champaign: University of Illinois Press, 2011.

Scammell, Michael. *Solzhenitsyn: A Biography*. New York: W.W. Norton, 1984.

Schmidt, Regin. *Red Scare: FBI and the Origins of Anticommunism in the United States, 1919–1943*. Copenhagen: Museum Tusculanum Press, University of Copenhagen, 2000.

Schrecker, Ellen W. *No Ivory Tower: McCarthyism & the Universities*. Oxford: Oxford University Press, 1986.

Shitov, Andrei. "Agent Del'mar vykhodit na sviaz" ["Agent Delmar Makes Contact"], *Rossiiskaia gazeta*, no. 4575, January 30, 2008.

Shitov, Andrei. "Geroi Rossii ostalsia grazhdaninom SShA" ["The Hero of Russia Remained a US Citizen"], *Rossiiskaia gazeta*, no. 4676, June 4, 2008.

Shtakser, Inna. *The Making of Jewish Revolutionaries in the Pale of Settlement: Community and Identity during the Russian Revolution and Its Immediate Aftermath, 1905–07*. Palgrave Studies in the History of Social Movements. London: Palgrave Macmillan, 2014.

Shteinberg, M. "Glavnyi atomnyi shpion" ["The Main Atomic Spy"], *Chaika Seagull Magazine*, no. 23 (106), December 1, 2007.

Shuman, Bernard. *A History of the Sioux City Jewish Community, 1869 to 1969*. Sioux City, IA: Jewish Federation, 1969.

Smith, Hedrick. *The New Russians*. New York: Random House, 2012.

Smith, Walter Bedell. *My Three Years in Moscow*. New York: Simon & Schuster, 1949.

Smyth, Henry DeWolf. *Atomic Energy for Military Purposes: The Official Report on the Development of the Atomic Bomb under the Auspices of the United States Government, 1940–1945*. Princeton, NJ: Princeton University Press, 1945.

Soldatov, Andrei, and Irina Borogan. *The Compatriots: The Brutal & Chaotic History of Russia's Exiles, Émigrés, and Agents Abroad*. New York: PublicAffairs, 2019.

Solzhenitsyn, Aleksandr I. *In the First Circle*. Translated by Harry T. Willets. New York: HarperCollins, 2009.

Solzhenitsyn, Aleksandr I. *The First Circle*. Translated from the Russian by Thomas P. Whitney. New York: Harper & Row, 1968.

Solzhenitsyn, Aleksandr. *The Gulag Archipelago. 1918–1956: An Experiment in Literary Investigation*. New York: Harper & Row, 1973.

Srebrnik, Henry Felix. *Dreams of Nationhood: American Jewish Communists and the Soviet Birobidzhan Project, 1924–1951*. Brighton, MA: Academic Studies Press, 2010.

Srebrnik, Henry. *Jerusalem on the Amur: Birobidzhan and the Canadian Jewish Movement, 1924–1951*. London: McGill–Queen's University Press, 2008.

Steinbeck, John. *A Russian Journal*. New York: Viking, 1948.

Straight, Michael. *After Long Silence*. New York: W.W. Norton, 1983.

Sudoplatov, Pavel and Anatoli Sudoplatov. With Jerrold L. and Leona P. Schecter. *Special Tasks: The Memoirs of an Unwanted Witness—A Soviet Spymaster*. New York: Little, Brown, 1994.

Sulick, Michael J. *Spying in America*. Washington, DC: Georgetown University Press, 2012.

Suvorov, Viktor. *Inside Soviet Military Intelligence*. New York: Macmillan, 1984.

Theoharis, Athan G. *Chasing Spies: How the* FBI *Failed in Counterintelligence but Promoted the Politics of McCarthyism in the Cold War Years*. Chicago: Ivan Dee, 2002.

Theoharis, Athan G., and John Stuart Cox. *The Boss: J. Edgar Hoover and the Great American Inquisition*. Philadelphia: Temple University Press, 1988.

Thomas, Charles Allen and John C. Warner. *The Chemistry, Purification and Metallurgy of Polonium*. Oak Ridge: Atomic Energy Commission, Office of Technical Information, 1944.

Thomas, Linda Carrick. *Polonium in the Playhouse*. Columbus: Ohio State University Press, 2017.

Tobias, Henry Jack. *The Jewish Bund in Russia*. Stanford, CA: Stanford University Press, 1972.

Wachman, M. J. *Why the Jewish Masses Must Rally to the Defense of the Soviet Union.* New York: ICOR, 1932.

Vaksberg, Arkady. *Stalin Against the Jews.* Translated by Antonina W. Bouis. New York: Knopf, 1994.

Van Der Rhoer, Edward. *The Shadow Network.* New York: Scribner, 1983.

Van Nort, Sydney C. *The City College of New York.* The Campus History Series. Mount Pleasant, SC: Arcadia Publishing, 2007.

Weinberg, Robert. *Stalin's Forgotten Zion: Birobidzhan and the Making of a Soviet Jewish Homeland.* Berkeley: University of California Press, 1998.

Weiner, Hollace Ava. *Jewish Stars in Texas: Rabbis and Their Work.* College Station, TX: Texas A&M University Press, 2006.

Weinstein, Allen. *Perjury: The Hiss-Chambers Case.* New York: Knopf, 1978.

Weinstein, Allen. *The Haunted Wood: Soviet Espionage in America—The Stalin Era.* New York: Modern Library, 2000.

Westcott, Ed. *Images of America: Oak Ridge.* Mount Pleasant, SC: Arcadia Publishing, 2005.

Whitman, Walt. *Leaves of Grass.* New York: Doubleday, 1940.

Zhukov, A. P. *Atmosfera deistvii: Zhorzh Abramovich Koval (1913–2006)* [*The Atmosphere of Action: George Abramovich Koval (1913–2006)*]. Moskva: RKhTU, 2013.

Zhukov, A. P. "Mendeleyevets v Oak-Ridge (st. Tennessee USA)" ["A Mendeleevite at Oak Ridge (Tennessee USA)"]. *Istoricheskii Vestnik RKhTU* 3, no. 5 (2001), 31–35.

INDEX

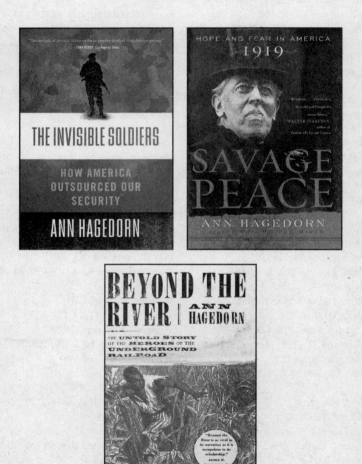
77662